A Town Called Perry

To Meryl
Best Wishes

Vivi Shirley
Perry Mayor
2008

A Town Called Perry

Midwest Life in Small-town Iowa

By Marjorie Patterson

Fullhart-Carnegie Museum Trust • Perry, Iowa

ISBN 0-9658341-0-7

Introduction to Marjorie Patterson's Book

Perry, Iowa, was born in 1869 when Harvey Willis convinced the railroad surveyor to put his tracks where Perry now stands. For more than 100 years, Perry was a railroad town. Then, in 1978 the Milwaukee Railroad went out of business, took up its tracks, and left a hole in the heart of the town. Things changed, but Perry lived on.

For as long as I can remember Mrs. Patterson has been the person to see if you had any questions about the history of Perry or its people. A railroad kid like me, Marge grew up to the sound of the whistle and the clikety-clack of steel wheels on steel track. She knew, too, what it was like to have her father called to work in the middle of a cold winter night. She knew the railroad life.

For years Mrs. Patterson wrote for the *Perry Daily Chief* where she catalogued the life of the town. One of my favorites was an interview she did with my grandmother, Selma Green. I learned things from it I would not have known otherwise.

Over the years, Mrs. Patterson has helped a great many people research a variety of topics that concerned life in Perry. At last, using the Perry Chief and her own research and experience, she has written her own account of Perry and its people, an account filled with humor and humanity.

Open the book to any page and read the stories of this small town. There are stories about people as they settled the town and came to grips with its growing population and everchanging needs. There are stories of Marshal Dave Willis who is a gentleman and hero. Then come stories of those brash and daring young men who took off for the Klondike Gold Rush. And, then come stories of courage as townspeople fought the fires that could mean the end of many dreams.

Here we have the unique perspective of a woman who has

lived most of her life in Perry, known the town and known its people. In these pages the story of Perry is Marjorie Patterson's story. You will see the town as she sees it.

Our hope at the Fullhart-Carnegie Trust is that this book will inspire each of us to ponder our own history and the history of the towns that helped to shape us and that we, in turn, shape. As with all memories, there are facts left to be discovered, others left to clarify. We hope Mrs. Patterson has whetted your appetite to discover more on your own.

We publish this book with the additional hope that A Town Called Perry will be the first of an occasional series of personal small town memoirs, accounts of a rich life with much to give to the world. Special thanks go to Bill Clark and Pam Jenkins, who saw the book through its design and printing. Most of all, we thank Marge Patterson for telling her story.

Roberta Green Ahmanson
9 April 1997
Newport Beach, California

Welcome to Perry

This is not intended to be a history of Perry, just stories about Perry out of history.

The material has come from more than 100 years of *The Perry Chief* files. From these old newspapers it can be learned how Perry began and how the town grew.

They tell of the many businesses which flashed into being, flourished for a while, then faded. This is about some of them. They tell of pioneers who led interesting and exciting lives as they played out their role in Perry's progress. This is about some of them. And it is also about conditions — the way they were.

Of course there were other businesses that survived and became the nucleus of later concerns. Their stories are not told. And there were other people just as illustrious, but not so flamboyant, who did not make the news. Their story could not be told.

When a block is mentioned, it is more apt to refer to a building than to the distance between two streets. The Fort Dodge, Rock Island, and M & St. L. are one and the same railroad. It just depended on the time of the event.

It took over 20 years of scanning the old newspapers to get these stories and many more hours to put them together. Some were easy. Some raised questions which might not be answered until years later in a different issue. Some will still leave the reader wondering what it was that was not reported.

There are many great stories hidden in Perry's past. It was not possible to tell them all.

— Marjorie Patterson

Contents

Chapter One
The Beginning

A Town is Born

Because D.J. Pattee was in business five years before there was a newspaper to chronicle events, it's difficult to know if this picture is of the west side of the Square or the north. Heaton rented an empty store in the building on the north side belonging to Pattee in 1879 for his store. The Perry Chief did report that Hubbell Pattee, Perry's first barber, sold his shop to Charlie Gale of Des Moines in April 1875. It was in December that Gale moved his shop to the front room of Haskins' restaurant which he had just opened on the north side of the square in a building formerly occupied by a saloon.

Across America Afoot

Harvey Willis, one of Perry's founding fathers, was born on April 15, 1831, in Wayne County, Indiana, of Quaker parentage. Until his nineteenth year, he served an apprenticeship on his father's farms and in a wool mill, with very little occurring to mar the monotony of his life.

At about this period (1850), the gold excitement broke out in California. The ringing news that Sutter and Marshall had struck it rich on the north or American side of the Sacramento River arrested the conservative, industrious plodding East. Farmers left their plows, artisans their tools, lawyers their briefs, doctors their patients, preachers their pulpits — all to make a run for the new Eldorado.

Young Willis, then just turning his nineteenth year, was among the first in his section to catch the fever and on the first day of April 1850, with a single companion, started for the far away gold fields. The two boys made their way to Cincinnati, thence by boat to Cairo, Illinois, where they reshipped to St. Joseph on the Missouri. The trip took a week. They remained in St. Joseph until the twentieth of the month, outfitting themselves for the long trip across the plains.

Forming a co-partnership with six others, Willis invested the money at his command into six yokes of oxen and two wagons loaded with provisions and supplies. Just as the grass began to look green, with faces toward the setting sun, Willis and his cohorts commenced their 2,000 mile tramp.

The trip across the plains and mountains was full of hardships and incidents. Many wandering bands of Indians were encountered and Willis told of many narrow escapes he had from being scalped. He walked almost the entire distance from St. Joseph to Sacramento and, at times, he would wander away from the train five or six miles and more than once came across Indian camps.

It was along in September when the little band, footsore and weary but full of zeal and hope, halted their oxen in the mining camp of Hangtown (now Placerville) on the American River. In a few days wagons and oxen were sold and, after a short pleasure tramp to Sacramento (about forty miles to the east), Willis returned to Hangtown and commenced placer mining in company with a capitalist who had taken a fancy to him. Willis looked after the camp and did the cooking as his share of the work, and received one-third interest.

At the end of eleven months, Willis was taken ill — the result of exposure. The doctor told him he must get out of the mountains or he would die. In the settlement of his stake with his partner, he received about $2,000 for his share. Willis went to San Francisco intending to stay until he recovered, then return to the mines. But, finding the expenses so high down at the golden gate, he decided to head home after ten weeks.

So, along the latter part of August 1851, Willis took passage on board the steamship Oregon for Panama, paying $300 for the ticket. Leaving the ship at Acapulco, Mexico, he began made his way down to what is now Panama where he decided to walk across the Chagres or Aspinwall. The walk across the isthmus was a momentous one, the trail led through tropical underbrush and required three days. The only persons he met were natives, very few of whom could speak any English. At Chagres, he witnessed his first prize, seeing Chris Lilly, the recognized champion of that day, soundly drubbed by a green, gawky Ohio River boatman named Taylor, who was returning from the mines.

From there Willis took a mail steamer for New York City, the passage costing him $150 and requiring two weeks' time. He landed with about $1,200, but he didn't leave the city with that much. He was still young in the ways of the world and, just after landing, fell into the hands of the harpies who infested the docks and lay in wait for the returning miner. Willis was buncoed out of about $600 of his hard-earned money.

Willis' money was all in gold dust. His boat landed on Sunday and the banks were all closed. Wishing to take a boat up the Hudson en route home at once and fearful that he would not be able to exchange his dust for money if he waited until he reached home, Willis inquired as to where he could sell.

He was directed to a place in a dirty, dingy basement where he found two men who offered him $2 more per ounce than the market price, and so, of course, Willis decided to sell. He unbuckled the belt in which he carried his wealth and emptied the contents into the scales they provided. They gave the weight in pennyweight and, while Willis was figuring the total, one of them emptied the scales into a large vessel in which there was a quantity of dust. When he discovered that they had given him weight for one-half of what he actually had, it was too late. He had no witnesses to the transaction and so was forced to take $600 for a good $1,200 worth of dust.

Leaving New York, Willis returned to his home in Wayne County where he remained only a short time before moving to LaPorte County, where he married Miss Eliza J. Webster. In 1859, with his wife and three children, Willis came overland to Dallas County, locating within a mile and a half of the site of Perry. When the trip was made, there were no railroads west of the Mississippi. The overland journey, made in wagons, took three weeks.

A Town Is Born

Perry, the largest city in Dallas County, owes her life, her location, even her name to a railroad. Three names played important roles in her beginning.

J. W. Otley was born in England in 1820 and educated there as a civil engineer. He and his wife came to America around 1848, settling later in Keokuk, Iowa.

D. J. Pattee was born in 1839 in Vermont and educated there. He took part in the Civil War and was taken prisoner. After being discharged because of ill health, he wandered west, drifting to Des Moines. He was employed there by the grocery firm of Rawson and Osgood.

The Willis brothers were already here. Harvey was born in 1831 in Indiana. His two brothers, John and Lindsey, were also Hoosiers. Harvey, with his wife and three children, came to Dallas County in 1859. Their first home was about one-and-a-half miles from the site where Perry was later built.

Around the early 1800s steamboats were the main support of the few towns along the Mississippi and other large rivers. The rest of the region depended upon the prairie schooner, pack horse, and stage coaches. The foot traveler was not rare.

In 1854, a group of men in Keokuk, who were far-seeing and progressive, decided to build a railroad up the Des Moines valley to Minnesota. They called it the Keokuk, Des Moines and Minnesota Railroad. It took ten years for the tracks to reach Pella, a distance of 116 miles. Thirteen miles of track were laid in 1865 and the line reached Des Moines in 1866.

Colonel Otley was employed by the newly formed railroad company to survey the route. He started out with a chain and compass and laid the line across the prairie as far as Fort Dodge.

D. J. Pattee, knowing the line was going to be built, came from Des Moines in 1867 to a spot on what is now Willis Avenue about one-fourth a mile west from First Street. He put up a building there and conducted a grocery store under the name of Rawson and Pattee. Later, he bought Rawson's interest. Then, the survey was changed.

According to the story, Harvey Willis bought 240 acres adjacent to his home in 1862, paying $1,800 for the land on which Perry was later built. For the first thirteen years, they lived in a log cabin which he had built.

It is alleged that it was through the untiring efforts of Harvey Willis that the line of the old Des Moines Valley Railroad was built through this section. He was out in his buggy one morning looking for cattle. Near Pearce's Point he noticed a group of men with flags and rode up to see what they were doing. He was told they were surveying for a railroad line. The direction was away from his farm. Harvey talked with the chief engineer and invited him to spend the night with him and his family.

The next morning, with the gift of a splendid horse, saddle and bridle, Harvey won the heart of the old English surveyor and secured the railroad.

After Pattee learned of the change in the survey, he put his store on wheels and moved it to a spot along the west side of the square. The land all about belonged to John and Harvey Willis.

The railroad reached here in 1868. The Willis brothers platted their land into lots and streets in 1868 and 1869. The first train reached Perry July 5, 1869.

Thirty-two years after starting at Keokuk, the line reached Fort Dodge. After Otley had surveyed to Fort Dodge, he started back along the route intending to return to Keokuk. But he was so pleased with the budding little village that he decided to make his home there.

The original plat of Perry was about 220 acres. Ten lots were given to the railroad for a depot in addition to twenty lots south of Willis. The name Perry was chosen for Colonel Perry of Keokuk, one of the owners instrumental in bringing the railroad west.

So, the town began around the angular line of the tracks and a vacant piece of land called a square because the street was closed on the south. Businesses sprang up along the east, west and north sides, interspersed with private dwellings. D. J. Pattee's home was on the north side.

The land in the center was a weedy patch criss-crossed with paths as people went from one side to the other. A few more daring merchants opened on Willis between Second and Third streets.

This is how Perry began. But, if the young town was to grow and prosper, a voice was needed to speak for it. And, that voice was found in a strong, long-lasting newspaper, *The Chief*.

The Strong Voice (1874)

It was early in the year of 1874 when two young men who were working as compositors in the office of the *Iowa State Register* in Des Moines decided to start a newspaper of their own. They were looking for a growing country town with bright prospects. The editor of the *Register* suggested they try Perry — "a little village up the Fort Dodge road a ways." They had no money, but each had knowledge of the printing trade and some journalistic experience.

They finally raised enough money for one of them to visit Perry and contact some of the prominent citizens — D. J. Pattee, J. H. Willis, Dr. Pangburn, attorney Cox, and others. But these men were wary. They had been approached before by strange men who had talked newspapers, and had given financial aid only to have the print shop and newspaper fail to materialize. The leading lights made it known that only when a printing office was opened in Perry and it issued a creditable paper working in the interest of Perry would they promise any support.

Returning to Des Moines, a conference was held and the two

Chief Staff of 1895

When The Chief was established the paper was turned out on a Washington hand press, and an 8" x 10" Gordon was used to get out the job work. The paper was applied by "kicking" the press. All type was set by hand and the paper cutter was an ordinary pocket knife. Only the day staff was on hand for this picture taken in 1895. From left to right — Allen Harvey; Fred Leonard; Den Snyder, foreman; Lotta Harris, typesetter; Fred Hoeye; and Frank Hoeye, editor.

young men decided Perry was going to have a newspaper. *The Oskaloosa Herald* had put in new equipment so the fellows were able to buy a portion of the *Herald's* old equipment and have it shipped to Perry. Then, they put in a full week of work in the Register office to raise enough money to pay the freight.

Through the kindness of attorney Cox, the new enterprise was allowed to occupy a storeroom in a two-story building near the railroad. Much of the necessary equipment was lacking, but there was an auxiliary printshop in Des Moines. When the two six-column forms were filled with advertising and paid local matter, they were locked and sent to Des Moines for printing.

Promptly on the day promised, fifty copies of *The Perry Chief* went out from their little office into the homes of the town. At least one of those original copies is still in existence, dated September 19, 1874. It is kept in a vault at *The Perry Chief* office. There was not a subscriber list and they had received no bonus of any kind.

The two men were John J. Jones and Edward D. Lunt. Jones wanted to call the little newspaper "The Mail." Lunt preferred *The Chief*. Because Lunt's choice of the name was the one finally chosen, the other partner's name was affixed first on the firm's name. Hence, it was Jones and Lunt of *The Perry Chief*.

Soon after the first issue appeared, true to their promise, representative citizens marched into the office and plunked down $100 in cash collected from new subscribers. This enabled the proprietors to buy a second-hand press and some type.

The boys had heard of printing offices so cold the devil would freeze to death while starting a fire, and that first winter, they had the experience of working in such a place. Snow drifted in on the floor and piled up on the stone. It was impossible to run a newspaper and be a Christian under those conditions. It was either steal coal or swear and, on occasion, do both. Because of blizzards, the paper was sometimes a delayed for up to two days. In spite of all this, the paper grew in volume, and twenty-four new subscribers were added to the list.

After seven months in the storeroom, in the last of April 1875, they, Jones and Lunt, moved their office to the northeast corner of the square, in an office over Clark's Hardware store. Still seeking the right place, they moved again in September 1875 to the Richardson Building on the east side of the square, next door to Otley and Slocum's real estate office.

Times were hard in the winter of 1875-1876 and it was necessary to reduce the size of *The Chief*. Scarcity of money, the inability to collect money due them, and the withdrawal of advertising, compelled the publishers to cut expenses.

Subscription rates were lowered to $1.50 a year, but advance payment was required. An additional ten cents postage had to be paid on all papers sent to the post office for out of county delivery. In spite of those reverses, circulation increased by more than 100. Several changes took place as a result. The office was enlarged and thanks given to Newt Beason, Sam Walker, Will Elder, W. A. Jones, W. A. Chappelear, Bart Smith, J. S. Walker, W. H. Phillips, and others for help in moving the press and the other heavy equipment.

In August 1876, the publication day was changed to Thursday. Then trouble overtook the young businessmen; the inability to meet their payments caused the plant to be absorbed into the mortgage. Publication continued, however, with George Harlan as proprietor. Harlan hired the former editor, Ed Lunt, to manage the paper.

With the change also came yet another change of address. *The Chief* was now to be upstairs in the building occupied by Cox and Hoyt on Willis. F. S. Stiles, Fred Griswald, Will Clark, J. H. Winsor and others were thanked for their assistance.

The subscription rate was raised to $2.00 a year with no apology given except that they couldn't afford to furnish the paper for less. Publication day was changed to Saturday.

After two or three months, Lunt was able to buy back the paper and plant for $600 on two year's time, and succeeded in clearing the debt when it came due.

Since that time, there have been many owners of *The Chief*, but there has always been a *Chief*.

Excerpts from Volume I, No. I

In that first issue of *The Perry Chief*, September 19, 1874, news from abroad mentioned the American polar expedition, the famine in India, mutiny among the crew of a British ship, and an ex-U.S. Consul at Lisbon being found guilty of swindling.

It told of bloody riots in New Orleans, of the annual state women's suffrage meeting in Des Moines, and of the changing of the name of Maudeville, a town in Butler County, to Allison.

And it gave the recipe for Saratoga potatoes, now known as potato chips.

On the local scene, the editor commented that he'd recently arrived here in the rain and, while plodding wearily up the street, thought bitterly of the man who put the walk below the surface of the ground.

About the scariest thing in Perry at that time was the lack of dwelling places to rent. Every house in Perry was occupied and the demand was increasing.

That next week, *The Chief* announced it would publish a full directory of churches and other societies of Perry and vicinity if the necessary information was obtainable.

The Chief reported that the Reverend S. Snyder, the new Methodist minister, had arrived from Moingona.

And why is there so much shooting at night in Perry? If it were absolutely necessary, all right. If not, in the name of suffering citizens, don't do it any more.

The Chief's Accomplishments: What a Newspaper can do for a Town

As early as October 1874, talk of the town incorporating was being heard and the very young *Chief* carried many editorials in favor of the idea. The editor believed that until the city did incorporate, there would be no sidewalks, horses and cattle would roam the streets at will, and mud holes and cess pools would assail the public nostrils.

The editor admitted taxes would be raised, but so would the value of property. The cost to run the town government should not be an issue as there were capable men willing to work for nothing and *The Chief* would print all proceedings and ordinances the first year free of charge — even longer if the town couldn't pay for it.

The election was held February 17, 1875, in the old school house and was a quiet affair, though both sides had worked hard. One hundred twenty votes were cast: sixty-three for and fifty-seven against, giving a majority of six in favor.

The articles of incorporation were executed in May 1875 and were in the handwriting of A.C. Hotchkiss. The petition to the court asked that a commission be appointed and a special election held to vote on the question. It was signed by L. D. Gamble and forty-five others. Dr. S. Pangburn and P. C. Rude made affidavit that the town contained 540 inhabitants. Judge Mitchell of the district court appointed A.G. Webster, L.D. Gamble, G. H. Rowley, Ed Lunt, and P.C. Rude as commissioners.

The first oficers were: J. H. Conley, mayor; A.G. Webster, recorder; Robert Ginn, B.F. Newport, W.H. Chandler, Wm. McLuen, and S. A. Capenter as councilmen.

Some members of the school board had opposed having the town election held in the school house, but they were accused by the newspaper of being less particular later, when the door had been left open day and night for over a week.

Having helped to secure incorporation, *The Chief* turned to other civic needs, such as a bank and helped in the search.

George Blakeslee of Brooklyn, Iowa, came to Perry on March 26, 1875, to look over the situation. Blakeslee told *The Chief* that he intended to establish a bank here. He later organized the First National Bank of Perry, a forerunner of the Brenton Bank.

Then came a drive to secure a mill. The appointed committee found a man who offered to put up a first class mill with all new machinery — if the town would give him the land and assistance to the tune of $1,000. But the project was left hanging so long that the man found another location with a larger bonus.

Then, Otis and Selby of Des Moines offered to put up a $12,000 mill under the same conditions, and they would not ask for a single dollar until the mill was operating. Land was secured from the Fort Dodge Railroad, Co., in June 1875.

By July, the railroad had put in a switch near the depot and the foundation for the mill was about completed. It was of stone and above it would be three stories built of heavy lumber. The steam mill started for the first time on November 5, 1875.

This mill had a large whistle attached to the boiler. The steam whistle was a relic and had been in use during the Civil War on the Confederate gunboat Florida. It was later dismantled and sold at New Orleans by the government.

In November 1876 it was doing duty at the Exposition building in Des Moines. It was blown morning, noon, and night to announce the opening and closing of that institution.

This whistle was removed from the mill boiler because it was too loud. It was eight-feet tall, and when there were 150 pounds of pressure in the boiler, that whistle could break windows.

Another pressing need, according to *The Chief*, was a tailor. Those who wanted clothes had to go to Des Moines. So, D. W. Payne and N. Edquist opened a first-class merchant tailoring shop in 1876. Their shop had three sewing machines.

And so it went. *The Chief* was always there as a spokesman for the growing town.

The editor was so pleased that the council was taking steps to stop the horse racing which had become so prevalent on the streets of Perry. And he said so in the pages of the newspaper.

In July 1875, *The Chief* again called the attention of the town authorities to the drove of colts that continually ran at large on the streets. They damaged trees, fences, and sidewalks, and when they formed in a line of battle and charged like a squadron of cavalry through the streets that there was great danger to the lives and limbs of the citizens, especially for the children.

He Didn't Like Perry (1868)

In 1868, F. A. Smith, who lived some distance northwest of Perry, turned some horses out on the prairie and they strayed away. He came down through the country, riding a bronco, looking for the lost horses. Smith rode into Perry tired and hungry.

Perry wasn't on the map then. It was Alton and consisted of one store and a blacksmith shop. Smith stopped at the store to get some crackers and cheese, all that he could get in the line of edibles. While eating he became aware that the natives were taking an unusual interest in him. They would talk together in groups, glance at him, and talk it over again.

When he finished eating, Smith went out to untie his pony and resume his journey. A man stepped up to him and began to ask questions which Smith felt were impertinent, but he answered them all in a civil manner. He was about to mount when the man announced himself to be the constable and asked Smith not to hurry away. The constable was looking for a horse thief and being a suspicious looking fellow, Smith would have to prove his identity.

There happened to be a man from Smith's own neighborhood in town, but to make matters worse, he had never heard of F. A. Smith. Smith, being a shrewd man, finally convinced the people that a man could not be identified by strangers and he had the constable accompany him to the neighborhood where even the dogs knew him. They met an old Quaker who knew both Smith and the constable, and Smith was allowed to go.

After that, Smith passed through Perry many times on the train, but never stopped here until September 1898. He was then Representative, the Honorable F. A. Smith of Scranton, and was on his way to the Republican convention in Dubuque. He had expected to make connections, but unfortunately, had to lay over for most of the day. He left on No. 3 to Madrid, preferring to wait there for No. 4.

Town Hall and Slocum

Towns need a hall for their council meetings. Of course, the very young Perry did not have such a place. Mayor J.H. Conley had resigned on August 15, 1875 and it was Mayor William McLuen who appointed a committee to secure a place. They reported that Mr. M.W. Slocum had offered the use of his office with fuel and lights for $15 a year. The offer was accepted.

M. W. Slocum began operating a drug store in Perry in 1871. By 1875 he was in business with Kirkpatrick. However, Slocum sold his interest to a Mr. Courtney in 1876 and became a loan agent.

Slocum's ad appeared in *The Perry Chief* on March 29, 1877, announcing money to lend in sums of $300 and up to any amount at nine percent interest. In May, a similar ad showed the interest rate at ten percent.

Residents of Perry in the early days had reason to remember M. W. Slocum. He had a narrow escape at the hands of an angry mob who took him from his bed one cold night and carried him several miles into the country in his night clothes.

Celia Covey was a longtime teacher in the Perry schools whose grandparents were involved in the incident. Her grandfather, A.D. Haskins, was the manager of the St. James Hotel and constable at the time. Her story, substantiated by a clipping from a Des Moines newspaper, was that citizens were angered by what they felt were shady dealings by the money lender. Unable to get justice legally, they took matters into their own hands.

The vigilantes traded and borrowed horses, and traded again and disguised themselves so that not one person knew the identity of the other. One man was sent to the hotel to keep the constable from interfering. Covey's great grandfather discovered something was afoot and rushed to the hotel to alert the constable.

A.D. Haskins surprised the man in the alley and ordered him to dismount. When he refused, the constable pulled his gun, but it would not fire. The man on horseback aimed his gun, but it did not fire either.

Meanwhile, the rest of the group had routed Slocum from

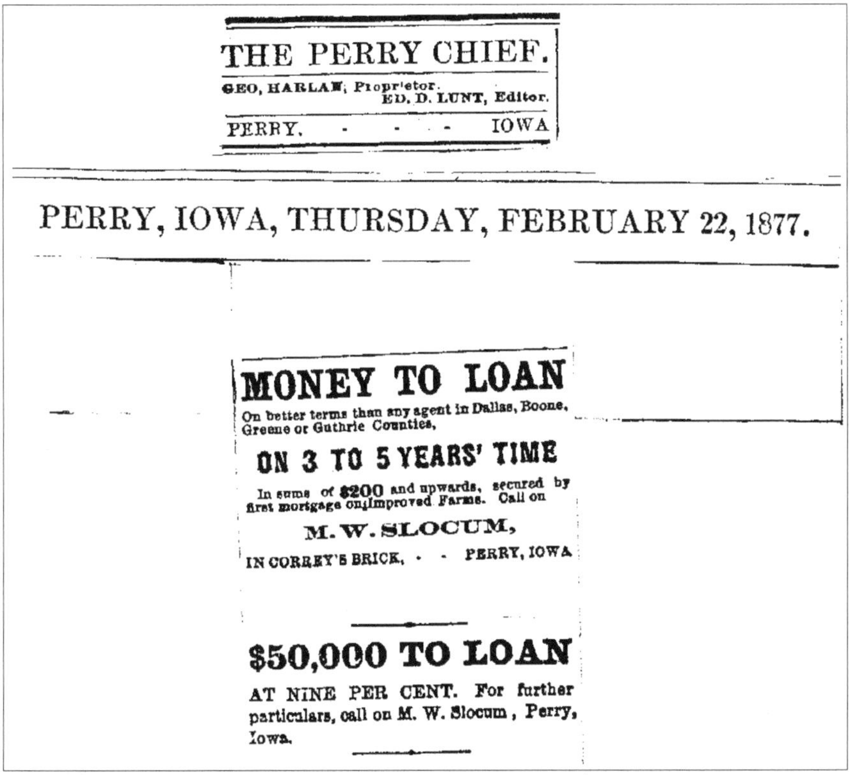

THE PERRY CHIEF.
GEO, HARLAN, Proprietor.
ED, D. LUNT, Editor.

PERRY.   -   -   -   IOWA

PERRY, IOWA, THURSDAY, FEBRUARY 22, 1877.

MONEY TO LOAN

On better terms than any agent in Dallas, Boone, Greene or Guthrie Counties,

ON 3 TO 5 YEARS' TIME

In sums of $200 and upwards, secured by first mortgage on improved Farms. Call on

M. W. SLOCUM,

IN CORREY'S BRICK, - - PERRY, IOWA

$50,000 TO LOAN

AT NINE PER CENT. For further particulars, call on M. W. Slocum, Perry, Iowa.

Slocum Gets into the Loan Business

Before going into the loan business in 1876, Slocum's drugstore ad appeared in the first issue of The Chief. He wanted people to know The Old Reliable Perry Drug Store, owned by Dr. M.W. Slocum was still at his old stand with a large and carefully selected stock of everything usually found in a first class drug store: drugs and chemicals, paints, oils and varnishes, perfumery, wall paper, pens, pencils, smoking and chewing tobacco, snuff and more. And in small print: "Presciptions carefully compounded at all hours."

his bed, strapped him to a wagon and set out for the "hanging tree." On reaching it, they dismounted and discovered one of the number was missing. Having second thoughts, they turned their victim loose to find his way back as best he could.

The next day, Covey's grandfather tested the guns and both fired the first time. She felt it was the hand of God which prevented three murders that night.

Slocum must have left town after that harrowing experience. An article from the *Chicago Tribune* appeared in the *The Perry*

Chief on February 11, 1887, reporting his death of a heart attack as he was stepping onto a street care in Chicago. He was forty-two years old.

Liquor — The Second Ordinance

The councilmen passed the first ordinance of the incorporated city dealing with sidewalks and the material of which they were to be constructed. Later these sidewalks returned to haunt them after several people filed suits against the city for injuries received from falls.

Perry's founding fathers were also determined to make the town dry — and to keep it that way. Two saloons in a town the size of Perry were just two too many. The amount of beer consumed was alarming and something had to be done about it.

Therefore, the second ordinance dealt with the suppression of intemperance, stating "no person shall manufacture or sell by himself or his clerk or steward, directly or indirectly, any intoxicating liquors, wine or beer."

In July of 1875, a call was issued to the citizens for a meeting in the Baptist Church to consider the question of licensing the sale of wine and beer. D. N. Kelsey was called to the chair and William McLuen was elected secretary. Chandler stated the object of the meeting and remarks were made by J. H. Willis, Myers, George Walker, Blakeslee, Reverend Mr. Simons, Campbell, Kelsey, Reverend Mr. S. Snyder, and Webster.

They came up with the resolution that to license the liquor traffic would be a covenant with the devil — an agreement with hell. The group found that the town council, for "excluding the sale of wine and beer," was entitled to lasting gratitude.

So, a beer saloon was established in a shanty just outside the corporation line west of town in the middle of July 1875. The first night the back door was broken open and a keg of beer stolen. The next night, one side of the house was torn out and the contents of the place badly "demoralized."

In the middle of August the saloon was torn down for the third time by the proprietor to make room for a larger and more substantial building. This was the notorious Blue Goose Saloon.

Colonel Otley (1876-1883)

Colonel J.W. Otley, for whom Otley Avenue is named, was born January 22, 1820, in Yorkshire County, England. He married Eleanor Janeson in London; they had one son who died in infancy. The couple came to Iowa in October 1856, settling in Keokuk. Colonel Otley made the first official plat of Keokuk and lived there for many years.

The Colonel did the survey for the railroad and decided to return to Perry after he had completed that survey rather than return to his home in Keokuk. It was soon reported that he had become the owner of much property.

He gave the Masonic Lodge in Perry its first set of jewels in June 1871 when the first officers were installed. In appreciation of the gift, they named their lodge the Otley Lodge. This was just one of many generous acts that could be traced to Colonel Otley.

The Colonel endeared himself to the editor of *The Perry Chief* by giving him a warranty deed to one of the finest residential lots in town.

As a large property holder, it was to his best interests to foster and encourage all enterprises which led to the improvement of the town.

Colonel Otley's own place was one of natural beauty, southeast of town. In the center of the forty-acre estate was a high knoll which afforded a view of Perry and the surrounding country. An unpretentious house stood there, but it was soon supplemented by a structure worthy of the location.

On the north and east of the house there was an orchard with many trees of a choice variety, and on the south, a long row of evergreens. There were also about three acres of strawberry plants and a vineyard containing several hundred of Clinton and Concord vines. Colonel Otley's cellar contained wines which were made on these grounds.

Otley had been in the real estate business with Squire Chappelear in 1876. When the firm dissolved in August 1882, he retired.

In 1883, Mr. and Mrs. Otley decided to move to Des Moines, and the Otley addition was thrown open to buyers. It consisted of his home, the orchard, and forty desirable lots lying west of the orchard and between it and the railroad. Dr. D. C. West pur-

Colonel Otley

The story was told that Colonel Otley promised to give a gift to the parents of the first boy born in Perry and named for him. Herbert Otley Taylor said he was the first boy, but his parents never received a gift. Taylor was a city councilman in 1949

chased the homestead and some residential lots for his father-in-law Dr. S. C. Goff.

Pure water was attainable at a depth of twelve to thirteen feet. A row of large Lombardy poplars marked the west line and three strands of barbed wire protected the young hard maples set out on every lot. An extension of Fifth Street ran between these lots and those maple trees, which have long been a beautiful sight every fall.

In 1883 a wide highway at the south end of Fifth Street connected with another avenue running north through the orchard, connecting with Sixth Street. This was a carriage drive unequaled for smoothness and beauty.

Otley retained kind feelings for Perry and continued to return for visits. He died in his home in Des Moines on January 2, 1888, at the age of sixty-eight.

The Chandler Building

One of the first hardware stores in Perry was that of W. H. Chandler and J. P. Spaulding. Chandler opened his business in Perry in 1871 on Second Street in a building listed as his. In the spring of 1875 he was considered to have one of the largest and best-stocked stores around — Champion reapers and mowers, Dixon stirring plows and sulkey rakes, both Brown and Quincy planters, Dexter and Weir cultivators. In 1876, Chandler bought out Spaulding.

Chandler continued in the implement business until January 1, 1893, when he disposed of his business. Henry Miller bought his hardware stock. Chandler then entered the Real Estate Loan and Insurance business.

Chandler's first building was erected in August 1883. Sam Heightshoe was the contractor; John R. Stewart's company furnished the lumber.

The second floor was made into a roller skating rink and a special wooden floor was installed. It was an ideal place — fifty feet by ninety feet without any obstructions. This building was burned in the fire of 1898 and rebuilt in 1899. The ground floor was occupied by Auspitz with the Grand Leader store. The upstairs was rented for an armory. The ceilings were much higher and built for the convenience of the militia boys and for balls and banquets.

One of the biggest deals in Perry business real estate was closed December 28, 1912, when W.H. Chandler sold the lot and store building on Second Street to F. H. Reid, which was occupied by Miller Brothers' Hardware and the Antler's Hall. Reid then moved his jewelry store into the building.

Chandler died in October 1922 in Los Angeles. His wife died at the age of eighty-nine in Los Angeles in November 1939. She was the sister of Mrs. C. A. Lee of Dawson and an aunt of Mrs. S. E. Doidge, west of Perry, and Bruce Kelsey of Dawson.

Skating Prodigy (1882)

It was in the winter of 1882-1883 that W. H. Chandler had a big run at his roller skating rink above his new implement store. Old and young got the fever and attendance was large every night. The excitement continued and in February 1884, Chandler leased the rink to W. E. Sidney, an engineer at Climax Mine No. 1 at Angus. Under Sidney's management, there was renewed interest in skating in Perry. John Dignan looked after a great part of the management for Sidney.

Sidney had a delicate boy less than four years of age whom he tried vainly to keep away from the rink. But John Dignan was the boy's friend and he cut down the smallest pair of skates in the rink for him, though they were still several sizes too large. It wasn't long until the little lad was darting among the skaters as gracefully as any of them. The first notice made of him appeared in *The Perry Chief* on April 11, 1884.

The four-year-old named Willie Sidney had developed a remarkable skill on skates and did many of the fancy figures with ease and teased to be taught more. A pair of his shoes were sent to the factory and a pair of skates made for him. With these the boy's skills developed rapidly and there was a call for him all over the United States.

In the Princess Rink in Chicago, Willie Sidney was awarded two costly medals, also in Denver, and everywhere else he went. His admirers in Perry presented him with a solid silver cup filled with coins. The presentation speech was made by Norris Brown while Walter Cardell responded for the boy.

After a tour of nearly a year, Willie was put in school at Frankfort, Indiana, where he was in 1895 at age eleven.

Chapter Two
The Liquor Game

The Union Block

This picture of the Union building was taken before November 1910 as there were no street lights or paving. The car was mired down on Second Street before the buildings, which were burned down in a spectacular fire in January 1920. They were located north of the First National Bank and north of the alley to Warford on the west side of the street.

Redfield Smashers (1866)

Forty-four years before Carrie Nation came to Perry to explain how and why she smashed saloons, the women of Redfield had already perfected the art.

In the year 1866, there was a saloon in Redfield which had a most unsavory reputation. The women of the community finally took it upon themselves to rid the town of the nuisance. They armed themselves with axes and hatchets and raided the place, smashing everything breakable. When they were through, it looked as though a cyclone had struck the place.

The saloon keeper filed charges and warrants were sworn out for the arrest of the women in the case entitled: *The State of Iowa v. Sarah Lawback and Others*. Twenty-six women were indicted and their husbands were present at the trial.

A change of venue was granted and the trial was moved into a Perry school house. Justice of the Peace Thornburg presided. The trial was held at the Potts school near the Thornburg home northeast of Perry. Captain J. Reed was the state's attorney; the women were represented by a Winterset attorney.

The crowd at the trial was so large that the floor of the school gave way, making it necessary to move the court to the Alton School west of Perry. The floor that gave way was but three or four inches from the ground, so the spectators go only a little bump.

After a week spent taking testimony, Justice Thornburg dismissed all the charges against the women. He ruled that the saloon was a nuisance and the women had taken the only available option in abating it. Reed was of the same opinion. The women were not even fined.

The Liquor Game (1889-1907)

From the time of the Blue Goose Saloon, liquor made for quite a game in Perry's early days. Like a child's game of cowboys and Indians or cops and robbers, it was the booze fighters trying to stop the booze sellers and booze guzzlers.

It had been some time since any effort had been made to enforce the Prohibition laws in Perry that summer of 1889, and the violators had grown exceedingly bold. The approaching Fourth of July celebration raised speculation that a goodly supply would be on hand for the occasion. So, law enforcement officers with civilian help held a surprise party on several joints.

Warrants in Justice Thornburg's court had been sworn out by four good and true prominent women — Mrs. A.S. Capen, Mrs. Goodman, Mrs. Hoyle and Mrs. Stephens — and were served by Constable Elliott. They were assisted by six equally good and true men — Cal Carhill, H.A. Hoyt, the Reverend Mr. Coffman, H.M. Townsend, R. Stephens and the Reverend Mr. Little.

Several places were raided on July 3, and the search uncovered about thirty cases of "Malt Mead" as well as some bottles "in use." According to the law, the liquor must be stored until a hearing was held.

The day before the date of the trial, someone with more thirst than respect for the law broke into the "secret" place of storage and stole the evidence. The contraband had been hidden in a cellar under the U.S. Express office.

The door at the rear of the DeLa and Oldham Marble Works had a glass out, boards nailed across it and propped shut. It was a simple matter to get into the cellar and through a door into the next room. The liquor was carried out and put in a spring wagon and taken across the first track of the Rock Island. This was easy to deduce as the culprits left their lantern on the track beside the path they made.

There were no condemnation proceedings in Justice Thornburg's court. The subject of the hearing was absent.

One day in July 1900, when it was rumored that "wet goods" had been shipped to Perry, the members of the Ministerial Association decided to do a little enforcing of the law themselves.

Several bills of information were sworn out before Justice Lee Thornburg and warrants placed in Constable Elliot's hands.

The first was for the seizure of a quantity of liquid alleged to be contained in a railroad car standing in the Milwaukee yards east of the city.

There was a delay because the bill of information did not have the number of the car to be searched. A trip to the depot was necessary to get this, but by then the fact that a search was about to be made had leaked out.

When the officers returned to the yard, the car wanted (along with two or three others) was being switched up and down the yards at a rate that defied a search. Finally, with the car in its train, the engine rushed passed the depot, over the crossing and on to points west. Thus the search was frustrated.

As early as 1902, it was said Perry was supporting from four to six saloons. Information on six places was filed before Justice Lods and six warrants were sworn out.

Sheriff Hanes came up from Adel on a Milwaukee train at noon. After dinner at the Stewart House, he called on Justice Lods for instruction and his papers, then summoned Constable Dave Willis, Marshal Resser, and Deputy George Greer. After a council of war, the four separated, going to different saloons. They found two had closed. A place on the Triangle was one of the ports of call for Sheriff Hanes and Marshal Resser. No one was there but a young bartender.

Meanwhile, Dave Willis had gone to a place over by the old post office. There, he found what the search warrant had called for and took possession of the goods. Willis secured Charles Maurer's dray and had the contraband loaded — twelve full cases of beer, one case partly full, and two half-pints of whiskey.

From this place, the dray was backed up in front of the place on the Triangle and one full case of beer was loaded there. Not liking all the publicity, the proprietor asked the officers to go around back, which they did. With Willis on the wagon and the sheriff in the place to see that all the contraband was loaded, they made quite a haul — eleven cases of beer and one quart bottle of whiskey.

The dray was taken to a place near Lane's Blacksmith Shop, as it was alleged that three cases a day were sold there. All were taken to Squire Lods' office to be stored until the time of the trial. The load of liquor attracted much attention as the dray made the rounds and was followed by a great crowd. This had been the sheriff's first experience in searching for liquor and he was proud of his success.

When the booze was placed on trial, no one appeared in its defense. It was given the death sentence. Sheriff Hanes came from Adel with Resser, armed with axes. They drove to Shotwell's little duck pond west of Standard Oil's place along the Milwaukee tracks where the sentence was carried out.

Though handy with axes, it was tiresome work — 500 bottles to be broken one at a time; twenty-three cases to be chopped into kindling wood and two barrels to be broken into pieces. The sheriff and his deputy took their time and rested occasionally.

In August 1907, ten barrels filled with bottles, three of them with the filled bottles packed in hay, were found in a shed just west of the Wolfe block. Constable Lee Thornburg loaded this merchandise onto a dray and took it to a secret place, which the newspaper duly reported was in the Citizens' Bank Building., The trial was set before Justice A.D. Haskins.

When the officers assembled in the bank building on the Saturday morning of the trial date to take up the case and condemn the liquor seized, it was found that it had been seized again. Friday evening, someone had entered the room where the liquor had been stored, lowered the booze from a window over the back post office window and carted it away.

L.A. French was the first to enter the building that morning and, seeing the hay in the hallway, asked Justice Haskins who had been feeding horses in the building. The Justice eyed the scattered packing, then made a dash for the keys to the booze room.

He didn't need a key; the door was unlocked and the barrels and the bottles were gone. Some dropped hay indicated that the team was driven east, but the early morning breezes erased the trail as thoroughly as the officers had hoped to erase the booze. The trial was postponed indefinitely.

And so it went. Each new administration promised things would be different. But, they never were — at least not in those early days when the subject was liquor.

Ladies Visit Saloon (1895)

The story was told about the time when in May 1895, twenty ladies of Perry visited one of the saloons all day long taking their handwork with them. As there were but six chairs, the saloon keeper rolled out beer kegs for seats and the ladies professed to be very comfortable and were very sociable. They stayed until dark, then some rogue covered the chimney of the building and smoked out the visitors.

But, anyway, the ladies had the fun of spoiling the day's sales in that saloon, for as each customer came rushing in and caught sight of the merry, chattering crowd of women perched on beer kegs, he backed out quicker than he came, slamming the door behind him, glad to get out of the locality.

Water Gets Him in Trouble (1901)

Mayor J.E. Wilson was an upright citizen and should have been a good mayor. But, he had problems once in office. Even his election was a near thing. In the election of 1901, there were only twelve votes separating Wilson and Frank Dodson.

Wilson's friends had circulated promises he'd keep the town clean of liquor joints, gambling houses and other resorts. And the work of cleaning up was begun within a week of the election. Several times the joints had been closed, only to open up in another location.

The keepers openly declared that they couldn't be kept from selling liquor, stating that their attorneys had said the ordinance passed by the council against such places was invalid. They threatened to go to court. Every fresh arrest would mean a fresh suit and that would cost the city plenty. The law wasn't clear. Saloons and joints seemed to fall under the official jurisdiction of the county.

If that were the case, the Mayor said, he would not attempt to prosecute under the city law, but under the state law. The state law was more severe and its legality had been tested. Hence, Marshal Resser notified the joints to close and stay that way. But, the joints didn't scare worth a nickel.

When suspicion became strong that there was beer being sold in a joint on Warford, Marshal Resser and Deputy Greer, armed with a search warrant, investigated. They found a case of suspicious liquid and sent it to Des Moines for testing. The proprietor said he'd have another case on tap in half an hour. The marshal said that if he did, he'd be back around to seize it. The joint keeper kept his word and so did the marshal. The proprietor of the joint swore to continue in business and the officials threatened to make it hot for him if he did.

For a time the liquor nuisance abated. The mayor and the authorities took out after Perry's gambling dens. There was no legal question concerning these. It took only the word of the mayor to close these and he gave the word. Some machines were removed, others were turned to face the wall.

Then came the wholesale seizure of liquor in December 1902, which created great consternation in the camp of the jointists. They didn't know what to do or what to expect. Their attorneys gave them no encouragement. They agreed to "be good," but leaders of the law enforcement crusade put no faith in their promises.

It seemed a strong band of men had agreed and pledged to see that the law was enforced. If the officers couldn't do it, they would. They gathered evidence and they proposed to convict the jointists of illegal sales and to secure permanent injunctions. Even the owners of the buildings would find themselves defendants in a suit.

Of course, this did not kill the liquor business, but it did lay dormant for a time. While Wilson was earning high marks for his fight against liquid spirits, it took pure water to get him in trouble.

For some years residents living near the waterworks had carried their water from the pump house, thereby saving water rent. The council had threatened to stop this practice and most property owners put in water connections. It so happened that the matter usually came up when the ground was frozen and it was impossible to put in city water at the time. Many, however, did as soon as the frost was out of the ground.

At a meeting in June 1902, the council instructed the water committee to shut off the hydrant on the east side of the pump house and not to allow families to carry water from there.

This triggered a series of letters to *The Perry Chief* signed "The Kicker" about how the council was making a fuss about a few poor people getting free water when the mayor was getting free water from the Milwaukee depot for his lumber yard. The mayor answered by saying that the grounds upon which his lumber yard were located were the property of the C.M. & St. P. Railroad and that the company furnished water for its tenant.

To this the Kicker retaliated by pointing out that the company had no right to furnish water without taking out a permit and paying for it. Furthermore, the Kicker added, the Neola Elevator Company, Standard Oil, and Shotwell and Davis were on leased ground on exactly the same terms as the mayor's lumber yard and they were paying for their water.

The newspaper never seemed to record how these little skirmishes ended. *The Chief* only noted that about a year later, in August 1903, Wilson sold his lumber yard to H.C. Modlin.

Mayor Wilson carried out another official function on December 3, 1902, at the request of Cupid. Wilson went to the home of the prospective bride at 3:30 p.m. and, in the presence of immediate relatives, he united in marriage Dick Lane and May Cannon. The groom was twenty-one years of age and the bride eighteen.

Raid on the Union Block (1903)

The Union block seemed to be the focal point in the liquor traffic. According to widely circulated rumors, there was a sleeping room where the goods were sold and one across the hall where they were stored.

One Tuesday evening in April 1903, Marshal Dave Willis swore out a warrant before Mayor Frank Dodson for certain rooms in the Union block. Willis went up the front stairs and Deputy John Mitchell to back. They broke into the room supposedly containing the stock, but found a supply of empties. They did find the arrangement by which the liquor was hoisted up the back of the building.

In less than a month the building was searched again, as rumors continued to circulate that liquor was being sold there. This time Sheriff Hanes came up from Adel for the express purpose of making a search of the premises. He was unable to get into the rooms — even after breaking the lock. Not proposing to be outdone, the sheriff took an axe and broke down the door. All he found were empties.

The sheriff returned to Adel, as nothing could be done without evidence. The hoisting apparatus discovered in the first raid was gone; evidently, other means had been found to get the liquor upstairs.

The officials refused to give up. If liquor was being sold,

they'd keep on searching until the rogues violating the law were apprehended.

Again, in the last part of May, Marshal Willis and Deputy Mitchell arrived with a search warrant, marched up the stairway of the Union Block for the third time. This search was instigated by a report that a barrel of beer had been taken to one of the rooms that very day.

The two officers made a thorough search but, as usual, could find nothing. They were convinced, however, that beer had been there because the room raided smelled of beer, and so did the empty bottles and glasses.

The officers became justly indignant when people began to make remarks to the effect that the searchers could just as easily seize liquor as all the empty bottles if they really wanted to. It was also hinted that the jointists had been "put next" so they might get wet goods away before the officers arrived.

Still, the lawmen continued. The sheriff came up again from Adel, this time unbeknownst to any local officers; carried out a raid — and bagged the usual empties.

Perseverance finally paid off in July, when a raid on the Union Block turned up 132 bottles of Schlitz beer.

C.D. Jones: Man of Many Trades (1904-1928)

Of all of Perry's prominent people of the past, C. Durant Jones had to be the most ambitious, energetic, and versatile. More newspaper coverage was allotted to him than to anyone else before or since.

He was a newspaper publisher and writer, a minister, a politician, an orator, and a lecturer. He owned a college, established a chautauqua, and operated a motor bus line. Jones owned a construction company and he dealt in real estate. He was also in and out of court — sometimes a winner, sometimes a loser. He made news.

Jones came to Perry in December 1904. He had been editor of the *Waukee American*, but since the *Perry Advertiser* had been "converted to the true religion," it was his intention to start a newspaper in Perry strictly for Democrats.

He bought the Adrian Cross print shop (it had belonged to

Lewis Griswold until he was elected county clerk). The type, machinery and stock were moved to the room formerly occupied by Marks Music House. The first issue of *The Journal* (a weekly) came off the press January 5, 1905.

For years booze was the cause of the battle in Perry, and the pros and the cons had many a skirmish. It didn't take Jones and his *Journal* long to get into the fight. He made the Journal an evening daily at six cents a week in order to help the cause of prohibition. But, after three months, feeling the mission fulfilled, he returned to the weekly edition. *The Journal's* end came in January 1906.

Due to his record as a temperance worker in Perry, Jones was chosen as superintendent of the Federation of Iowa Law and Order League in February 1906. He gave up newspaper work to devote full time to the League. His headquarters were in Perry, but the new job required traveling all over the state to lecture and organize leagues. Not only did the organization deal with liquor, but with gambling and other vices as well.

Jones organized a league in Woodward in March 1906 for the purpose of fighting drug stores there. In April, a league was organized in Perry at the Presbyterian Church. Reverend Mr. Coakwell, pastor of the Christian Church, was the only minister able to attend.

April 1906 was also the month that Jones launched *The Pilot*. According to the editor, it was going to be a corker, so much of a corker that it would cork all whiskey barrels and bottles wherever it would circulate, with the expectations to make it a statewide publication. Jones, meanwhile, expected to donate all his time to the Perry Normal College, which he bought in May 1907 in order to keep it from being moved out of town.

Through it all, he was constantly on the trail of alleged liquor nuisances and gamblers, bringing charges against any and all regardless of whom they might be. He also was doing substitute preaching in the pulpit of the Christian Church.

Jones entered the political arena as a candidate for mayor of Perry in March 1909. He headed an independent ticket using the platform of governing from a prohibition standpoint, along which lines he'd been so active. He lost that race to Mayor H.C. Modlin.

In August, Jones left on a speaking tour which was about the time that *The Pilot* issued its last edition (August 27 1909). By March 1910 he had made so many speeches all over the state, that it was evident that there had been an awakening of the Prohibition Party. The post office also gained due to all the mailings which had been made.

Jones rose to prominence in the Prohibition Party and was named chairman of its Central Committee in 1911. He also rose in prominence in Perry during the 1911 race for mayor. This city election went down in local history as being a "turn 'em out campaign." In every ward, voting was fast and furious. With one exception, the entire Peoples Ticket headed by Jones was elected.

For Jones, being mayor was no ho-hum experience. He single-handedly cleared the Milwaukee depot of the army of hoboes that had camped there during cold nights. They stretched out on the floor and benches until travelers could not reach the ticket office window without kicking a sleeping man.

Jones answered a call one afternoon in March 1915, when a gang of tramps was reported to be molesting the children near the Washington School. The men were ordered out of town and, when four of them became obnoxious, the mayor and the marshal escorted them to the tracks. When near the depot, one fellow stepped behind the mayor and delivered a knockout blow. The marshal attempted to capture the assailant, but he escaped. Jones was picked up and the heavy flow of blood was stanched as well as possible. The wound was cared for at Drs. Nellie M. and Theodore F. Johnson's office.

During the time he was serving as mayor, Jones was also a candidate for governor of Iowa on the Prohibition Ticket. He left September 30, 1912, for Washington, Iowa, where he joined the party's presidential candidate and both started out on a speaking tour.

In one week, he made thirty-seven speeches from the back of his car. The faithful old Maxwell car, finally protested to this rigorous campaign and broke down twice near Mason City. Jones had pushed the old car all over the state, speaking twice at every village and discussing the liquor traffic at every hilltop.

Then the news of his business ventures began to overshadow his other interests. He started the manufacture of various products in his auto company building. He purchased the Cement Block Products business from receiver H.M Shively. Along with this went nine lots the company owned on Railroad Street, eight of them utilized for the building and storage yards. Jones also got the small parcel of land at the corners of Otley and Railroad streets in the angle of the electric light plant and Waters garage.

On May 15, 1913, Jones announced that a new garage was to be built on Railroad Street just north of the Shotwell and Davis plant. Ground was broken on May 17 for the building just south of the cement works. The next venture was to build concrete residences. By December, he had twenty-six buildings under construction and more than 100 men on the payroll. He signed a contract with Henry Wiese for the construction of a two-story block building on the west side of Wiese's lot on Lucinda, opposite Lester's Livery barn. Along with this there was also the Jones Realty Company.

A motor bus line was added to the city on January 8, 1914. The car left from the north Jones garage at 6:20 a.m. and every hour after that until 9:20 p.m. The line ended at First and Park on the north and the Dilenback addition to the east. The fare was ten cents; children under five, free; and children from five to ten years of age rode for five cents. The cars were designated by flags and stopped anywhere on the scheduled route.

Patronage the first day was hardly sufficient to justify the continuance of the service. The first passenger was a resident of the Dilenback addition and his destination was the new roundhouse, but the service to the roundhouse had not yet started, so it was necessary to get off at West Ninth and walk the rest of the way. That was the sole passenger of that first day.

The second day reports showed three times the number of patrons, and arrangements were being made with the Shorthill Steel and Ironworks to arrange a time for the benefit of the workers there. Only one car was in service, but a second one was kept constantly at the garage in case of an accident or break-down. After an advertisement in *The Chief* on February 25, there seemed to be no further mention of this business.

Overwork and poor health forced Jones to take several vacations and he began to ease out of some of his activities. The chautauqua was still operating, he was still active in "dry work," still going on lecture tours, and writing columns for various newspapers.

Jones apparently left Perry in 1928. In 1931, he took up radio work in Amarillo, Texas. He had been invited to host a program and the public showed so much interest through calls and letters that he was given a weekly program. Jones lived out the rest of his life in Amarillo. He died January 15, 1966, just a few weeks before his ninety-first birthday.

Unique Bonfire (1905)

In November 1905, there was a unique bonfire that differed from all others. This one was fed by wet fuel and made a very hot fire.

Marshal Dave Willis piled the five barrels, the cases and two boxes in a circle, with an opening in the center in which he placed the two kegs of whiskey. He smashed the heads of the kegs, touched a match to it, and away it went.

The bottles popped and the flames leaped high in the air. The fire was still smoldering the next morning when Mr. Curler went out to dig a hole for the remains of the fire.

Witnesses at the official cremation — in addition to the Curler family — included Doc Resser, Andy Maxwell, and J.H. Moore. The scene was in the Curler garden at their home at Fifth and Otley. This location later became the site of the Christian Science Church.

Carrie Nation, the Smasher (1910)

Carrie Nation, the notorious hatchet swinging Kansas reformer and temperance agitator, came to Perry in September 1910 and gave one of her famous speeches. She came under the auspices of the local suffrage group.

The lecture was given at the Methodist Church; admission was twenty-five cents. A large crowd filled the auditorium. Many attended out of curiosity to see the woman who had been in the limelight for so many years; others came because they believed the woman was earnest and sincere in her crusade against vice in all its forms.

The subject of her talk was: "How I Smashed, Why I Smashed, And How You May Smash." She was introduced by Rev. J.H. Thuresson of the Methodist Church. After a prayer by the Reverend Mr. Burleigh, the audience sang "America the Beautiful." Mrs. Nation, as usual, led in the singing.

The address was a strong denunciation of the liquor business, the tobacco users, the church members who did not live up to their teachings, and the Republican Party — especially the latter. There were a few good words for the ministers, but the Republican Party was hopeless. Everyone from the Republican mayor of Perry to the Republican president of the United States came in for a roasting.

President Howard Taft was an "infidel;" Speaker Gannon was a "bulldog;" and Theodore Roosevelt the biggest hypocrite of them all. The Republican newspapers were recipients of a few pot shots; the Republican preachers, who talked temperance but did not vote that way, were also scorched.

Mrs. Nation spoke in support of the Prohibition Party. When she called on those who wanted to see a Prohibition government to stand up, most of the audience rose to their feet. Then she asked those who wished to see a Republican government to stand; no one moved. When she asked those Democrats present to stand up, Mayor Sol Johnson of Rippey was the only person who did. Mrs. Nation said she was glad to see one man with the courage of his convictions.

After she had paid her respects to the Republican Party, she went after the tobacco users, saying: "Hell is the last smokehouse for some of you fellows." She then denounced pool halls.

Mrs. Nation told the story of her life; how after suffering for a long time because her husband was a drunk, she took matters into her own hands. She told of how much money she had made and what she had done with it. She said she had been in jail thirty-four times. She had her autobiography for sale, as well as little gold hatchets. One of those hatchets is preserved in the Hastie Museum.

During her discussion, Mrs. Nation paid tribute to motherhood and expressed sentiments on the subject with which everyone agreed.

Fire: The Final Raider (1920)

On January 26, 1917, D.D. McCall and E.D. Carter purchased the block just south of William Wolfe's Union block from the Goff Estate. These buildings were on the west side of Second

Fire of 1920

A mysterious fire had occurred in the Union Block in January 1909. Smoke issued from Allan's China Shop for two hours before the fire broke out in Reid's Jewelry Store. Total loss to the William Wolfe Building in that fire was $10,000. Damage from that fire paled in comparison to the disastrous 1920 fire in the same block, the results of which are shown above.

Street, from Warford south, the Union block on the corner and the Carter-McCall block south of it to the alley.

J.C. Atkins bought the buildings the first of January 1920, and took possession January 15.

Businesses in the Union block in 1920 were: W.W. Pope Drug Store, Mission Pool Hall, Keenan Cigar Store, Reith's Tailor Shop, Express Co., and Dr. H.E. Cobb, dentist.

Businesses in the Carter-McCall block south to the alley were: Perry Candy Kitchen (Gus Poulos); Olympian Candy Kitchen (Athens George); Schaeffer Grocery Co.; Nolan and Olean; Jones Brothers; and Dr. M.M. Lynch.

A disastrous fire broke out shortly after midnight in late January 1920, with an estimated loss of $140,000.

Before the flames were under control, the buildings were in ruins. Officer J.E. O'Malley first saw the smoke issuing from the second floor of the Union building at the northwest corner, the fire apparently starting in an empty room. O'Malley turned in the alarm and both trucks were on the scene in a few minutes.

The buildings were originally frame structures, but had been veneered with brick, so the flames spread rapidly. The Keenan Smoke House and the Mission Pool Hall were soon a fiery furnace. The Candy Kitchen caught a few minutes later. The W.W. Pope Drug Store next door south was ablaze in ten or fifteen minutes.

It was thought that the firewall here would contain it. However, there was no firewall between the two buildings. The flames soon broke through.

Thousands of barrels of water were thrown and the pumps kept working on the LaFrance truck at a rate of 800 gallons a minute.

Nearly every other business block in the neighborhood was threatened. The Phillips, Tiernan and Sherman Store was besieged with sparks. Several small fires started on the roof, but were extinguished by the use of chemicals. The Gamble Furniture Co. and the Rude Garage were protected, but the firemen and the patrons of the Hotel Pattee had a bad scare.

Athens George, proprietor of the Olympian Candy Kitchen, had a heavy loss because so much of his stock could not be carried out. W.W. Pope saved a few valuable fixtures and his books. The Schaeffer Grocery Co. got out a few things in addition to the contents of the safe.

The loss to Roy Keenan of the Mission Pool Hall and the tailor William Reith was almost total; much of the contents of the Express office were lost. Dr. Cobb saved part of his office equipment, as did Dr. Lynch. Nolan and Olean and Jones Brothers, who had offices on the second floor of the Carter-McCall building, saved nothing.

The members of the fire department worked steadily for twelve hours before being relieved. They were in danger on numerous occasions. They suffered from the cold and the soaking, but stayed on with only a few minutes off in relays for breakfast and lunch. Restaurants and individuals furnished hot coffee, dry clothing, and mittens throughout the night.

The American LaFrance truck, purchased only three years earlier, proved its worth. Pumping began at 12:15 a.m. and continued until afternoon without as much as a skip of the cylinders. Verne Council was kept busy carrying gasoline and cylinder oil, but that was all the motor needed.

A humorous little story circulated the streets of Perry in the aftermath of the fire. It was rumored that five or six Perry men had a narrow escape from the burning building. They only talked about it amongst themselves, but enough conversation had been overheard to piece together a sensational story.

It seems that some men had gathered around a card table in a back room of the Union Block when the fire broke out in another part of the building. So intent were they on the game that they did not hear the crackling of flames nor smell the smoke until someone opened the door.

Money was forgotten. The one thought uppermost in the minds of all was to get out and the one way to get out was the window. They made a rush and went through it much as the fellows went over the top in France.

From the window to the first landing place was a small jump and then by leaping from the first shed to another, they all managed to get away safely. When they struck the alley pavement, they "lit running."

The truth of the story was borne out by the actions of several fellows poking around in the ruins the following day.

After J.C. Atkins of the Atkins Land Company had purchased the William Wolfe property known as the Union block, he said he intended to tear down the old buildings and put up a new, modern, fire-proof structure three stories high. The Carter-McCall block was also transferred to the Land company; so they had possession of the entire tract from Warford to the alley.

Charles Grilk, of Davenport, purchased the burned out area in March 1922. An announcement was made in 1926 by Mrs. C.W. Bice and Mrs. Jennie Jensen of plans to erect a new brick building on the corner to be occupied by the J.C. Penney Company.

Chapter Three
City Government

The Old Engine House

The Old Engine House with its "tin horn" fire bell. Perry City Council meetings were held upstairs in this building for many years.

Jail House (1877)

The city fathers realized early a jail would be needed, and one was built the week of June 10, 1877. It was fourteen feet by sixteen feet of two inch by six inch lumber, spiked together. It was located west of the railroad tracks on Willis, handy to the Blue Goose Saloon, and just in time for the Fourth of July trade.

After the town hall was built in 1880, the jail was moved to this structure. In August 1886, it was refitted to stop leaks. Prisoners could almost blow out of it. In 1892, the jail was moved back of the city building and put into better condition.

About 2 a.m. November 22, 1900, the fire department was called out to save the city calaboose. A tramp housed there built a hot fire, and the roof was nearly burned off. After the fire, the tramp couldn't be found. The jail was re-roofed and re-chimneyed and the work was rushed along to accommodate the holiday trade.

It was reported in June 1903, that the city prison was such a disgrace no respectable hobo would stay in it five minutes. He wouldn't have to — even a cheap pocket knife was sufficient to make a get-away. As the jail became a more popular place, the general feeling was that it should be made more substantial.

Therefore, in 1904, the city decided to build a jail in the rear twenty feet of the new fire station. The council appropriated $750 to the fire department for this project in April 1905.

It was often said that the county jail should have been in Perry because Perry had sent more men to jail than any other town in the county. It was not known if that was because there were more bad men or a better police force.

On a Monday afternoon in September 1904, Dave Willis, with the assistance of one of the Milwaukee detectives, rounded up a half dozen suspicious characters who were drunk. Between the time they were jailed, which was about 5:30 p.m. and dark, one or more of their cronies stole a crowbar from the Rock Island section house and gave it to the men in jail to make an escape.

Willis was about as spry as they were, and stationed a night watch at the jail to be on duty till daylight with orders to shoot the first prisoner who attempted to escape. He did not have to use the rifle, however, as the temperature became quite chilly before morning and the fellows were content to remain in jail where it was warm while the night watch patrolled the beat in the cold.

Tuesday morning they were taken before the mayor on charges of intoxication. All gave a name, except one man who put up a plea of being deaf and dumb. When the mayor wrote on a piece of paper that the un-named man had been sentenced to thirty days in jail, he grunted loudly. All the accused were found guilty and all got thirty-day sentences.

Perry's jail was not always a safe place. A lone prisoner had a bad scare in November 1914, when a small plug in the radiator blew out and he was forced to climb to the top of the cage to keep out of the hot water.

The man was a prisoner of Sheriff George Ross. Chief of Police Pat McGoeye discovered the prisoner's predicament and rescued him from the top of the cell. The accident was not all bad: the jail received a much needed scrubbing and had hot water for the job.

Harry Markress of the Rall Shoe Store was jailed the afternoon of December 12, 1924, by Chief of Police Ed Trouth. No charge was filed against Markress; the only reason they placed him in jail was to take some moving pictures of him behind bars. Markress was just one of a big cast of local people who were taking part in the making of a moving picture, which was cast in Perry. After taking the pictures, Markress was released from jail.

"Careless Gus" was the name of the movie being filmed. Clyde Edmondson was chosen to take the title role. The picture was being made under the supervision of O.D. Tinley of Corning. Tinley had taken a number of photographs in Perry some years earlier.

Council Meetings In Old Engine House (1880-1904)

Perry's Town Hall, erected in 1880, became a sorry looking place over the years. It was feared that some day the plaster would fall on the city fathers' heads. In February 1893, as feared, the plaster did fall. The way the whole ceiling played tic-tac-toe on the rough floor was beyond *The Chief*'s power of reporting. Three years then elapsed with the city hall question dormant.

Records of 1894 show the hall was a room over the hose carts and was a little longer than the carts. A long table and seven chairs occupied the center. A homely old stove, an empty coal box, and a chip basket stood in one corner. What impressed the reporter present for the meeting was the absence of chairs for the public. None for the visitors or the public — and worst of all, none for the reporters (which might explain why *The Advertiser* and *The Reporter* did not cover the meeting).

At the October 1894 meeting, *The Chief* reporter sat "on the verge of despair, first on the window sill; then on the coal box; and then, leaned against the wall. Marshal Willis grew tired of being hung on the wall and he moved the council to secure more chairs, but the motion died for want of a second."

The agenda for that meeting was a long, but interesting one. Explosion insurance on the waterworks was considered, but it was decided that the city didn't want it. Two more arc lights were ordered; one for Second and Pattee, the other for First and Willis. Licenses for Willis' Hall were fixed at $12.

Mayor Allen Breed suggested an ordinance ordering all boys under seventeen and all girls under sixteen off the streets by 9 p.m. When it was mentioned that enforcing this curfew would require hiring an extra policeman, the matter was dropped.

As the final matter, Mr. James Wimmer reported that the new waterworks house was completed at a total cost of about $1,170. The report and the building were accepted.

The death knell for the plans for a new city hall sounded in 1902. In November, the council was still meeting in a room better suited as a robbers' rendezvous. Against such gloom and evidence of poverty, it was no wonder the council always felt the town of Perry was poor.

That night the mayor and all councilmen were snugly ensconced in overcoats, collars turned up, hands in pockets, and heads turned toward heaven to see when the next piece of plaster would fall. The room was heated by a stove pipe and lighted by two dim lights.

At the December meeting, the council decided the old weather-beaten, worn-out, dilapidated building had to be repaired.

The mayor appointed the street and alley commission to look after it, and gave the commission the power to act. That did not include the power to tear down the existing city hall, according to the city solicitor in response to a query by the mayor.

Later that month, the council held an adjourned session in the "new" old town hall. It was the same old location; same old steps; same old door, but with a new spring lock. The same old floor was in evidence and the woodwork had new paint on it. Two more electric lights were put in and broken windows repaired. A stove that cost $8 was provided. The table and two benches were painted and sixty cents worth of oilcloth attached to the table with fifteen cents worth of brass tacks. The old walls were covered with paper costing twenty-five cents a roll; fourteen rolls were used. The labor came to $12.30.

Relief finally came for the councilmen. In August 1904, they moved their quarters to the library basement where they could grind out city business in style. The firemen decided to erect a building for themselves.

Police Required at Voting Precincts

A special meeting of the council in 1886 was held to appoint two policemen for each voting precinct as required by law.

Fred Griswald and A.J. Flinn were appointed for the First Ward; N.E. Hart and A.W. Parmenter for the Second Ward; and J.C. Sides and William Hunter for the Third Ward.

City Suits (1891-1900)

Using the courts to settle disagreements is not new. The young Perry often found itself on the receiving end of a damage suit and at considerable drain on the treasury.

When Ed Willis discovered the flowing well in Perry he started a bath house. Then the city put in its water system and used the water from these wells. This interfered with Willis' business and he offered to settle for $65. Mayor Allen Breed and some of the other council members thought it would be in the city's best interest not to pay him even that much.

The matter was taken to the District Court and the city was defeated. A new trial was secured which resulted in a judgment of $450 in favor of Mollie H. Willis. The city appealed to the Supreme Court, where the decision of the lower court was upheld. The judgment and costs amounted to $1,050.

The mayor and all members of the council met in special session on December 20, 1894, for the purpose of providing means to meet that judgment. The case of *Willis v. Perry* had at last been settled but at a heavy expense — a special tax was necessary to pay the judgment.

A tax of two mills on the dollar of the assessed valuation of all taxable property in the corporation was levied. At that time the assessed value of property in Perry was $516,534. The two mills brought in a little more than $2,000 and, since it was levied in halves (half in the spring, the other half in the fall) the council thought the ordinary property holder would scarcely notice the additional tax.

The results of suits against the town were not all negative. It was the result of several suits against the city which gave Perry its fine system of cement sidewalks. The old plank walks around Perry had become a real hazard. In many places the stringers were rotten and the boards loose and warped.

In early January 1897, Mrs. J.E. Grace met with an accident while walking along west Second Street. She was with a little girl who stepped on a loose board, causing the woman to fall on her face. Her nose was broken and she was otherwise badly bruised.

Not quite a week later, in the early afternoon, Hannah Townsend fell at the first crossing south of the Triangle and was badly bruised. Later the same day, at the same crosswalk, Mrs. Earnest Lester fell and was also badly bruised.

At their regular meeting in February, the city council received a communication from Mrs. Grace demanding payment in the amount of $2,000 for injuries received in her fall, claiming impairment of sight, hearing, sense of smell, and breathing. The letter was referred to the city solicitor. Notice was served on the mayor that a suit had been filed.

The case was set for trial on a Tuesday afternoon in April. Shortley and Harpel appeared on behalf of the plaintiff, and Cardell and Giddings and Edmund Nichols represented the city.

The jury returned a verdict of $350 damages, a compromise which satisfied neither party. The city had hoped for an award under $200 which would have thrown the costs on the plaintiff. Attorney fees were expected to be between $400 and $500.

In September 1897, another verdict was rendered against the city because a man stubbed his toe on a warped board. The previous March, C.B. Mecum had caught his foot on a loose board near the Ginn property on First Avenue and was somewhat injured.

He sued the city for $8,000 and the case was decided September 3, in District Court, resulting in another $350 verdict against Perry. Shortley and Harpel conducted the case for the plaintiff, while City Solicitor Giddings and Nichols represented the city.

The city fathers were getting tired of these suits. An ordinance went before the council in late 1897 which prevented putting down plank walks. Temporary walks could be made of gravel or cinders.

In July 1898, the council passed the long-expected resolution providing for the construction of cement walks covering practically the whole city. This brought about a hassle between Perry's newspapers.

The Perry Advertiser accused *The Perry Chief* of beating the tom-tom when it brought up the subject of the council skipping the Milwaukee right-of-way when ordering the walks. It was pointed out that the walks were ordered, but neither the Milwaukee nor the Rock Island had complied. The superintendent of the Milwaukee had been in town in the summer of 1899 and informed the council that it could not force the railroad to lay cement, but he courteously agreed to put in plank walks and keep them repaired. The offer was accepted.

By August 1900, the cement walks were being put in. The following summer, many other cities were preparing to follow Perry's lead. The mayor and councilmen of Manilla, Harlan, and Marion came to inspect Perry's splendid system.

Residents on Willis west of Frog Creek had no sidewalk, so they constructed their own cinder paths, then began complaining loudly because others took to driving cattle and horses on the path instead of the road. Perry's sidewalk system was again improved and lengthened under Works Progress Administration project in 1941.

H.A. Chappelear (1876-1897)

Some of the pioneers having a prominent role in the history of Perry had their contributions to the town commemorated through the naming of streets, parks, or buildings after them. And some have descendants of the same name who still live in Perry.

The name of one pioneer emerges from the past has had no street, park, building, or lodge named for him. His descendants, if there are any, do not have his name. Yet he was well known in the early days. His influence was felt and his life was interesting and varied. Even his name was intriguing.

Henderson Alexander Chappelear lived in Ohio and was in

Henderson Alexander Chappelear

his 40s before coming to Iowa and Perry in 1869. His name appeared in an 1876 issue of *The Perry Chief* as being a partner with Colonel Otley in the real estate and insurance business. This partnership lasted until 1882 when Otley retired. It is said Chappelear built the ninth house in Perry.

Chappelear was named a Justice of the Peace sometime in 1881. As such, his name flared into prominence through the various trials reported in the newspaper. His court tried a variety of cases — assault, wife beating, fights between women, fights between hack drivers, forgery, and many causes in which the defendant was beer.

After one trial in which a man had sued another for services rendered, the high-strung loser called his honor a liar. The Squire was quite an old man, but at this insult all his youthful vigor returned and Chappelear physically rushed the man from his office. The Squire was a good man, but he was also an angry man when his dignity was insulted.

Once while a forgery case was in progress, the U.S. Marshal from Des Moines appeared in Chappelear's court and literally snatched away the defendant who was also wanted for robbing the mails. The trial ended abruptly as the U.S. Court was bigger than Squire Chappelear's.

In fourteen years as a justice, he married more than sixty couples, which was quite a record considering the number of other justices and ministers in town. In 1896, he had the distinction of officiating at the first Negro wedding to take place in Perry.

There was one scheduled wedding the Squire almost missed. A couple had made arrangements to be married at 8 p.m. in his office, but events of a busy day put the appointment right out of mind. When the evening church bell sounded, as was his custom, Chappelear made his way to the sanctuary, removed his coat, seated himself, settled back to listen to the services. Suddenly the eight o'clock appointment flashed to mind. Chappelear rushed to his office, made two people happy and returned to the church in time for the sermon.

Suave and debonair in manner, Chappelear was a gentleman of the old school and wore his years with dignity which won him the respect of the community. Frequently during his public career he sought to return to private life, but his friends, appreciating his integrity, refused to give consent.

The office of coroner was given him in 1871, and in 1893 he sought election to the post, feeling he should ask for it in the regular manner. As coroner Chappelear was called upon to investigate many tragedies. There was death by black damp in a well, by runaway horses, by drowning in the river, by train accidents, and even death by unknown assailants — all recorded in *The Perry Chief* in precise and horrible detail.

Chappelear's wife, the former Ruth Newton whom he had married in 1841 while still in Ohio, died at their home on First Avenue in 1893. That winter he stayed downtown, taking a sleeping apartment in the Masonic block and his meals at restaurants.

Then, in a surprise move, in 1894 the Squire went to Chicago and there married Miss Bessie Stem on June 23. Chappelear brought her to Perry to live. But the following January she, too, was dead.

On May 1, 1896, Chappelear went to Kansas City and on May 15 he was again married, this time to the former Mrs. Mollie

Ebhart. The couple returned to Perry to make their home.

That year, Chappelear became the victim of a long illness, but rallied and was able to walk downtown and to perform the duties of his office. Also that year Chappelear was a candidate for coroner.

In June of the following year, he was taken ill again and, after nine weeks of paralysis, died on August 4, 1897. He was seventy-nine. Three of his children survived him: a daughter (Mrs. Hall) who lived in Perry; and two sons who lived in the western part of the country.

The Squire was at one time an exhorter in the Methodist Church and was a charter member of the local church. During his years in Perry he contributed much to the early establishment and growth of the Methodist Church. He was a spirited public official, a businessman, and a member of the Masonic Lodge.

On April 11, 1898, Chappelear's widow moved to Des Moines, taking all her household goods to open a boarding house there.

No Night Watch (1904)

When Night Marshal John Mitchell handed in his resignation in April 1904, Perry was without night protection for the first time in many years. Mitchell had been working nights just to accommodate the mayor.

The businessmen of the city had been paying the larger part of his salary, but most of his time was utilized by the city. This was the cause of the dissatisfaction. The businessmen asked the city to pay the marshal a larger salary and relieve them of the burden for which they received no results.

The matter was hotly contested in the council chambers and the city council decided in a unanimous vote that they would not pay more than the $20 allowance which had been granted for several years. So, the businessmen hired a block man whose sole duty was to look after their interests at night and let the city employ a policeman at whatever salary they saw fit to pay.

Then the mayor called a special council session to reconsider their action. Mitchell was urged to take the businessmen's offer, but he refused. He didn't like the idea of going around to the businessmen each month and collecting sums varying from 25 cents to a dollar. Mitchell stated he would, however, be interested if the city would pay a reasonable salary.

Numerous disturbances at night impressed upon property owners and businessmen that something had to be done. The council moved first, increasing the salary to $30, but finally agreed to pay $45 a month. With this pay plan in place, the mayor appointed W.J. Pryor night watchman.

Superior Court (1907)

Most likely the Superior Court was organized in Perry as a matter of convenience. In the early 1900s Adel was not easily accessible and the District Court terms were usually overloaded with cases.

The question of a Superior Court came up in the 1907 city election after a strenuous effort by the Perry Commercial Club. It was necessary to get the state legislature to amend the state law in order for a new court to be established.

The Superior Court superseded the mayor's court. Any civil suit in equity or at law (except divorce matters) could be brought before the Superior Court from any part of the county. The new court was in operation most of the time.

The question of quarters for the court became a primary concern. Those who were trying to get the court established appeared before the library board and asked that the basement room (then unoccupied) be set aside as a courtroom. There was considerable opposition, but the use of the room as a court was granted through January 1, 1909. Governor Cummins appointed Judge Fahey to the new position and he was sworn in at Adel on April 12, 1907.

The first session began on May 21, 1907. It was nearly 10 a.m. when Marshal Pat McGoeye called the hearing and the judge took his place in the little coop built for him. City Clerk Adrian Cross served as the clerk of court. Miss Burleson was the court reporter. Janitor E.A. Moore continued in his position, but his salary was now paid by the town instead of the library board. Moore also doubled as bailiff. The city paid half of the judge's salary, the county the other half.

On opening day, the furnishings were of a temporary nature. Charles Timeon completed and delivered the courtroom furniture on June 10. The benches for the audience were of oak and were painted green. Each of the twelve benches accommodated nine persons. The jury chairs were comfortable. Timeon even built an oak cabinet for the clerk's room.

When Judge Fahey, preferring to go back to his law practice, refused to be a candidate for re-election, he was succeeded by Judge John Shortley. Judge Robert S. Barr, a Dallas County lawyer, was appointed to the court following Shortley's death.

When the time for use of the room was up, no action was taken by the library board to seek removal of the court. The room was still not needed by the library. However, by 1912 that changed and in November of that year, the library board presented the city council with a request to relocate the court.

The request applied only to the court; the city clerk could keep his office in the library because council meetings were held there and the space was not needed by the library. The library had given the council use of the room in June 1904. The city had used the room rent-free that entire eight-year period. The city did pay for heat and light, or had those services donated by the respective companies. Once or twice the council had to appropriate money towards the maintenance and upkeep of the building when the library board's funds were exhausted.

After the first request for removal in 1912, the court was given sixty days to find new quarters. None could be found, so the council waited sixty days, then another sixty days because no course of action was presented. The council's position was that until a legitimate city hall was built, there was no place to move the court without it costing more to rent such a space than Perry could afford. The council wanted to work out a time sharing plan with the library board.

Jack Bruce was first elected mayor in 1913 and it soon became apparent that the new mayor was not one to be taken for granted. He objected strongly to the way cases were being dismissed in the Superior Court. He expressed his views strongly and directly to the judge, declaring that it was useless to try to secure law and order when offenders were turned loose.

Mayor Bruce's criticism of the court was sparked by one particular case. In it, a man was arrested on the Interurban car and held for intoxication and drinking in the car. He had liquor with him. The court held this was insufficient evidence inasmuch as a physician had testified that the liquor had been ordered for medical purposes for the defendant's wife. The man was liberated.

Bruce vowed that he would gather statistics to show the court was a burden on the taxpayers and serving no purpose at all as far as the city was concerned. Still, it was a surprise when on October 19, 1914, a petition bearing 544 names was presented to the city council calling on it to abolish the court. Two councilmen were absent, delaying the council meeting for a day. On October 20, the council voted to submit the court question to a vote of the people at the next city election.

Those favoring the court went to work. W.W. Cardell, who had repeatedly been asked to accept the nomination, consented to be a candidate for judge. Because of his indecision, Cardell would have to be a write-in candidate, while Judge Barr's name appeared on the ballot. Judge Barr contested the validity of the election after Cardell's win, citing a number of points of law.

Judge Cardell presided at his first session on November 17, 1914. He conducted the business of the court as if he had been doing it all his life. He dealt with three men brought before him and disposed of the cases without any friction.

Then Barr appeared and made formal protest against Cardell exercising the duties of judge, contending that his own term did not end until January 1 — and then only if the courts decided Cardell had been legally elected. Cardell showed the commission given him a few days before by Governor G.W. Clarke which read that he was empowered to act as judge on and after November 11.

The first hearing in the election controversy started by Barr was held December 10, 1914, by a three-man trial board. The board, which consisted of H.W. DeLa, W.H. Winegar, and D.H. Miller, announced the case would be taken under advisement and a decision rendered later.

The trial board met on December 21, and, in a unanimous vote, declared that Cardell was duly elected. The only surprise was that Mr. Miller of Adel, who had been chosen as Barr's representative on the panel, said that he, too, was of the opinion that Cardell had been duly elected and should serve.

In 1920, Judge Cardell announced that he would not be a candidate for re-election. The feeling was that the court would be abolished by the first of the coming year. A canvass of the lawyers in the city revealed that none wanted the judgeship. Perry was then the home of a District Judge, which simplified matters for attorneys.

When the superior court was abolished, cases went back to Adel and a mayor's court was reinstated to handle ordinance violations. A resolution opposing the re-opening of the superior court and the appointment of a judge was adopted by the council and a copy sent to the Governor in October 1920. The councilmen declared there was no demand for the court and it was only an expense to the taxpayers.

The Bloody Third (1908)

Years ago it was said that politics were corrupt and that each ward vied with one another in its underhandedness. The north ward seemed always to outdo the others when it came to spilling blood. It was dubbed the "Bloody Third."

That slang expression accurately described conditions in parts of the ward as late as 1908.

Some suggested the root of the problem was that Perry's two policemen both lived in the north ward and devoted most of their attention to the people in Perry's other two wards.

For whatever reason, most of the blood shed in Perry was shed in the Bloody Third.

Blue Laws (1911-1920)

Blue laws were the first printed laws of one of the Colonies, so called because they were bound in blue paper. Later these laws were designed to enforce morality as the lawmakers saw it. Most of these laws related to Sunday activities. Perry had a number of blue laws on the books, but it was the difficulty authorities had enforcing them that was best remembered.

Shortly after C. Durant Jones was elected mayor in 1911, he issued an order closing all businesses on Sunday. Because many didn't care if they opened on Sunday anyway, the order was generally obeyed — except for John Dignan, who opened his store on Sunday as usual.

Mayor Jones and Officer Hart arrived at the store at 8:12 a.m. and formally ordered the proprietor to close. He refused. The officer told him he was under arrest. W.E. Norwood, the head clerk of the store, was also arrested.

Dignan refused to comply with the closure order until he was served with a warrant, which the officer did not have. After consulting with his attorney, Dignan went with the mayor and the officer to the city clerk's office where legal papers were made out. Bond was set at $300 and Dignan provided it. No more goods were sold, but Dignan remained open until noon, as was his custom.

The courtroom was crowded on the morning of May 3 when the case was called before Judge John Shortley in Perry's Superior Court. The trial lasted until noon when the judge announced he'd give a written opinion the following day.

The trial ended in acquittal. County Attorney W.H. Winegar represented the state and H.A. Giddings and E.J. Kelley the defense. Dignan's defense was that the goods sold were necessities for the customers. The judge ruled that no law had been violated. Little attention was paid to the mayor's orders after that trial.

Dignan was arrested a second time in October for keeping his store open on Sunday. This action differed from the first in that warrants issued by Justice of the Peace A.D. Haskins based on sworn information provided by Mayor Jones were served on October 16 by Constable Lee Thornburg.

Dignan immediately appeared before the justice and was released without bond. As before, Dignan fought the charge. Giddings was again his attorney. A change of venue to L.B. Thornburg's court was sought and granted.

The case was tried November 10. After introducing testimony by the mayor and a brief exchange between attorneys Winegar and Giddings, the action was dismissed and the defendant discharged.

Perry turned a deeper shade of blue in 1917. It was possible to buy a Sunday paper, a loaf of bread and some gasoline, but that was it. No ice cream, root beer, cigars, or shoe shines.

The Perry Candy Co., Dooley, Anderson and Daw Drug Stores, Shoe Shining Parlor, and Dignan's Double Header closed. The Helvetia Lunch Counter was open, though no cigars, tobacco, or soft drinks were sold. There was some question if the ice cream could be ordered with a meal. The garage sold gas and oil and all necessary supplies for auto travel.

Athens George reported he'd planned to stay open and it was said the Idle Hour Smoke House sold cigars. So, on June 3, the police arrested Athens George, L.R. Keenan (proprietor of the smoke house), James Konidaris of the shoe shine parlor and F.R. Patterson, news stand operator, for staying open on Sunday.

On June 6, Judge W.W. Cardell heard the evidence against Patterson and Konidaris; the latter was fined $1. The state was represented by County Attorney F.H. Don Carlos and the defendants by Harry Wifvat. A lengthy opinion of twelve typewritten pages was filed by Judge Cardell on June 9. It covered every detail of the case and gave all the points of law involved. He discharged the defendants, saying the law had not been violated.

Again in March 1920, it was the councilmen who dipped their fingers into the blue ink. At an adjourned meeting at which a crowd filled the chambers and overflowed into the city clerk's office, hall, and anteroom, the council first took up the matter of closing the movies on Sunday. The week before, the city solicitor had been instructed to prepare the ordinance, and, when the mayor announced that action would be taken, a petition containing the names of 1,500 objectors was filed.

No attention was paid to the petition, and the council immediately moved it be laid on the table.

The second ordinance was read by the city clerk doing away with pool halls in the city limits after April 1, 1920, with a fine not to exceed $100 or thirty days in jail for each offense. This was immediately read three times and adopted unanimously by the council with no discussion.

The third matter was an ordinance relating to public dance halls and applied to the dance halls, schools of dance, or similar business. An annual license of $100 or $10 for each single dance was assessed, along with a set of drastic regulations.

No one under eighteen was allowed without a parent or guardian, places must close promptly at midnight, no person of immoral character was to be allowed admission, patrons were not allowed to leave the hall and return without paying a second time, and an inspector was engaged to visit all public dances. All violations were $100 fine or thirty days in jail. This, too, was adopted after three readings.

In compliance with the ordinance, both pool halls closed; the first time in Perry's history that such a condition existed. Rumors were soon afloat that this would change, and by July the lid had loosened.

At the council meeting of July 19, the lid had all but come off. The ordinance undoing the ironclad regulations which tied up the pool halls and Sunday movies was repealed just as mechanically and smoothly as it had been enacted four months earlier when the reform bug bit the councilmen.

Protecting the Morals (1913)

It used to be that Perry authorities looked after the morals of the citizens and took prompt action to keep them pure.

It was the custom in early 1913 of two women (one from Des Moines, the other from Sioux City) to make weekly visits to Perry. After receiving numerous complaints, the mayor investigated them thoroughly. He had an hour-long interrogation, noting the accusations they made regarding a number of Perry people. At the end of the session, the mayor told the women they had an hour to get out of Perry. They didn't actually leave until the next day.

Sioux City Sue first came to Perry under the pretext of looking for a husband who had deserted her. She even appealed to the mayor to help her in her search. She didn't find him that trip, but came back several more times supposedly searching. It became apparent that this was only a blind.

The Des Moines woman was a habitué of a chop suey joint and had been coming to Perry on Saturday nights for weeks. Most of her time was spent in a certain building never known as a rooming house.

She came up as usual the evening before the investigation and an effort was made to arrest her. She eluded arrest that night, but was found the next morning.

The women admitted their ways were questionable, but they liked Perry and mentioned to the mayor that a number of people liked for them to come to town. It was said that one man lost his job based on what they told the mayor, and a number of others nervously wondered what to say when the mayor called them in to answer a few questions.

The mayor's investigation also drew attention to the two

places which served as the respective headquarters of the two women. Booze had apparently been dispensed, and action was started to close these places.

After the two women had been ordered out of Perry, they went to Madrid and were greeted at the depot by the city marshal, who had been informed of their arrival. The marshal allowed the women to stay only until the train to Boone arrived, and he saw to it that they did not leave the station until then.

Meanwhile, the Madrid officers notified the Chief of Police at Boone, who formed yet another welcome party for the women, this time at the Boone depot. Finding out they were not wanted in Boone, the women took the Interurban to Des Moines. They reportedly took in more than $100 their last night in Perry.

Jack Bruce: A Militant Leader (1881-1930)

Not only was Jack Bruce a prominent businessman in Perry, he was also a militant leader of the town and often in the news.

Bruce was born in Scotland and came to America with his parents when he was two years old. They first lived in Canada, then in Michigan, before coming to Perry around 1881. His father was an engineer on the Milwaukee Railroad.

In 1886, Jack Bruce opened a first class bakery, one of his earliest ventures. Everyone predicted much success for this young man who was so full of bustle. Later Bruce went to work as a salesman in Leonard's butcher shop along with Will Case. After a few months they formed a partnership, going into business for themselves in January 1902.

Their shop was located in the north room of the Boyden block, corner of Second and Pattee, now the address for *The Perry Chief*. Their shop made the fourth meat market in Perry, but as both of the men were reliable and experienced, they were confident of receiving a good share of the town's business.

Bruce had a simple way of advertising. Every few days his delivery team took a tour of the principal streets on their own. Then he traded horses and really treated the residents on First Avenue to an exciting exhibition — a runaway team. On reaching First Avenue, the runaways suddenly decided to turn north while Bruce went out of the buggy in a southerly direction. Children

Bruce's Snowball Market No. One

The old Bruce Building, large enough to store five carloads of potatoes, was erected in April 1915 near the M. & St. L. tracks. In 1922 he opened a market on Railroad Street south of Otley in a building formerly used as a garage which later housed the Shackleton Construction Company. In 1930, Bruce built a new building which was connected to the Snowball Market. Bruce handled every-thing from food stuffs to farm implements.

scampered to safety and oncoming teams took to the lawns. The runaways' badly damaged buggy finally came to a stop against a tree in front of the Bruce residence.

His interest in the shop was sold and sometime later, Bruce opened another market in the old William McLuen building at Second and Lucinda. The store room was torn down in 1905 to make room for a new cement block building on the corner.

In December 1909, Bruce sold the business to his brother Harry, who had been a traveling salesman for an Omaha packing house. Jack then devoted his time in the produce and wholesale market in addition to the buying and butchering for the shop on Second Street. He was in and out of the market which he started on Railroad Street. In November 1911, Bruce and his brother bought the building from McLuen and that became the location for their meat market.

In spite of his enterprises, Jack Bruce found the time to court a Des Moines girl and they married in 1908. He purchased seventy-two acres of land in 1910 at the foot of Sand hill. He planned to build a home, barns and — since his slaughter house just west of the stock yards had burned down — an up-to-date slaughter house and rendering plant were also included. At this time, he sold his three lots and ice house at the corner of Lucinda to the grocers Rathburn and Cleveland for $2,500.

In 1915, Bruce leased land near the M & St. L. tracks and put up a building large enough to store four or five cars of potatoes. In 1930, he contracted with D. Chrystie to erect a new building on the little triangular lot at the intersection. This was an oddly shaped building with no right angles and connected by a large double door to the old building, which was then used as a stock room for his Snow Ball market.

For all his industrial and commercial accomplishments, it was during his years of public office that Bruce made the most news, starting with his election as mayor in 1913. Bruce's victory was decisive, taking more votes than his two opponents combined. A large crowd was present in the Superior Court to witness the change of administration.

He assumed a new role as mayor in September 1913, when he performed his first marriage ceremony as a city magistrate. A Des Moines couple came to Perry thinking it was the county seat. They had no acquaintances here and it was with difficulty that they were identified. The bridegroom was a motorman for the Des Moines Railway system. He found someone at the Interurban Depot who could provide the necessary affidavit. The city clerk then telephoned Adel and the deputy clerk came to Perry with the license. The happy couple went to the Superior Court room where Mayor Bruce was summoned and the ceremony performed.

Bruce was re-elected mayor in 1915 following a bitter three-corner fight. Papers were circulated attacking the character of the candidates. Dozens of automobiles were engaged in hauling voters to the polls. For the first time in years, the results were known within fifteen minutes after the polls closed.

After the results were officially announced, a celebration was held in Bruce's honor. A rope was secured and the water wagon manned by his constituents who paraded around the business district. Bruce had promised a "dry" platform and this was symbolic of what was to come. In the crowd were a number of small boys and they were gathered together and escorted to an ice cream parlor for treats.

In a few short weeks, the dry campaign netted a quantity of beer and whiskey which was kept locked in a cell in the jail. One night, as the mayor led the way to the jail, his officers formed the rank and file of a devastating army. They took the barrels, cases, and bottles of booze out back of the jail and shattered every one of them.

So many cars were being sold and so many inexperienced drivers were behind the wheel, that the mayor next attempted to regulate traffic and promote safety on the streets. A circle was painted on the pavement over a manhole on Second and Willis, and a police officer stationed there to see the proper turns were made. If not, the drivers were called back to do it right, and not released until they did. A warning was issued calling for orderly parking on Second Street. Traffic was to be confined to the right side of the streets at all times.

In the winter of 1919, Perry was hit by a coal shortage during a bitter cold spell that was punctuated by many blizzards. To alleviate the suffering, Bruce offered free wood from his timber one mile west of town to anyone who wasn't too lazy to go out and get it.

Bruce was defeated in the election of 1921, losing to Adrian Cross. Bruce died in June 1930 at his home at the age of 59. A blood clot formed in his leg above the knee, and death came following the emergency amputation of the left leg in an attempt to save his life.

Dog Daze (1914)

Frank Miller, the official dog catcher, instigated a rush on the city clerk's office on April 2, 1914, by people wanting to renew their by then delinquent dog licenses. When the weary clerk trudged home that night, he'd issued 150 licenses. The method was hard on the dogs, which were picked up on Miller's rounds, as they were promptly dispatched to dog heaven.

The morning catch wasn't so great, as Miller left his wagon standing back of the Grand Theatre while he went to buy meat for dinner. A sympathizer raised a board in the end of the box and all the dogs escaped. There was a chase, but the dogs had had enough of the wagon and did not dally.

The afternoon catch didn't have the good Samaritan to release them. Release for this group was by the spirit route. A few which the officers thought someone would show up with a dollar to redeem them were held over. One dog with a tag and license mixed it up with the officer and sank his teeth in the officer's leg. That dog was not spared either.

The work continued, but after the first day, every Fido, Rover, Fannie, Gyp, and Sport were safely tied until the owners could get to the clerk's office and purchase immunity for them.

Though he was only doing his duty, this episode was indirectly the cause of Miller being hauled up before Judge Barr of the Superior Court on May 14, 1914, charged with attempting to do great bodily injury. Lee Clark, an employee of the Globe Mfg. Co., was the complaining witness.

While Clarke was passing Miller's house the night before, he made a remark about a man who picks up dogs, which Miller resented. In the argument Clark picked up a couple of bricks and Miller drew the gun allowed him by officers for the dog dispatching business. The men were separated before any damage was done to either. After listening to both of them, Judge Barr dismissed the case.

Perry's Silent Policemen (1915)

In 1915, Mayor Jack Bruce had warning lights placed at the intersection of the principal business streets. These signals were four foot posts set in cement, painted red, and bearing signs "slow" and "turn right." At night they were decorated with red lanterns which were filled and cleaned by the officers without any added expense to the city.

Since there was not enough money in city coffers to hire officers for these intersections, this plan did more to correct the hazards of street travel than anything else tried.

Almost immediately there were six arrests. Those arrested made contributions to the city for turning on the left side of the posts and five more posts were added to intersections where traffic was heavy.

In March 1916, two more "silent policemen" were installed. Sometime between then and 1919 the posts were reduced to cement mounds in the intersections.

We know this because a traveling man representing a Cedar Rapids concern was in the city on December 18, 1919, and called at the city clerk's office asking for a settlement of a repair bill for his automobile which was damaged considerably when he ran into one of the cement mounds in the street without a signal light.

The man told the clerk that two weeks earlier, when entering the city from the west, he collided with the obstruction. He said it was not in the center of the intersection and that it had no light of any kind on it as a signal.

The car, a Ford, had the crank shaft thrown out of line as a result of the collision and, after a short drive, the man also found two main bearings were burned out. Besides losing two days of work, the repairs to his car set him back $43.55.

No word as to how the claim was resolved.

Bum is Honored (1917)

Although he did not realize it, old Bum, the mouse-colored dog that was a familiar figure on the streets of Perry, was accorded an honor perhaps never given to another canine in the country. A *Chief* representative tried to interview Bum on May 17, 1917, but he was so sleepy and indifferent to a little thing like glory that he did not even wag his tail in answer to questions.

For years, Bum had slept days and been wide awake at night. His odd sleep schedule made him a friend of the night police force and the various men who served in that capacity accepted his presence gratefully.

A blue uniform and a star looked better to Bum than a big meal and he adopted the officers as fast as they were put on the force. Every night he accompanied them on their rounds, poking his nose in the dark places of alleys and scaring many a real bum from his sleeping quarters.

When the crusade against untagged dogs was started in the spring, Bum's case became one of interest. Because he had adopted the police department and refused to leave, Bum was really a member of the force even if he did work without pay.

Mayor Bruce settled the matter on May 16, 1917, when he officially declared that Bum was on the force and ordered the city clerk to issue a tag for him. Tag number 125 was furnished and was attached to the leather strap which took the place of a collar. Bum was, therefore, a full-fledged patrol dog, with all rights and privileges of other dogs and some that others of his breed could never hope to enjoy.

Motorcycle Division (1919-1920)

Those who think they have a complaint about a citation for a motor violation should be thankful they were not driving a car on the streets of Perry in 1919 and 1920. The police department had added a motorcycle division. There was only one cycle, but that one made news while it lasted.

The cycle, a Harley Davidson capable of going up to eighty miles an hour, arrived and an officer was assigned to it. Patrols over the city began immediately and the first results were known by July 8, 1919, when nine motorists either paid fines or promised to do so.

About two months after its introduction to the town, the officer and the cycle, a Ford car and a new Chevrolet mixed it up on Wolf Hill just southwest of the city. The cyclist was the only one hurt. He was testing the pulling power of his cycle and had just passed the Chevrolet when he met a Ford coming down the hill. The driver of the Ford lost control when he struck sand and collided with the cycle. The officer was thrown off and badly bruised. The driver of the Chevrolet, in an effort to avoid another collision, went into the ditch and toppled over.

The presence of the motorcycle cop on the streets had made believers of the motorists but, come spring, the tendency to speed resurfaced. Again, the services of this branch of law enforcement were needed. The officer and the cycle were back on the job on June 4, 1920. Two offenders appeared in court the next day and paid a fine of $5 and court costs.

Six more were apprehended on June 5 and 6. On the seventh, six more who forgot to keep their speed on city streets within the limits proscribed by law ran afoul of the motorcycle cop. A total of $60 and costs went to the clerk on that day alone. People began to get restive over the officer's exuberance in making arrests.

Five prominent Perry citizens were among those ticketed on June 8th and all protested. One claimed that he had been stopped when the speedometer registered 17.5 miles per hour. Superior Court Judge Cardell said he would fine all speeders regardless of who they were, but not until he had a statement from the solicitor regarding the validity of the speeding ordinance. The assistant solicitor had said the ordinance was void because the speed limit was not posted on the streets.

There had been many complaints against the radical methods used to stop speeding. When the speedometer showed a mile or two over the fifteen mile limit, they were naturally incensed at being stuck with a $14.95 ticket for reckless driving.

One motorist was stopped near the high school and his speedometer registered fifteen miles per hour. He was told by the officer to go to Thompson's Cafe or the Pattee Hotel. The motorist said he'd appear in court the next morning and, when he started his car, the officer shot a hole through his fender.

A special meeting of the council was called that evening by the mayor to take up the traffic ordinance. The meeting was a real delight. The preliminary bout was more exciting than the main go, but there was more than enough action to keep a big crowd there until adjournment. The court room was filled as was all the available space in the hall and the windows.

The city could not make laws conflicting with state laws and the city had failed to post proper speed limit signs according to state law. A new ordinance read at the previous meeting was ordered re-read and the clerk waded through four or five pages of typewritten copy so drawn as to make it impossible to make a wrong move in an auto and escape punishment.

The mayor asked if the council wanted it enforced to the letter and was told that this was the idea. The mayor warned that he didn't want anyone to come yipping to him if every man in town was soon in jail.

A councilman declared that if an officer used common sense there would be no trouble. Another said the mayor should appoint another officer and, if he refused (which he did), the council would have to do it. The result was that the motorcycle cop was fired after five days on the job.

Then it was moved that, since the fines imposed and collected were contrary to state law, they should be returned. That motion carried. A bill was presented for the repairs made necessary when the motorcycle cop shot a hole in the fender. This caused more arguments.

The now ex-cop got into the scrap by saying that he had had orders to do everything he had done — to bring drivers in if they were going faster than fifteen miles per hour. A councilman asked him if the order was to bring them in dead or alive. The repair bill was finally allowed.

After that the meeting cooled and the motorcycle cop was no longer news for the rest of the summer. A different officer was made the motorcycle cop in 1921. There was a noticeable decline in speeding. No arrests were made, but many were warned.

When the city administration changed in 1922, the mayor was instructed to sell the old cycle if a buyer could be found. By that time, the motorcycle had been out of order for a long time.

A Bell Was Heard (1920)

George Mills, a former legislative reporter and political writer for the *Des Moines Register* published a book in 1972 entitled "Rogues and Heroes from Iowa's Amazing Past." Perry has an amazing past, too, including rogues and heroes. Many short stories were written about people who were neither heroes nor rogues. It's just that the rogues' side was more interesting, such was the case in "A Bell Was Heard."

On the morning of March 12, 1920, F.M. Bell was at city hall to register a kick against officer W.E. Sanford who shot his dog the night of March 10. The Bells were out of town and their dog, not being able to get into their home, went to the produce plant on South Third and howled to be let in. This was Bell's business establishment.

The dog's "appeals for admission" brought the officer instead. Bell said a license had been paid for the dog's protection and that he had a tag as receipt for payment. He was further incensed because two cases of eggs were stolen from the plant the night the dog was shot, which he felt would never have occurred had his dog been on watch. The shooting brought forth considerable discussion and feeling.

City Clerk Cross stated on March 13, that the books showed no license had been issued for the dog in 1919. In 1917, he had tag number ninety-one and in 1918, tag number seven. Bell claimed he had tag number seventy-eight, but had mislaid the receipt. The clerk's books showed number seventy-eight was issued to Ray Folsom, but his dog had been killed by officers because of a complaint that it had bitten a child.

Bell filed suit and it was heard in Superior Court on March 15. Bell had been arrested for an altercation with the officer and was charged with using obscene and blasphemous language. After questioning a number of witnesses. Judge Cardell fined Bell $50 and court costs.

Wild and Woolly Council Meetings (1926)

Some wild and woolly meetings were held in the Perry council chambers in the days when the newspapers sought to know and told all.

There were seven men in the city jail in January 1926, and all the information the authorities would give out was that they were arrested by city officials. The men were picked up at the rooming house operated by Otto Tingwald at 1314 Otley Avenue and were sitting around the table on which the arresting officers declared there was money. Those arrested were: Harry Dodge, Otto Tingwald, Guy Doty, Harry Danoff, Frank Briggle, and Elevator Vasque.

Rumors on the street were that a man hired by the city had gained the confidence of some poker players and sat in with them in order to get evidence.

It wasn't rumors flying at the February council meeting. During the routine business segment of the meeting, when the bills were reported, J.I. Kelley raised his usual objection to the bill of $297.50 for the special police and one regular policeman. He asked the council to take action on the matter of paying bills not allowed by the council. This included two city warrants of about $300 paid without having council approval.

Kelley also objected strenuously to hiring spotters to come in, drink free whiskey, and squeal on gamblers. He was for getting the gamblers, but objected to the method used.

Charges that the affair was being kept under cover were borne out when city officials refused to allow a *Chief* reporter to look over the list of warrants issued and refused to answer questions. So, *The Chief* did its own investigating. They discovered the name of the stool pigeon and the amount of bills never presented but paid contrary to law. The amount was almost $700 for police in the month of January.

Mayor W.W. Phillips, on February 6, decided to give out the facts, declaring that when the fines were collected and Perry received her share, the cost of cleaning up the city was only about $11.50.

He accused *The Chief* of not trying overly hard to get the particulars because he, the mayor, was there at the time and was not contacted. However, *The Chief* would not retract its statement that the clerk's office refused to give out any information and asked that nothing be published concerning the warrants.

The law provided that all city council meetings be open to the public, but the one held on February 8, 1926, was closed. The mayor stated that there was no business to be transacted of interest to the public. Before the council chambers were cleared, however, spectators got in on an interesting discussion over previously contested bills and warrants.

The contested bills previously passed without council approval came up for allowance. Councilmen Kelley and Kibby were out voted, and the bills were approved. Then Kelley moved that the bills be rejected because they were illegal. The out-of-town spotter was a poor character for police work. Kibby seconded the motion, stating he had affidavits that he gave away whiskey, which Kibby assumed was paid for with city money. Kibby said the spotter also asked two women to drink with him, that he'd tried to start a poker game, and that this didn't seem the correct way to spend taxpayers' money.

After such a discussion, the motion to reject the bills was voted down with the comment, "You have to hire a scamp to catch a scamp."

The business the mayor didn't want the public to know about was his discussion with the council about some phases of the appointment of an officer to take policeman M.O. Storm's place. Storm was relieved of his star because of an incident in which it was charged that he struck Albert Ferguson.

Storm, night policeman, had been arrested by Deputy Sheriff Glen Council on charges of assault and battery.

Ferguson was the complaining witness and, according to his allegations, he was hit over the head with a billy club wielded by policeman Storm.

Ferguson drove to the front of the American Legion building and honked his horn for some people who were waiting for him. They evidently didn't hear him, and he honked again. At the time, Ferguson alleged Storm opened the door of the car and asked him what he thought he was doing, and then hit him over the head with the club.

Storm was taken before Justice of the Peace L.A. French where he plead guilty to the charges and asked for a continuance of the case. The hearing was set for the next day and Storm remained on the force. He plead guilty to charges on February 10, 1926, in the court of Justice Heiss, and was fined $15 and court costs. The case was prosecuted by County Attorney Blake Willis.

At the February 17 council meeting, Weise presiding in the absence of Mayor Phillips, councilman Kelley made a motion to retain Storm until the next meeting. On February 23, Mayor Phillips appointed Wilbert W. Nicholson as night policeman to take Storm's place. The position had been temporarily filled by Roy Metzger.

Chapter Four
With People Come
Schools and Churches

The Washington School

This is the site of the present Post Office Building. The teaching staff in 1877 was composed of Mrs. Lindsay, Miss Ballentine, Miss Lombard and Miss Newbury.

Washington School (1876-1917)

In 1876 Perry boasted of two small frame school houses, but talk was being heard of erecting a new school on a high hill in the northeast part of the town plat.

The editor of *The Chief* felt this was entirely too far from the thickly settled part of the town, being about three-fourths of a mile from the majority of the families.

At the election of the directors on March 13, the people voted on the question of issuing bonds in the amount of $8,000 for a new school and to levy a tax of 24 mills for school purposes. The newly elected directors resolved themselves into a committee to select a site for the new school.

It did not take long to get the project rolling. By April a site was chosen: six lots on the east side of Second Street between Pattee and Bateman were purchased for $1,000. The house on the site was sold to P.C. Rude for $80.

Excavation for the foundation began the last of June, and work was pushed forward rapidly in order to have the school completed by the first of October. The cost of the fifty feet by sixty-feet, two-story building was $11,500.

In November of that year the ladies of Perry arranged for a costume party and banquet in the new school, the proceeds to go for the purchase of a bell. The first one proved too small and was soon replaced by a new 800-pound bell.

Two big fires in January 1904 (a Chicago theater burned leaving 546 dead and 115 missing, and the immense loss when the Iowa capitol burned) made city officials safety conscious. Fire Chief Knell conducted the first fire escape drill at the high school in the Washington building and was encouraged by the interest shown by the students in the exercise.

At a signal, ranks were formed and files passed out into the main halls and down the stairways to the campus in fine order, considering that it was the first exercise. The rooms were emptied of nearly 560 young people in a short time. The drills were to be continued at the Fire Chief's pleasure. After fire escapes were installed (at the Chief's recommendation), officials believed the building to be as secure as it could be.

Schools had trouble with vandals in those days, too, though they were called pranksters then. In 1910, someone strayed into the engine room in the basement and turned the water into the boilers. This resulted in the opening of valves in all the radiators; as a consequence, the floors were flooded.

Henry Miller of the school board was notified of the trouble about 4 p.m. and, with the aid of George Shenton, soon had the trouble corrected. Little damage was done, since it was the close of the school day and no inconvenience suffered due to the flooding.

The last high school class to graduate from the Washington building — and, at twenty-nine members, the largest — was in 1910. After that, the building continued to be used as a grade school.

In 1914, the old Webster, Otley, and Washington buildings ceased to be used for school purposes.

Many feared that with the passing of these schools the notes of the old bell would be heard no more. But a contract was awarded to John Knosby for the lowering of the bell from its time honored tower, transporting and raising it to its new position in the belfry of the Willard building at Seventh and Lucinda streets.

A hard-fought, three-hour battle with fire occurred November 26, 1916, when flames started in a shed on the east side of the building and spread to the roof of the main structure. The big tower caught in a short time and was almost demolished. Firemen poured water from several lines into it and saved the main part of the building.

The building — exclusive of plumbing — was sold at public auction in April 1917. There were two or three bidders, but none of the men seemed anxious to pay much. The winning bidder was F.P. Weinhard at $25. Wildman and Conway were the auctioneers. Under the terms of the sale, the structure was to be torn down, the basement filled, and everything taken off the grounds.

Two wings had been added to the original building: one on the north, one on the south. Each was two stories high and gave an assembly room to the high school, more rooms for grammar grades and a library. After it was abandoned as a school, it was used by the Globe Manufacturing Company for about a year.

The grounds were seeded in May 1921 and the site was made an uptown park. The 1937 school board donated the use of the grounds to the city for a public parking lot which would accommodate about 50 cars. In 1947, the city purchased the grounds for $8,000.

The Perry City Council, by a 4 to 1 vote in 1962, decided to give the General Service Administration an option to buy the north 170 feet of the community parking lot at Pattee and Second streets. Although the representative would not give any indication, it was assumed that a post office building would be constructed on the land.

A Note on an Early Revival (1876)

In an article from *The Chief* in 1876, we learn that not all revivals in Perry were successful. It seems that an Elder Adams came to Perry for a few days to assist in the revival meetings at the Baptist Church, did not stay long. Adams got disgusted over poor attendance at the first two or three meetings "and shook the dust of Perry from his feet after giving the church and its people a piece of his mind in language more emphatic than courteous."

Graduation Exercise (1883)

The first commencement exercise at Perry High School took place at Union Hall on June 7, 1883. Members of the graduation class were: Hattie Bollen, Clara Kenworthy, Mollie Ross, Nettie Blue, Lettie Mowrer, and Thora Warren.

The graduates were the recipients of many handsome bouquets which, along with many other testimonials, convinced them that they had acquitted themselves in a satisfactory manner which was appreciated by the the public and the patrons of the school.

The 1884 commencement was held in the Methodist Church in April. The church was filled to capacity and many failed to gain admittance.

The graduates were: Ernest Thornburg, Mary Brody, Lizzie Dugan, Emma Lane, Kate Mowrer, and Arch Newport.

On June 1, 1909, the twenty members of the senior class at Perry High School appeared in caps and gowns at graduation ceremonies; the first time the garb was worn here. The innovation came courtesy of Superintendent Whaley and met with the approval of everyone. Dr. McBride, who gave the principal address, appeared in the robes of his office at the university.

Unitarian Church

By 1884, there were in Perry six church organizations: Methodist, Catholic, Baptist, Christian, Congregational and Presbyterian (which met every other Sunday at the Christian Church at the corner of Second and Lucinda).

Only the Congregational Church is no longer in Perry, but their building still stands. The Presbyterians have a building of their own and the other four are presently in their third or fourth church home.

Many might not know there was another organization which had a beautiful building. For about ten years, they did very well in Perry. That was the Unitarian Church.

On an evening in 1883, a number of citizens from force of habit met in Parks Book Store and discussed religion. None of them belonged to a church, although they all were religious. They were barred from membership in existing churches because they were too conscientious to subscribe to a belief they could not understand and which seemed wrong.

On this particular occasion they noted that moral and business integrity were not monopolized by the churches and they were criticizing the churches as well as their members. Finally, the proprietor spoke up suggesting that if they had something better, why didn't they do something about it. This put the matter in a new light, so they began checking to see if there was a church or society they could belong to without compromising their beliefs.

Liberal lecturers were brought to Perry from time to time. Ethical cultural societies, spiritualists, and others were investigated, but none seemed to fill the need. They had heard of the

Unitarian Church, but dismissed it without investigation, thinking it was only another orthodox church.

Finally, in the fall of 1889, an old gentleman gave two lectures in Perry to the great satisfaction of this liberal group. After one of these lectures, Parks asked if he knew of a church they could attend. The lecturer thought the Unitarian filled their needs and after a short correspondence, a representative, J.R. Effinger came to Perry and preached in the Congregational Church on June 23, 1890.

In April 1891, Rev. Mr. Thomas P. Byrnes of Humboldt preached in the Congregational Church on a weekday evening. A few weeks later, Miss Safford followed with two large meetings in the Opera House. At those sessions, a subscription paper was started; $300 was raised to pay the expense of twelve meetings to be held the succeeding year, with the state conference agreeing to furnish ministers.

A temporary organization was established and plans made to hold regular services every Sunday with some members of the society reading a published sermon when no minister was present.

The meetings continued through the year, first in private homes, then in Redmen's Hall and, later in Union Hall. The first lay meeting was held at the residence of B.H. Campbell.

In April 1892, the state Unitarian Conference Committee met in Perry, and at the close of the sessions, articles of association were adopted by the society and it was duly incorporated under the laws of the state.

A deal was closed for the purchase of the Frank Carpenter lot at the corner of Third and Lucinda. The house on the front was moved to the rear and improved, with work beginning in September 1894.

Entrance to the church was in the northeast corner, directly under the tower and steeple. The audience room was large enough to seat 200 and the arrangement of the pulpit and choir was such that the speaker and singers could be seen by each listener. The estimated cost of the building was $2,000.

One afternoon in November of 1894, the cozy audience room of the new church was crowded with friends and citizens, old and young, who came to see the church interior, to eat lunch, to listen to music by the Mandolin Club and to have an hour of social enjoyment.

One of the features of the event was the voting for the most popular lady in Perry, the winner to receive a fine silk quilt. Among the candidates were Mesdames. P.C. Rude, A.L. Longshore, Allen Doss, and A.F. Stevens, the latter getting the most votes.

The receipts of the two evenings' entertainment were more than $80, which the ladies felt well repaid them for their efforts.

The service of dedication took place on December 16, 1894, at 10:30 a.m. Every seat in the audience room was taken, plants decorated the platform, and the organ music was by Mrs. Walter Cardell.

At the 7:30 meeting, a large audience more than filled the room, and the attendance and interest shown were very gratifying to all the friends of the new religious movement. The new seats for the church arrived on the 17th, just one day too late for the dedication services.

The church was also well-filled on the night of November 25, 1903, with a happy crowd of members and friends who had assembled to rejoice because of the payment of the church debt and to witness the burning of the church mortgage.

Sometime during the next two years services were discontinued, but beginning September 2, 1913, the church which had been without a pastor for sometime was re-opened for meetings. Rev. Mr. Thomas S. Pierce of Des Moines delivered a series of sermons, but the end was near.

After 1915, it was announced that a deal was closed whereby the Unitarian Church and residence were transferred to the Catholic Church. Rev. James Cleary stated that it was the intention of the members of this congregation to use the property for school purposes.

However, the Assembly of God members began renting the former Unitarian Church in 1916. In September of 1929, the pastor, Lionel Hitchcock, announced the purchase of the property. That group removed the old belfry, remodeled the entrance vestibule, refinished the basement for Sunday School, and held religious services there for the first time on January 1, 1930.

This church then moved to a new structure in a new location and Dr. Frank Wilke purchased the old church property in August 1948. He received a permit to remodel the church into a clinic. Succeeding occupants were Drs. Laverne Utterback and Jerome Zartman. The Perry State Bank parking lot now covers the former Unitarian Church grounds.

Celia Covey: A Home Grown Product

Perry has had many wonderful school teachers. Celia Covey was truly a home-grown product.

Born in Perry on March 26, 1887, her mother, who had named her Vivian, died when she was a week old. The grandparents, the Haskins, who reared her, gave her the first name of Celia, which had been her mother's.

Her father was George Covey, a railroad man. When he transferred from Perry, he did not try to take his daughter from her doting grandparents.

She went to grade school, high school and the Jones College in Perry, before taking classes at Cedar Falls and Drake.

Twenty-four of her fifty years of teaching were in country schools. She walked three and one half miles morning and night when she taught at the Davey Hall school which was located two miles west of Alton School and was along the Milwaukee tracks.

Crossing the bridge west of town was always frightening because there was only a narrow plank on which to walk. In the spring, when the ice was breaking up and churning against the bridge pilings, the crossing was a harrowing experience. She would pray, "Lord, I'll pick my feet up. You put them safely down."

In those days the rules were not so stringent and she could ride on the switch engine if one came along at the right time. When she taught at Oak Grove School east of town, she sometimes rode out on the switchmen's hand car.

Twenty three of her fifty years of teaching were in the Perry system. She guided hundreds of youngsters through the maze of fractions and down the exciting paths of geography.

Once she was asked if she had any famous pupils. She replied, "Yes, lots of them," and proceeded to call of the names of local people. She told how Ned Willis, on an European trip, sent her a card saying he was looking at the places she had told him about in geography and that they looked just as she had said they did.

It was things like that which she said were her reward for the years of her life which she had given to the children of Perry and vicinity.

A College Town (1892-1909)

Perry "used to be" a college town. In the summer of 1892, H.C. Wahl, who had taken shorthand in Des Moines, came to Perry and organized a summer shorthand course. This was the nucleus of the Perry College.

That fall, his business college was doing very well. It had opened with 28 students, but more came every day. He had secured splendid instructors and new furniture which added greatly to their comfort. In fact, due to the rapid growth, Wahl was compelled to add three new typewriters to his stenography department. They were Smith Premium and cost $100 each.

Edwin D. Hulley

Just where it began is not clear, but in December that first year, Perry College moved into new quarters in the Gamble block on Warford. The fall term of 1893 began in the upstairs rooms in the Diddy block, which were especially fitted for the college.

Ed Hulley, who had been educated in the commercial school at Shenandoah, came to Perry in the fall of 1893 and became associated with Wahl.

The first commencement exercise of the Perry Business College was held in April 1894, at Breed's Opera House. It was reported that "an intelligent audience greeted the classes." Most of the young ladies wore the regular white dress and took front seats, while the boys preferred to remain in the rear. Professor Hulley presided at the exercise and, at the close, gave the class good advice along with diplomas.

After about two years, W.M. Tarr secured control of the school. Wahl went to Omaha and later on the road as a traveling salesman. While on a trip to Vinton, he became seriously ill and died. When last heard of, Professor Hulley was in the newspaper business in Elliot, Iowa.

In December 1898, the Perry Business College was being called the Perry Normal School, yet it still taught business courses. Tarr was the principal of the business college and was a native of Dallas County, while Professor A.L. Lyon, formerly superintendent of the city schools, was in charge of the normal department.

The Normal School was incorporated in August 1900, and was owned by thirty-one citizens. S.E. Carrell was president; F.L. Rogers, vice president; Wm. Tarr, secretary; and J.M. Woodworth, treasurer. Directors were Carrell, W.E. Rall, D.J. Pattee, L.V. Harpel, and Tarr.

The winter term was opened on November 20, 1900. Carpenters had been hard at work on the Diddy building, making room for the influx of students. All of the upstairs was used and part of the downstairs. A partition was run through the building, and M.L. Diddy and Bro. occupied the west room, while the east room was fitted to accommodate the large commercial classes.

The second commencement, after the reorganization, was held in June 1902, one night being class night, the next night the commencement. On both nights, the Christian Church was filled by friends of the graduates and patrons of the school.

That fall it was announced that another college would open in Perry, The Central Iowa College. It was reported to have five strong financial backers. The Frush building on the west side of the Triangle, then occupied by O'Malley Brothers, was leased for three years. The entire building was to be used: the gymnasium in the basement; commercial department on the first floor; and the normal department on the second. M.M. McMahon was the principal and promoter, and H.H. Rangeler, formerly a resident of Perry, was his associate. November 24 was affixed as the starting date.

Then it was announced that Professor Rangeler had withdrawn because of his wife's illness. Hard on the heels of this, came the news of a sudden change of affairs at the college. Where there had been two schools vying for patronage, there was left only one, the Perry Normal School.

It was told on the street that the schools had consolidated, but the details of the transaction were not made public. Professor McMahon said the serious illness of his mother caused him to give up the enterprise. It was also learned that he had a well-paying position offered him. At any rate, the students, who had enrolled at Central Iowa College, headed by the principal and his assistant, marched in a body to the Perry Normal building.

It was the sentiment of Perry businessmen that the field was not large enough for two colleges anyway, so they were pleased by the turn of events. The Perry Normal School took over the students, the furniture and books which could be used. As for the lease on the building, rumors were a new furniture store was to be opened there.

A change of ownership in the Perry Normal College was announced in February 1905. Tarr sold an interest in the school to Professor G.E. Weaver of Mt. Morris, Illinois. In March, Professor F.L. Meek, principal of the Madrid schools, became one of three equal owners.

In 1906, Tarr took a position with Highland Park College in Des Moines. Weaver disposed of his interest in 1908, but remained in Perry. Professor Meek signed a contract to take charge of the Minburn schools and disposed of his interest.

While this institution had been in Perry for fourteen years, it was about to be moved away. While everyone was wondering about what would happen to the college, a deal was being made with C. Durant Jones who took over from Professor Meek in May 1909.

Jones sold his newspaper in order to devote more time to the college, though he was never on the faculty. As soon as he gained control of the college, Jones began an advertising campaign with hopes of doubling the school's enrollment.

Jones' campaign must have been successful, for in July of 1912 work was begun on a new college building.

Willard School (1900-1967)

The need of a new school building for Perry was talked about for over a year at the turn of the century.

The need was pressing. A primary room was in the basement of the Second Ward school. The Salvation Army barracks, which were being used to house two seventh grade classes, were ill fitted for use as a school. There were no playgrounds and the proximity of back alleys and out-buildings made for a bad situation.

The decision to build was finally made on April 20, 1900,

The Willard School

This school did not go beyond the sixth grade. Seventh and eighth graders went to either Webster or Lincoln School. Teachers in 1910 were: Ada Melick, Emma Huffman, Bessie Dundore, Grace Barnard, Veva Aylwood, and Ruth Hall.

and the lots of James Wycoff and Peter Munsen at the northeast corner of Seventh and Lucinda were secured. This location wasn't the first choice of the board, but it was the only desirable one that could be secured at a reasonable rate.

Two of the lots were fifty feet by seventy-seven feet; one went for $800, the other for $550. These prices would have been considered high for vacant lots, but there was a house on each lot which could be sold and moved off.

The firm of C.C. Cross of Des Moines (who drew the plans for the Christian Church built in 1898) was employed as architect. J.J. Courtney was awarded the construction contract.

Plans called for the outside wall to be of Van Meter pressed brick and the basement of Anamosa stone. Limitations of the board's finances made it impossible to erect an elaborate building, but it did contain six classrooms — three on each floor — with a high basement available for recitation rooms or as a gymnasium.

At the time the finishing touches were being put on, the board of health ordered the old "rookery" — a row of frame flats located on Eight Street near Lucinda — condemned. These apartments, which were occupied by a number of families, were declared unfit for habitation by the city. The city physician, Dr. A.W. Trout, took steps to have them abated. The city solicitor was also ordered to secure the removal of the inmates, either to the county farm or some other institution.

The opening of school that fall was late for all. In anticipation of an opening the first of September, the Salvation Army Hall had been given up and the Second Ward school remodeled; at least four classes were without a home. To avoid confusion, all classes started at once sometime after the middle of September.

Shortly after the completion of the new school, the teachers there asked to have it named, suggesting Willard, and the board agreed. This was the only school in Perry with a name.

At a special meeting of the Board of Education on April 11, 1906, a course of manual training was adopted for the seventh and eighth grades. The work was commenced in a small room in the Willard Building. If it proved desirable, there was an excellent opportunity to extend it by outfitting a room in the basement.

On October 19, 1906, the rooms were opened for school board members and teachers to view the manual training department. The superintendent was arranging for three visiting days when all interested parties could visit the workshop.

The health officer did not give Willard a good report in February 1913. The rest room conditions were bad and the ventilation system not good, but the report said, that with some changes and repairs, the building could serve its purpose well.

Willard's demise came a little at a time. In 1928, the walls were condemned and then fixed using tie rods as supports. A few years later, the stairs were condemned and an architect's report recommended the upstairs not be used.

The school authorities then considered removing the top floor of the building, making it a one story structure; but they were told by the architect that this would make the walls dangerously weak.

In 1940, school directors took official action on closing the Willard building for school purposes and, that winter, used it for a NYA project.

Subsequently it was converted into a recreation center for boys and girls. Finally, the building was snubbed by school young-

The First Webster School

Fred Knell had been given the contract to erect the Third Ward school which was named the Webster School in hopes of inspiring its students. It is located at the northwest corner of Fifth and North streets and was converted into an apartment house in 1920.

sters and the school board. It stood silent waiting for a bidder to claim it.

Two bids were rejected as too low. The school board wanted $1,200 for it. Money was needed to pay for permanent bleachers at the athletic field. Mark Hanlon finally bought the property in 1951. The building had stood empty for over twelve years and had fallen into decay. Only the occasional footsteps of school custodians echoed through the building as they went for supplies stored there.

The building was torn down in February 1967.

Willard had served the community less than forty years when it was abandoned. There is nothing now to show there ever was a school there.

Of all the public school buildings — the Washington, the first and second Webster schools, Otley, Lincoln and Roosevelt — only the first Webster building still stands. Fred Knell had been given the contract to erect it on May 11, 1893, for a grand total of $1,619. It is located on the northwest corner of Fifth and North streets, and was made into an apartment building in 1920.

Schools Named

Willard School was named shortly after its completion in 1900. The other schools were not named until 1904, when the school board voted unanimously to name the Second Ward school Washington.

The names of the other two were left to Fred Knell and John Diddy. Their reports were approved at the May board meeting that year.

It was voted to call the First Ward school Otley, after Colonel Otley, a Perry pioneer. The Third Ward school was christened Webster in the hopes the pupils would turn out as bright as Noah or Daniel.

Jones College

The Perry Normal College was to have a new home. Work was begun on July 9, 1912, but like everyone else with a building

The House That Jones Built
C. Durant Jones took over Perry Normal College in 1909 and renamed the institution Jones Business College after it moved into its new building in 1913.

projects that year, Jones had trouble finding laboring men. There was so much construction work in progress, that help was extremely hard to hire.

The new college building was described in August 1913 as one of the most handsome structures in Perry. It was constructed of reinforced concrete of artistic design and the interior was of solid oak. The college and Chautauqua offices were on the first floor. The second floor was devoted wholly to college purposes.

Franz M. Fazel of Mitchell, South Dakota, had charge of the commercial department. The shorthand department was handled by Miss Ava Richards of Joliet, Illinois; the music department by Mrs. Cara Gregg.

Many other organizations used the college facilities. Jones opened the assembly room in February 1914 for lodges which could not find a meeting place. In 1920 the Christian Church met at the college every Sunday morning, and in 1921 a series of gospel meetings was held by representatives of the Church of God. The Christian Church also held its annual meeting in the college building.

Sometime after 1921 the college was closed and the building remodeled into six apartments. Hard times had come and bank failures touched many. It was reported in *The Chief* in May 1927 that a fifteen percent dividend would be paid to depositors of the closed Security Savings Bank as the court had approved the sales of the Jones apartments on Otley. Mrs. Charles Repp of Perry was the buyer; the price was $11,200.

Christians Make War on Satan (1896)

The Christian people of Perry decided to join forces and charge the battlements of Satan in a way that would make that cloven-hoofed individual feel sick.

A meeting was held in February 1896 by delegates appointed from the various churches and the matter was talked over. The pastors were pushing the matter with all their might and the congregations could be depended upon to aid them. The revival couldn't be held until winter departed, but during the interim every detail was arranged so that when the meetings began, it would be with an impetus that assured success.

The preliminary arrangements were completed by May 1896, and everything was in readiness. The meetings began on June 12, and were conducted by Rev. H.C. Cordner of Chicago, assisted by E. Burnett, one of the best revival singers in the country at the time.

The meetings were held in a large tent located on Third and Bateman, just south of the Milwaukee tracks. Two thousand chairs were provided and the tent was lighted by four arc lights. A committee of 20 women began taking a religious census of the city.

Reverend Cordner was unable to reach Perry in time for the opening services on a Friday night, but the local pastors spoke and outlined the work proposed.

Cordner was present the next night and his first sermon was what he termed a get-acquainted talk. Sunday services were like the old-time revivals. The tent would not cover the crowds that gathered. The people hung around the edge like a fringe and sat in buggies beneath the blazing sun, paying close heed to the speaker. Sunday night looked stormy and the crowd was not so large as in the morning. The evangelist was greatly annoyed by people leaving and said that they had better think more about their souls than their Sunday clothes.

The meetings closed the first of July 1896. Cordner made many friends in Perry and a few enemies. And the Christian people loved him all the more for the enemies he had made in Perry.

On the last Sunday morning the churches were crowded to their fullest capacity. Sunday afternoon, the church people had a big parade. Marching eight abreast, singing songs, led by Grand Army veterans bearing the post flag and keeping step to the Salvation Army bass drum, the Christians made a procession three-blocks long. During the three weeks of meetings, nearly 400 enlisted under the banner of the cross.

The revival meetings actually closed in a blaze of religious glory on a Thursday night. The heat was intense and a thunder storm threatened, but that did not keep the crowds away. The big tent was crowded and hundreds stood outside.

Cordner had to take the 10:40 p.m. train to Chicago, so the closing service was cut short. When he went to the depot, he was escorted by a vast crowd and, while waiting on the platform, good-byes were said and salvation songs were sung with a will. Tears flowed freely when the train bearing Cordner and Burnett pulled away.

Sunday Meetings (1898)

The Reverend Billy Sunday was invited to conduct evangelistic meetings in Perry in March 1898. The executive committee decided the Opera House was inadequate, so a committee was appointed to solicit subscribers to buy stock in a tabernacle association. The response was so favorable that the project seemed assured of success.

It was decided to erect a board tabernacle which would seat 1,500 people and the committees were appointed to look for a location and to evaluate building costs. The location committee favored the same lots used for the Cordner meetings two years earlier at the corner of Third and Bateman.

Lumber was purchased at the end of February for the 80 feet by 120 feet tabernacle. About 43,000 feet of lumber was put in place by donated labor in less than three days. Besides the chairs available in Perry, 1,200 were shipped in from Des Moines for use during the meetings.

The building was completed on March 4. The roof was covered with paper and a galvanized chimney put up. Paper was put around the inside and a stage erected. Flags, bunting, and suitable pictures were solicited for decorations. Four large stoves furnished the heat, and arc lights were installed. These meetings were sponsored by five churches: Congregational, Methodist, Presbyterian, Christian and Baptist. They opened on March 10.

Professor Oliver had charge of a 150-member choir for the services. Reverend Sunday, who arrived on the day the meetings began, was described as a "hummer." The crowd was rather small the first night, due to disagreeable weather. But at other services the attendance was estimated to be at least 1,500.

During the four weeks of meetings a variety of weather tested the comfort of the tabernacle. It ranged from disagreeable to ideal spring weather, from wind and storms and threatening rain to blustering wind and severe cold. People were surprised that such a barn-like structure could be so snug.

Reverend Sunday's sermons hit sin hard and knocked the props from under the complacent. His talks were calculated to separate the sheep from the goats. He hit at the backsliders, saying the Chief cause was dancing and card playing — cards having been invented as the plaything of an idiotic old king. He hurled hot shots into the liquor traffic and all who sided and abetted that evil. He was an entertaining speaker and won friends wherever he went. He also made enemies by this firm denunciation of sin and sinners.

A free will offering was taken the last week for Reverend Sunday's services. It produced almost $600, the largest sum the evangelist had ever received for such services, and more than he made playing on the baseball team he left to do Christian work.

Sunday closed on a Monday. His discourse on that evening was short as he had to leave on No. 4 for Chicago. He was accompanied to the depot by a large choir and others — an estimated 3,000 were there. The choir, led by Mr. Oliver, sang sacred songs as the train left.

The tabernacle was sold to the highest bidder and A.D. Haskins' bid of $425 was accepted. Expenses of the meetings included the rental of chairs and pianos, lights, fuel, etc., and came to about $350. This was met by the basket collections taken each evening. The tabernacle had been erected through a special fund and cost about $750. The total costs of the meetings were about $1,300. There was between $125 and $150 left on hand which repaid the stockholders twenty-five or thirty cents on the dollar.

On April 8, 1898, demolition of the tabernacle was under way.

Tabernacle Revival (1924)

Tabernacles and revival meetings have had far-reaching results for Perry, but the one that touched more people in a different way was the one held in 1924.

A member of the Fairfield Gospel Team came to Perry in January and appeared before the City Council with a request to erect a tabernacle on Second Street on the lots made vacant by the 1920 fire that burned the Union and Carter-McCall buildings. The location was on the west side of Second Street from Warford south to the alley.

Permission was granted to erect the temporary structure with provisions that it be thirty feet north of the east-west alley, that the roofing be of at least one-ply composition, and that it be approved by the fire chief. The churches agreed to keep a watchman on duty day and night as a protection against fire.

A formal announcement was made on January 9 that the forty-two-man gospel team would be in Perry during February to take charge of a six-week interdenominational revival. A plea went out on February 9 for 100 men with hammers and saws to donate a few days' labor to assist in building a tabernacle large enough to seat 2,000. Their only compensation would be dinner and supper served at the Methodist Church by committees of all churches participating in the meetings.

Contractor Peter Johnson was in charge of the workers and the task was practically completed by February 12. A raised platform for the speaker and chorus was at the south end of the shed. Stoves were installed for heating.

The meetings began February 24.

Novel ways of getting greater attendance were employed. One was the shipment of twelve-foot-high balloons to be turned loose on Saturday afternoon. They were weighted to travel low and a cross was attached to one. The person bringing the cross back to the tabernacle was presented a leather-bound Bible.

The meetings were brought to a close on a Sunday morning in the fore part of April after a successful evangelistic effort which netted 635 Christian decisions. Hundreds pressed forward at the close of the meeting to say good-bye to the men of the team.

Those converts present at the final meeting formed a great unbroken line along the south wall in front of the platform, while others present marched around the building taking each convert by the hand. There had never been a more thorough work of grace than the campaign just closed. Emotions ran high and caused far-reaching waves.

On the afternoon of the closing services, a gospel team was organized for the purpose of conserving the results of the revival with meetings to be held each Sunday afternoon at the various churches.

The next day, the result of this religious zeal became apparent. The city council passed the first reading of an ordinance prohibiting Sunday theatrical shows, exhibitions, vaudeville shows and performances, and motion pictures. Stiff penalties for violations were imposed.

At the second reading an effort was made to suspend the rules and pass it on to the final reading and adoption. That effort failed. A large crowd filled the council chambers. The second reading of Ordinance 165 was passed.

On May 1, an election was held to consider the closing of the movies on Sunday. It was a lively contest, with one of the largest votes ever cast. Of the 2,376 votes, 1,397 favored closing. Though the actual closing was up to the council, council members agreed to cast their ballots in accordance with the election results, and so did pass Ordinance 165 to its third and final reading. All council members were present and Mayor James Peters presided.

Petitions asking the council to repeal the ordinance and allow Sunday movies began to circulate. More than 1,200 names were affixed to the petitions when the city council met on March 22, 1926.

A crowd that packed the chambers to the limit was on hand at that meeting. However, the council members tabled the Sunday movie question, ostensibly for investigation, but from their attitude, it was evident that they intended to ignore the petition entirely.

At a subsequent meeting a committee of businessmen was present and asked what was being done in regard to the petition, but the council did not seem ready to answer the question.

Ignoring the wish of more than 1,200 voters, the council at its April 5 meeting voted to keep the ordinance prohibiting Sunday movies. The council, in so acting, was within its legal right, but the general feeling was that the council had used arbitrary methods in so handling a petition which contained the names of almost half the voters, including more than 100 businessmen.

Realization came that the only recourse open to the advocates of Sunday movies was at the next town election. An organization was soon begun to elect a council pledged to reinstate Sunday movies.

The city election of March 1927, was one of the closest mayoral elections in the history of Perry, with one of the largest votes ever cast. J.I. Kelley was elected mayor with 172 more votes than his closest opponent.

A crowd of citizens packed the council chambers later that month when the new slate of officers took over the reins of the city. The mayor made a strong plea for unity, touching on the Sunday movie question.

The council finally set the date of November 18, 1927, for a special election to determine if Sunday movies should return. The two theater men, William Youngclause and C.J. Latta, agreed to pay the expense of the election.

Perry voters signified their approval by a majority of 261 votes. It was the largest total vote in Perry up to that time. The final count showed 2,583 ballots cast.

At their next meeting, the council members passed two ordinances, one repealing the disputed ordinance and one outlining the rules concerning the class of shows to appear on Sunday. Theatricals and vaudeville performances could not be held, but musical entertainment or motion pictures were not deemed theatrical performances.

And so Sunday movies returned to Perry.

Chapter Five
City Strives
to Modernize

Electric Plant Goes Bang

Henry Draper, night operater at the light and water works, was just going to work when the plant blew up. After the acident, Draper took a job at the cemetery where he produced a landscape second to none. For a time, only he knew where the 900 or so dead were buried as the cemetery plat had been destroyed.

Electricity Comes with a Bang (1884-1894)

The drive for an electric power plant really began with a request for street lamps. In 1884, several citizens and businessmen of Perry on both sides of Willis from First Street to Eighth Street offered to erect street lamps near their premises, providing the city would pay the expense of lighting and furnish the oil. Nothing ever came of it.

At their regular meeting in October 1889, the council decided not to get any street lamps but to let people find their way home after dark by lantern light or feel along the fences as usual. The proposition put to the council was to light the city by means of double jet burner kerosene lights, but it was laid on the table by an "almost unanimous vote," according to *The Chief*.

This really upset the editor, as there was not one street lamp within four square miles of the corporate city limits. This was a "deplorable fact, one that we dislike, but cannot deny. The use of kerosene might not be so elevated in tone as electric light, but one is available and one is not. Light is what we need."

Talk of an electric plant continued. Steele Kenworthy canvassed the city to see if there was enough interest to put in such a plant. He suggested the dynamos and machinery could be placed in the mill, convenient to all businesses. He was convinced this venture would pay, but it was going to be too expensive for him to handle alone. It would have to be a company.

Finally, on October 20, 1890, the City Council met in special session to discuss the question of whether or not to authorize construction of an electric plant or waterworks, or both. The council sent the question to the voters in a general election in November.

The Chief did not tabulate the votes, but did report that "a goodly number of citizens attended the polls and cast their votes." Although the First and Third Wards defeated the light plant by narrow margins, the Second Ward carried it with such a majority that it passed citywide by twenty-five votes. Each ward approved the waterworks which carried by 211 votes.

Through the efforts of E.H. Richardson of Manson and Henry Hock the light plant became a reality in 1892. By September, they had nearly all the poles in place and the work of wiring business houses and residences was commenced. Most of the machinery arrived by October. The lights were turned on December 7, 1892. The light plant and the water plant were in the same city-owned building on West Warford.

One week later, a fire alarm turned in from the waterworks power house. Fortunately, the fine machinery of the light plant was not badly damaged. Superintendent Hock, who had been working day and night to get his plant operating, was not discouraged. By 9 a.m. on December 19th, he had everything running again.

About a year later, on a Sunday morning in December 1893, something about the engine at the plant gave way and, in a very short time, the engine was a wreck with large pieces of it flying around. Engineer Henry Draper started to shut off the steam, but when a chunk of iron struck the throttle and bent it, he concluded the boiler room was good enough for him. As a result, streets were in darkness and the cost of kerosene lamps was way above par. A new engine was ordered. Manager Hock expected to have the plant running again in about ten days.

A coal famine in May 1894, caused by striking coal miners forced the power plant to shut down temporarily, but by the end of June, lights were on again all night.

Then, in July 1894, a terrible explosion occurred. The day had been an intensely warm one, and all welcomed the approach of evening with its shade and cooling breezes.

At 7:15 p.m., while many were seated in their homes, a strong shock and horrible explosion was felt and heard almost simultaneously. Then the clang-clang of the fire alarm, the rattle of the hose carriages over the streets and the surge of running feet in the direction of the light and water plant pointed to the site of the calamity.

The plant was located in the western part of a fifty-feet by fifty-feet building containing boilers, dynamos and other machinery. At about four o'clock on the fatal afternoon, the fireman fired the machinery, as was the custom, the machines apparently being intact and in good condition. Mr. Hock, one of the proprietors and general superintendent, was also present. A short time after 6 p.m., Hock relieved the engineer for supper and it was during this period that the explosion occurred.

Mrs. Morehead, a woman living in the vicinity, was at the building just a moment before, having gone for a pail of hot water, which neighbors were in the habit of getting the barrel into which the exhaust emptied. She did not reach her home before the shock came.

The north boiler exploded and was literally torn wide open. The building was completely demolished, fragments of planking, iron and bricks were hurled in every direction — the air was thick with missiles.

Hock was blown from his position near the engine and through the north end of the building where he was found immediately by Mr. Dugan, who lived across the street. Hock was lying on a pile of debris, terribly wounded and gasping for breath. He was moved onto a stretcher improvised from a couch and taken to the St. James Hotel where Drs. A.J. Ross and A.W. Trout did all that was possible for his relief. Hock died at 11:10 p.m.

Several neighboring buildings were damaged by missiles. Mrs. E. Everett was slightly injured when hit in the arm by a brick. A piece of iron tubing weighing about 100 pounds was thrown more than 300 yards, passing over the residence of Lew Griswold, and into a pasture, plowing earth for thirty feet before burying five feet of its length in the ground.

An old gentleman, W.E. Griswold, was sitting on the front lawn, and he compared the sound of it passing through the air to the whistling of a mortar shell. A piece of piping fifteen feet in length fell in the front yard; a safety valve struck the ground and half-buried itself within ten feet of where the old man was sitting.

E.H. Richardson, principal stockholder of the company, arrived in the city for the purpose of selecting a lot to rebuild and to settle with the city for damages. The city had owned the old building which sustained at least a several thousand dollar loss.

At the time of the accident, the city owed the light company $500 on one of the boilers. In the settlement made on August 2, the light company cancelled the note they held against the city, turned over to the city the coal they had on hand, including a carload on the tracks, and furnished the city free lights for three months and two arc lights for one year. This amounted to the equivalent of $1,000, which the city received in damages.

The light company bought the lot (on which an old warehouse stood) on the south of the Triangle from H.J. Holmes for $750. The first load of brick for the new building was hauled on August 3. The company said it expected to be able to furnish lights in time for the District Fair.

There had been talk of the city buying the lot opening Second Street through to the south, but talk was all that came of it. The foundation for the electric company's new plant was laid by August 1894. In September, the boiler inspector was in the city — the dynamos and engines were ready for a trial run.

On the evening of the fifty-eighth day after the explosion, Manager Gus Hindert said, "Let there be light" — and there was.

Waterworks (1891-1927)

Perry's first waterworks were installed in 1891 at a cost of $20,000. It was said the water was slightly mineral, slightly soft, free from lime, and pleasant to the taste.

A fire was reported in December 1892 at the department's power house. The heavy brick walls and iron roof kept the flames down but also hindered the firemen from getting at the fire. The power house was shared with the Electric Light Company and the fire started behind the boilers in a room containing light company supplies, burning through to the light company machinery room. Fortunately, the machines were not damaged.

The loss to the city came to about $100 but the light company's loss was about $1,000. The light plant had not yet been put in operation.

Water pipes were distributed along the west side of First Avenue early in 1894, and the work of putting the mains in on Third was progressing. By October of that year, Perry had a complete waterworks system. The pumps had a capacity of 750,000 gallons and the standpipe held 60,000 gallons. Water was taken from three artesian wells from 116- to 126-feet deep. The plant was city-owned and cost approximately $19,000.

When the terrible explosion shook the light plant in July 1894, because the water plant was in the same building, the town water supply was knocked out, too.

The boilers at Shively's Mill were removed and placed in position on the old foundation and connections made. The smoke stack was erected late in the evening, and, after getting up steam, the pump was worked for some time without producing any water. By July 28, the standpipe was only partially filled, and the thirsty people about exhausted the supply. The smoke stack was too short and barely furnished enough draft to keep steam up.

The city at once began to erect a suitable building on the old lot, while the light company bought a lot from H.J. Holmes where an old warehouse stood. By September 1894, the roof was finished over the building and there were twelve applications for the position of engineer.

For some years it had been the custom of Perry residents who lived near the waterworks to carry their water from the pumping house, thereby saving on their water bill.

At a meeting in June 1902, the City Council discussed shutting off these parties' water priveleges, an action they had often talked of before. But the matter had always come up when the ground was frozen, making it impossible to lay new water lines. Many property owners had put in water connections that spring, just as soon as the frost was out; now the council proposed that the rest do the same.

The water committee was instructed to have the hydrant on the west side of the water building shut off and not allow families to carry water from the pump house. The hydrant was shut off June 11, 1902, and those who had not taken steps to install water lines had to rely on the generosity of their neighbors.

In January 1905, the council expressed the city's intent to place meters every place in town where water was used carelessly. The meter at the Milwaukee Railroad showed they had used $205 of water in December. This was the "high water mark" and showed how much the city would gain by installing the meters.

The plant had been improved from time to time, and, after the installation of a new boiler and smoke stack in April 1905, the next move was the extension of the mains.

At a meeting in December 1904, Mayor E.F. Edmondson presiding, the council decided to make a gift to the churches in the form of giving them free water. Just what caused this freak of charity by the city fathers was not known. Mr. W.K. Graham made the motion that the city would not charge the churches;

when it came to a vote, the council deadlocked in a tie. That left the deciding vote with Mayor Edmondson and, as he was of the Baptist persuasion, it was a foregone conclusion that he would cast his vote in favor of the gift, which he did.

In the summer of 1927 there was a typhoid scare. The council met in special session to discuss the matter and warned residents to continue boiling their water until further notice. On August 22, 1927, the council voted to purchase a chlorinator. Councilman C.A. Knee left for Chicago the next day on a mission to secure the new equipment. It was installed and made operational by 8 p.m. August 28. By the thirtieth, all homes were receiving thoroughly chlorinated water. Boiling was no longer necessary.

On October 12 that same year the council decided to make the standpipe more sanitary. A contract was let for the placing of a lid over the top.

Mayor E.E. Clothier reported on December 12, 1941, that in line with defense efforts and precautionary moves, the city waterworks was closed for the duration. No visitors allowed. The doors were barred with the employees being issued keys.

Sewer System Hard to Complete (1905-1907)

Perry was soon to have a sewer system, according to the news in 1905. There were a few private lines run at various times, but no system was ever put in. Plans had been drawn a number of years previously, but it never went beyond the paper stage.

A sewer system had been assured for Perry in 1903. It was badly needed, since the city no longer depended on individual wells for water. A company of citizens was organized to build the outlet and lay lines along certain streets.

Private citizens would have the privilege of hooking on upon payment of a certain price each year. The city was to get free service and the chance to buy out the company at a reasonable price whenever wishing to do so.

At a meeting in July of 1904, B.C. Dilenbeck read a report of findings of the special sewer committee. The council directed the committee to get a survey and specifications; the council would decide between a septic tank and a river outlet.

The contract for the sewer was awarded to M.A. Earl, a

Chicago engineer. Earl was in Perry in January 1905, to submit his report.

The City Council acted to push the matter to completion. Bids from cement and clay outlets were placed and the city proceeded to buy or condemn the right-of-way for an outlet. There was little money, so fancy prices were out; and, if the property owners were so inclined, the land was to be condemned and assessed by a jury.

Some lively City Council meetings were held over the sewer project. Because of difficulty in obtaining the right-of-way, the committee decided to change the route of the outlet.

Dr. W.P. Mowrer was in attendance at the June 1905 meeting and made a liberal proposition if the new route were taken. It would mean almost a quarter mile farther, but all iron pipe and grade would be avoided, and the possibility of damage suits done away with. The engineer was sent a telegram to come at once.

The new route went farther south on First Avenue. The engineer estimated that the new route would cost $1,500 more. When Dr. Mowrer saw the expense was going to be so much, he suggested the septic tank site be moved closer to the river. He did not object to the sewer crossing his land, but he did object to having the septic tank in the middle of his farm and only a short distance from his house. It was recommended that the outlet be taken to the river.

The council let the sewer contract to Regan Construction Company of Des Moines on August 2, 1905. The bid amounted to approximately $32,995 for the sewer proper and $38,000 for the entire project. Work began on August 21, where the sewer crossed Frog Creek and progressed toward the city. Nothing could be done on the outlet until the right-of-way matter was settled.

The city fathers had trouble as well as business on their hands at their September 25, 1905 meeting. Nathan Mowrer served notice that he was seeking an injunction to restrain the city from building a sewer through his land as contemplated. The route was changed to get a better crossing under the Interurban Railroad and he said the change was to his injury. Damages in the amount of $500 were sought.

Judge Edward Nichols refused to restrain the city from constructing the sewer. However, a temporary injunction was issued preventing the city from using the sewer until acquiring a legal right of way by purchase or condemnation.

Jacobson and Chrystie of Perry, contractors in charge of building the septic tank, completed their work in November 1905. The lower part was six feet deep and built of solid cement. It stood eight feet above ground, built of cement blocks with four doors and two windows.

The Regan Construction Company had to quit work on December 19, 1905, for the winter because of difficulties. They finished the outflow sewer and Group One. They received pay for the outflow, but Group One was not accepted by the council. The ditcher used on the project was calculated to dig through fourteen inches of frost, but when it encountered rock on First Avenue, work was abandoned. The ditches were refilled and work was at a standstill until spring. The company maintained their offices in Perry and one person from the company was present at all times.

In December, a jury appointed by Deputy Sheriff Lee Thornton and comprised of T.J. Gilbert, G.F. Roddan, W.B. Robinson, H.J. Holmes, J.M. Woodworth, and L.A. French, investigated the sewer line dispute over which Nathan Mowrer had gone to court. They found the new route took almost five acres more land than would have been used in the original layout and for which Mowrer received compensation. The jurors returned to the city and met in the Giddings and Winegar office to assess the damages and formally condemn the right of way. The decision was that the city should pay $700, less the $150 already paid Mowrer. The W.P. and P.A. Mowrer tract had already cost the city $1,200.

By January 1906, Group One of the sewer still had not been accepted by the city, much to the construction company's disappointment. There was too much sand in the pipes according to the council. Regan prepared to flush the sewer. Long rods were used, coupled together until they reached from one manhole to another, with wire brushes on the end to loosen sand and mud.

Another test was made prior to the February 1 council meeting. Still, the council did not accept the work, saying there was too much water running through the lines. Regan said he was not getting a square deal regarding the acceptance of Group One.

At a special meeting of the council in May, the acceptance of Group One was again considered, this time the council accepted the work. The contractor was ready to quit and turn the contract over to the bondsmen. Acceptance meant there would be no lawsuit.

All work on the sewerage system was about completed by July. Tiling under the Milwaukee tracks and pavement at the depot was not difficult, but the Regan Company had encountered more delays on the Perry job than on any other it had worked on.

A muskrat was used to clean the lines. The Isenhart boys had a tame rat to which they tied a string and started it into the sewer. The end of the line was closed, causing the animal to head for the first opening dragging the string behind him. If it didn't show up in a reasonable time, the workers knew there was an obstruction, and they'd let the animal return to the starting point. The length of string let them know where the obstruction was. When it ran through to the next opening, the rat was caught and the string used to draw a rope through the pipe, and then chains, thus getting out the sand.

The last of November 1906 brought a serious question before the city. Was the sewer system serviceable and sanitary, or was it improperly and poorly built? The portion designated as Group One was accepted some time before and there were steady complaints that it was completely blocked.

On November 15, the Regan Company notified the city that Group Two was ready for acceptance. It appeared to the company that the council was dragging its feet and that property owners were being denied use of that phase of the new system. The company declared that it had waited long enough and that the city was inviting a law suit by failing to accept the work.

The belief was that the Perry contract had been taken for about $10,000 less than it should have been, and, with all the delays, the company would not make a dollar's profit on the deal. Visiting engineers from Des Moines examined the outlet and, while they criticized the specifications, said that Regan had built it properly.

In December 1906, the first legal document relative to the sewer matter was served and executed. A Kansas bank was the first to start trouble. The city accepted Group Two and began inspecting Group Three. The last of December, the city accepted more of the sewer based on a report of the engineer at a special meeting. The business district was soon to have use of the much-wanted sewer. In January 1907, workmen completed the task of cleaning the fourth and last group, which the city accepted at its March meeting.

Matters finally ended up in court, when the city council

proved unable to determine the rights of claimants in the dispute. Contractor Regan made an assignment of Group One to Peoples Bank, Groups Three and Four to D.J. Pattee, and had a subsequent assignment of $5,000 to a bank at Clyde, Kansas. Judge Applegate held all money and certificates due Regan on the various phases of the project, including the assignments.

Two local men brought suit in Superior Court against the city for $300 in wages due them for their work at the outlet. When the Regans made a settlement with the city, they claimed all these claims had been settled.

Sheriff Pat McGoeye auctioned off the Regan Company's cleaning tools at the order of the court to settle a claim made by Robinson's Clothing Company to satisfy a judgment. The clothing company took the tools and was expected to sell them back to the city after court proceedings were complete.

By the last of September 1907, City Clerk Adrian Cross had issued permits for 164 people to tap into the sewer.

The end of a threatened flood of litigation was reached in October. C.E. Maurer and J.E. Meyers settled their claims for $75. As expected, the city bought the cleaning tools from Robinson Clothing Company in April 1908. They were as good as new and valued at $250, but the city struck a bargain and got them for $75.

Contracts for storm sewers were awarded in June 1910.

Seeking the Great White Way (1902-1914)

By 1902, with a new electric plant in operation, it would seem that street lights — so long desired — would soon be in place. Not so. More years brought more disputes, more meetings, and more concessions were needed before the Great White Way became a reality.

Two arc lights were installed, one at Second and Pattee, the other at the Rock Island tracks on Willis. This was a welcome change from darkness.

Then, a very warm council meeting was held on March 3, 1902 with Mayor J.E. Wilson presiding. The question was more light on the streets. Councilman E. Nichols moved that two more lights be placed on First Avenue near the Rock Island tracks. Councilman W.E. Ginn opposed it, and said the people there could

The Great White Way
The top picture was taken after December 5, 1912, and before November 29, 1913, because the street has gas lights. The bottom picture shows electric lights which were turned on after November 29, 1913.

wait for lights, just like they had to do in the First Ward. Council-man C.E. Dixon got warm and so did Nichols; both claimed the lights being sought by the First Ward were seriously needed and declared that they would never get the lights so long as Ginn chaired the lights committee. Nichols' motion failed.

Another informal discussion took place. Nichols and Dixon agreed that if a street was worth putting cement walks on, it was worth lighting. Though they put up a fight for their constituents, they failed to convince their fellow councilmen on their point. No lights were ordered.

At a Commercial Club meeting in November 1909, members discussed the proposition of lights on Second Street and came up with what they felt was a workable plan. Each business house and property owner would pay a certain amount until the cost of installation was settled. Their only thought was electric lights.

When the club members approached the light company, they felt the price was too high and the terms unsatisfactory, so the merchants asked the gas company to submit a bid. That bid was accepted. The club members talked to the businesses along Second Street and they agreed to pay $2 a month for five years.

The Perry Gas Company put up the poles for $2,700. The equipment was installed and accepted by the merchants. The manager of the Electric Light Company attempted to secure some of the lighting but finally withdrew and put his name on the subscription list.

Work by the Gas Company started in September 1910, tapping the mains near Second Street and Otley Avenue before the paving was laid. This contract was for Second Street only. The Light Company, however, installed electroliers from Second Street west on Willis, south to Otley and into part of the residential district. Theirs was the first to be turned on and, on September 27, the business district in the vicinity of the library was lighted, presenting a beautiful appearance and giving the people an idea of what Perry would be like when the system was completed.

The middle of November came and Second Street was not yet lighted. Citizens were asked to be patient, reminding them that it took six months to get the streets paved after 25 years of getting ready. The Great White Way finally arrived on December 5, 1910.

Vague and conflicting rumors about the Gas Company's financial condition and its future began circulating. In October 1911, the company went onto the financial rocks.

The Gas Company was comprised of local men who had banded together in an effort to give Perry the one utility it lacked.

When the stockholders discovered that they had been victims of a patent that would not work, they investigated more, bought new machinery, and changed the method of making gas which would furnish light. Then, when the lights were on and could bring in extra revenue, the plant blew up. Temporary repair of the building was made, but the stockholders had reached their limit.

John Reed of Cedar Rapids purchased the gas plant in October 1912 and began work on the lights at once. Each lamp was taken down, washed and new mantles and glassware put on. But, a bigger threat was afoot.

In August 1912, the manager of the Light Company offered the city council a proposition which, if accepted, would mean changing the street lights on Second from gas to electricity. With three exceptions, property owners and businessmen favored the change and the manner of paying for it. They signed an agreement to pay 1.5 cents per street frontage foot for five years; after that, the poles would belong to the city.

Reed wanted to keep the contract which had two years left on it; the contract had been listed as one of the Gas Company's assets when he bought it. He also had a plan to present the City Council which would not ask for one cent from the property owners. He further promised to refund twenty-five cents a light a night for every light that did not burn. The proposal sparked a long debate between the two companies.

A Second Street businessman called at the gas works and came away with the impression that the gas company's plan would provide a higher level of customer satisfaction while the electric company's plan would be more expensive and had no provision for burned out lights.

A representative of the Gas Company asked the businessman why, if the light company believed there was no possibility of lights burning out, did the light company itself maintain three gas arcs in their own plant at the foot of Second Street?

The Light Company's response as to why merchants would have to pay them a monthly fee to cover the price of the poles was, in essence, their poles were more expensive and were worth more. The service alone, the light company maintained, was worth the difference. A light company representative clinched his argument by asking the merchants if they would rather see a man go to each post and turn it on, or climb a ladder to light the gas lamps if the pilot had gone out, all down the block.

The fight between the two companies was expected to come to a head at the October 1913 council meeting, but it was called off when one side conceded defeat. The manager of the gas company announced he had decided not to compete for the street lighting in the business district. So, the council signed a contract with the Electric Light Company.

The first lights of the Great White Way were turned on November 29, 1913, from Warford to Lucinda on the west side and, if all went well, another block would be brought into service every two days. But, all did not go well.

Because the cost had gone beyond the reach of the city levy, Mayor Jack Bruce refused to sign the contract presented to him on December 1, 1913. He said the lights would cost $800 more each year than generated by the levy. But the manager of the Electric Light Company said this was not the case since the block from Pattee to the Milwaukee Depot was not equipped and wouldn't be as the owners failed to sign for the cost of the equipment. He maintained that this brought the cost for the system within the means of the city levy.

Rather than calm things down, the statement that the lights would not go north of Pattee started considerable discussion. The city didn't have enough money, the Electric Light Company had a great deal of equipment on hand not being used, and the businessmen were insisting that the lights extend to the depot. Many council meetings were held in attempts to settle the issue. Finally, a plan was developed which seemed to satisfy all concerned. The mayor signed the contract at the end of March 1914.

City Hot Water Heat (1889-1932)

It came as a surprise to the community when the new light plant changed hands in 1899. John R. Swearingen and Frank Dodson purchased the plant for $20,000. The new owners took over on March 1, and they had in mind the installation of hot water heating for the town.

The council met in June and passed the ordinance granting them the right to lay a system of mains and by July, the big pipes were distributed along Second Street. The work of laying the mains and installing the machinery was pushed.

The plan utilized the steam from the electric plant and carried the water heated in the boilers through the mains in the streets. These were tapped and hot water carried to circulate through radiators. The circulating system consisted of two wrought iron pipes laid side-by-side, one for the outflow of hot water forced by the pumps, the other for carrying the cooled water back into the suction end of the pump. The same water was used over and over again. The only other such heating plant in Iowa was at Missouri Valley. This heating system was turned on September 28, 1899.

A change in the screw vents had to be made because of the enormous amounts of water taken from the radiators, causing the company great expense and preventing them from supplying sufficient hot water for heating during winter. It had been the custom for users to open the vents and draw out hot water for household uses. Floors had been scrubbed, even washing done with water thus taken. Some older houses in Perry still had the hot water heat using these old registers.

Agitation for all-day service began in 1903, continuing for two years. It wasn't until March 1907 that the electric plant announced it would run days. This permitted people to run electric motors for their work and to do the ironing and cooking with electricity if they so desired.

In July 1912, the plant was purchased by a group of Cedar Rapids capitalists who were buying up plants all over Iowa with a plan to link them into one huge electric system. Clyde R. Lyon was the owner prior to this deal. James A. Read of Cedar Rapids and C.A. Hoffman of Des Moines came to Perry in August to close the deal making the Perry plant the property of the Iowa Railway and Light Company.

The company completed plans for a new power plant in March 1916, located on the Interurban tracks facing Otley Avenue. Three lots were purchased. The big smoke stack of the new plant towered almost 200 feet into the air. Estimated cost of the building was $100,000. Completion was set for September 15, 1916. With this move the way was left open for the city to open Second Street south, which the city council did in 1919.

The Iowa Railway and Light Corporation changed its corporate name in May 1932, to the Iowa Electric Light and Power Company, which was very similar to the original name under which the company was incorporated 50 years earlier.

Second Street a Through Street (1902)

After the light company put up a new plant in a new location, the City Council voted in December 1919 to open Second Street through the location of the former plant. The city clerk was instructed to notify all property owners to be at the December 15 council meeting.

The plan was to open the street to the full 70-foot width which meant two or three buildings would have to be altered. Property owners on South Second agreed to paving if the street were opened properly.

At the meeting objections and comments were heard. Attorneys for the M & St. L said it would mean six crossings in four blocks. G.W. Smith of Pomeroy, who paid $10,000 for the property housing the Ballentine Garage had no objection if the city paid for the damage to his building as a considerable portion of it extended into the street.

There was no representation for the Ryan McDonald Garage which also extended into the street. W.H. Winegar, attorney for the light company, stated it would be OK if the company received market value for the two small pieces of its triangular shaped lot involved in the street opening. Charles Dixon, speaking for the property owners in the south part, said they were anxious to get the street opened.

Ordinance 110 was passed unanimously; the street and alley committee was given power to assist in the purchase of the land, decide upon damages sustained by cutting through buildings and carrying out condemnation proceedings.

In June 1920, the council approved a report of the committee composed of James Ross, J.H. Stevenson, and W.R. Grant that the expenses be paid from the general fund. Total cost was $18,900: $4,200 to Smith; $1,700 to Iowa Railway and Light Company; $4,000 to the owner of Lind and Hoffman's Garage; and $9,000 to the M & St. L.

City officials were served with a notice of appeal from a decision of the sheriff's commissioners in May 1920. The papers were served on the mayor, the city clerk, and the solicitor. Smith of Pomeroy claimed the $4,200 allowed him was too little. A September hearing was scheduled to resolve the dispute.

However, in August the Smith Building was sold to A.D.

Looking south on Second Street.

For years the electric plant blocked Second Street at its south end, keeping it from being a through street.

Allgood who had a flour and feed store. Sheriff Stacey was in Perry at the time to give Smith the $4,200 awarded him by the Sheriff's jury as damages. The corner of the building was cut off to conform to the other buildings and prevent a jog in the street.

By September workmen were busy remodeling the Lind and Hoffman Garage building and the Allgood property. They tore down parts of the building which were to be moved and made improvements in compliance with the rulings. Pearson and Son were contracted to remodel the garage. A strip was taken from the west side and brick and hollow tile used instead of cement blocks of which the building was constructed.

Trouble was experienced in removing old footings and the foundation of the former light plant. It was necessary to blast them out with dynamite.

The task of widening Railroad Street was begun on October 7, 1920. A strip of ground fifteen feet wide was taken from the west side of the library grounds and the northwest corner was cut off. Since that time, many changes have come to Railroad Street.

Street Names

There used to be a Fitzgerald Street. It extended from Third Street to Fifth Street and was north of Park Street.

It was First Street until August 1896, when the residents there became high-toned and requested that the council change the name to First Avenue, which they did.

It was Edna Street until the residents there were struck by patriotism. They petitioned the city council to change the name to Dewey after the hero of Manila. This was done in June 1898.

In the early days, there was a North Street and a North Avenue — the avenue, ironically, was in the south of town. When plans were made to institute free mail delivery, it was feared that this might cause a problem. In June 1907, Councilman Diddy was given the honor of deciding what North Avenue should be called; he chose to name it Iowa Street.

Chapter Six
The Fire Department

Building a Fire Station
Members of the Perry Fire Department shown excavating for a new engine house in 1905

Woes of an Early Fire Department (1879-1909)

Fire is a public enemy and every town, business, or home is vulnerable. There was a time when Perry had no means to combat this enemy.

In the beginning all the buildings were built of wood, stood close together, some with stove pipes running through the roof. Portions of the storeroom were used as dwellings.

Perry's first fire fighting organization was the old bucket brigade. The idea of an organized fire company was conceived by A.W. Otis, who owned the mill, and Fred Knell, a jeweler. The organizational meeting was held in February 1879 in the old blacksmith shop of F.M. Hain on Willis Avenue. A fire department with a membership of fifteen was organized. Otis was elected the fire chief and served for one year. He was succeeded by Knell. The department had a hand engine and 300 feet of hose. Four big wells were dug in different parts of town to furnish water to use to fight fires.

By December 1884, Perry had a town hall, a fire engine, and an engine house located on city lots on First Street.

The first fire call for the department after the engine had been bought came in January 1884. Fire broke out in the one-story Van Norden building on the east side of the square housing Del Loomis Grocery and Warner's Shoe Shop. The department was on hand promptly, but as soon as the water struck the valves of the pumps, they froze; it was twenty minutes before a stream could be thrown

Fearful that the pumps could not be made to work and the fire get out of hand, a call was sent to Des Moines. The mayor there ordered out his department and the superintendent of the Fort Dodge Railroad had a special train ready to bring the equipment to Perry if needed.

Luckily, the fire didn't amount to as much as the extreme exposure the firemen endured in the 20-below weather, the coldest since the winter of 1856-57. Knell was badly frosted and both he and Arthur Willis of the hose company were completely covered with ice — face, ears, and hands.

Generally, it took two men to handle the nozzle on the hose, but in this instance Jack O'Neill did it alone, scaling the gable of the building to direct the water where it was most needed. Though not a member of the company, he was cheered by the excited and appreciative crowd.

It was in 1886 that the city council appointed a committee to locate and build six wells for the use of the fire department. They were located at the northeast corner of Willis and West Second, southeast corner of Otley and Fourth, southeast corner of Sixth and Otley, northwest corner of Sixth and Lucinda, southeast corner of Fourth and Warford, and the southeast corner of Fifth and Edna (later Dewey). Each was to contain five feet of water.

The next important step came in August 1888 when the city council authorized the purchase of a steam fire engine. The equipment cost $1,800, with the last payment of $300 due January 1, 1892. This was in a day when milk was three cents a quart.

The fire engine was delivered from St. Paul and immediately tested as to its capacity to throw water. This proved to be twice as high as any building and in sufficient amount to drown any fire. But, of course, the demonstration was by those whose business it was to show the engine at its best.

A few weeks after acquiring the steamer and just as lamps were being lighted, the cry of fire rang out. It was in the large front window of W.H. Croft and Son's store on the west side of the square. Before the fire engine reached the well, the fire was out, but it was decided to try out the steamer anyhow to see how it worked. It didn't. The test was a failure. Too much time was required to get up steam and, when the steam was in full force, it would not throw a drop of water.

When the Moody and Son building caught fire in 1893, the steamer was called out. Since the installation of the water system, it had not been kept in condition, but the fire was across Frog Creek, out of reach of a hydrant. It took 30 minutes to get the machine in operation and by that time the whole structure was burning fiercely. Just when the flames were being contained, sand got in the valves, and the steamer was shut down. The building was destroyed.

From the day it arrived, the old steamer was in the news, whether fighting fires or setting idle. Of necessity, the fire engine and the steamer were stored somewhat off the beaten path in the old fairgrounds which were at the west edge of a much smaller Perry. One day, the Des Moines police contacted Perry officials. Some fellow had offered a quantity of old brass for sale there and the prospective buyer was suspicious.

Marshall Dave Willis and Fire Chief Tom White went to Des Moines and identified the brass as belonging to the city fire engine. The would-be seller was arrested, but was able to convince the officers that he had not stolen the brass, but had bought it. The real culprits turned out to be five or six small boys living in Perry. The damage amounted to several hundred dollars, but for some unknown reason the boys were never arrested.

Word got out that the steamer was an easy mark at the faigrounds, other scavengers got into the act. At the big Shotwell and Davis fire in which the buildings were destroyed, it was discovered that the brass couplers on some sections of the hose had been cut off. In addition, some of the couplings which had been taken from worn out hose and stored had also disappeared. These couplings were valued at $35 each.

In November 1899, a year after the big fire, Fire Chief Knell appeared before the city council to explain the need for a hook and ladder truck. The burned out section had been rebuilt with three-story buildings and the department had no means to fight a roof fire or to rescue people on the third floor. Chief Knell thought a good outfit could be purchased for about $400, but the grading necessary for the cement walks had depleted the treasury. A first-class Seagraves truck with full equipment and several trussed ladders was purchased in January 1900 at a cost of $610. The longest ladder was fifty feet.

The next problem was where to keep it. The engine house was too small and the fairgrounds not safe. The new truck arrived in April and was a very showy affair. The department escorted it from the Milwaukee Railroad to the engine house, drawing it on the cement walks in order to avoid the mud in the street.

The engine house and city hall had become unusable. After the Library Board offered the city the use of a room in the basement, the fire department decided in 1904 to build a new home for themselves. And they did.

Almost Died (1886)

The Perry Fire Department almost died a-borning in 1886. They held a special meeting and the question of disbanding was thoroughly discussed. It was their annual ball which became the straw that broke the camel's back.

The "fire boys" went to great expense planning their ball. They rented a hall and hired an excellent orchestra. They mailed out invitations and, so no one would be missed, issued a general invitation through the columns of *The Chief*.

Tickets were a dollar with proceeds going to improve the department and not to any individual member. Music was by Professor Gordon's orchestra and was very good.

But, just as it was with so many of their other attempts to raise money, this one, too, was miserably supported. Attendance was meager. In addition to the department and their special guests only about half a dozen businessmen and a handful of residents attended the ball. This was really shabby treatment.

So, the firemen held a meeting. After considerable deliberation, the members decided to stick together. City officials agreed to contribute $5 each to reimburse the firemen for their loss, but the offer was rejected.

Year after year, without one cent of reward, the firemen held themselves ready to protect property and sometimes under the most trying circumstances.

After publicizing the indifference of the people, it was hoped the lack of public spirit would end. And it did. Perry's Volunteer Fire Department has proven itself a credit to Perry.

Firemen Exempt from Poll Tax (1887)

Until the late 1930s every man in Iowa had to pay a poll tax or work a certain length of time on the roads, cutting brush, etc. in order to have the right to vote.

In March 1887, a list of fire department members was submitted to the city council as being in good standing and, thus, exempted from the poll tax.

The exempted men were: Joe Thornburg, George Sipes, John

Albright, Newt Hart, W.W. Cardell, A.E. Willis, P.B. Baker, W.J. Cole, Joe Hager, Frank Smith, Harry Smith, Jim Daugherty, J.M. Condon, W.H. Carmody, J. Ballisorer, C.L. Ashcroft, Sam Lee, Russ Smith, J. Wilcox, J. McMichael, Ross Green, Al Parmenter, Tom Mott, Miller Sipes, and L.N. Carrell.

Tin Horn Fire Bell (1894)

When the Perry Bottling works located on West Willis caught fire in November of 1894, the operator at Woodward could see the fire and telegraphed the dispatcher in Perry asking what was burning. The Perry man replied that there was no fire. All the while, the little tin can of a fire bell was ringing its best. Even some of the firemen were surprised next morning to learn that there had been a fire.

The bell then serving as the fire bell on the top of City Hall was about the size of an ordinary dinner bell. When Perry only had about a dozen houses huddled together it might have sufficed; by this time it was little more than a joke.

At the December 1894, City Council meeting, the fire alarm was discussed and it was decided to replace the bell by using the whistle at the electric plant. A fire committee was formed and authorized to purchase the necessary valves for the whistle. A code of signals was established. The new system was tried in April the next year and worked satisfactorily.

Building a Fire Station (1904)

When the old City Hall and engine house became unusable and the City Council took up the Library Board's offer to set up shop in the library basement, the Fire Department was left out on a limb. In July 1904, Chief Knell suggested that the department build a home for itself.

The firemen proposed to use city-owned property just south of the Heightshoe Carpenter Shop; to proceed they needed the city council to set aside the ground for that purpose. The old City Hall building was formally turned over to the Fire Department

The New Fire Station
Three hose carts, a hook and ladder truck, and an abundance of hose and other paraphernalia were kept in this building in 1910.

to be used as material for their new fire hall (if needed).

During the winter, the work of making the doors and window frames was carried out by the firemen. This enabled the firemen to get a jump on the new building when spring arrived. The new building had forty-two windows, with six needed for the jail, which was to be located at the back of the fire station. The contract for the joists was let to Modlin and Company who bid the work at $255.

Work began on the first of April 1905, under the supervision of Emery Wilcox.

In January, Chief Knell had asked the council for direction as to what the city wanted with regards to the jail. Mayor Edmondson appointed a fire committee to confer with the department, get estimates on the cost, approve the plans and bring in the bill for the city's share of the expense. The committee was also authorized to secure cells for the jail from the county board of supervisors, who were favorable toward the new jail.

After a thorough investigation of building materials, the committee decided that the new engine house should be built of brick. The contact was awarded to the Perry Brick and Tile Works. This company was not making any new bricks at the time, but the supply on hand was thought to be sufficient for three sides of the

Ready for Action

Hook and Ladder trucks in front of the new engine house.

exterior of the building; fancy brick was to be used on the front of the building.

Quite a number of spectators were on hand as Fire Chief Knell presided over the solemn service of laying the cornerstone on April 15, 1906. Enclosed in the stone was a bottle containing a history of the fire department, of the work on the building (as far as it had gone), a copy of the subscription list of the building fund, and the latest copies of the *Perry Advertiser* and the *Perry Chief*. Judge W.H. Fahey was expected to give the address, but he was called to Adel at the last minute, so a short talk by Allen Harvey was substituted.

There really wasn't any cornerstone. There were two columns at the front corners of the building which were built of brick and strengthened by iron pillars. The sealed bottle was lowered by a cord into one of these columns.

The building was thirty feet by eighty feet and two stories high. The front was rock-faced brick and an octagonal tower added greatly to the building's appearance. The tower was used to hang the hose to dry.

The task of constructing an engine house debt-free was not an easy one. In May, after a call for help through the columns of *The Chief*, a large sum of money already subscribed was paid into the fund. One to whom the firemen would forever feel a debt of gratitude was D.J. Pattee. Pattee went to the building site and was surprised to see the progress made. He sent a check for $100 to enable the firemen to get the building under cover.

Despite the coolness of the evening in May 1905, the people were willing to attend an ice cream social to help swell the building fund. The ladies auxiliary held the social in the new building, but the cold weather cut into the proceeds. It could be said that the new fire hall had been formally opened at this point, though without a floor or a roof.

Perhaps the most unusual fund-raising event was the banquet which the firemen arranged to entertain the people of Perry on August 1, 1905. The building would be nearly completed by that date if enough tickets were sold in advance. The banquet was also to double as the dedication service.

Bad weather came to Perry the night of the banquet. The rain began early and many who had tickets were either unable to attend or arrived very late. The ladies auxiliary served an elaborate meal. D.J. Pattee was master of ceremonies and the toast program was carried out as planned. After the banquet, the guests went to the armory where a dance had been arranged. Perry's orchestra rendered its usual solid performance.

The firemen set aside Thanksgiving Day as a time for saying thanks for all the help they had received in the building of the new fire station. The firemen spent the day in the new engine house with their families. Two hunting parties organized by T.R. Phillips and Henry Miller secured the meat, with the losing team providing the trimmings. The ladies cooked and served dinner. The afternoon was spent in games. That evening there was a private dance to cap the day.

In the beginning, the second floor was fitted up as a club room and office for the department, while the first floor provided ample room for a team of horses. In the rear was the jail, for which the city council appropriated $750 for construction. The completed building cost around $5,000 and was debt-free.

Even though this building was named to the National Register of Historic Places in 1978, that was not enough to save it from destruction. It belonged to the city and, since no federal funds were involved, they could do with it as they pleased. And they pleased to sell it and see it demolished.

Firemen's Tournaments (1885-1915)

Firemen tournaments were popular spectator events in the "olden days." The first such event was held July 29-30, 1885.

In June 1886, the tournament was held in Perry. A purse of $100 was offered for the best hose team; $35 to the second best; and $20 for the third place winner. Similar purses were at stake in the hook and ladder competition. A track for the contests was made on Railroad Street, reaching from the Willis Avenue corner to the junction with Third Street.

Great preparations were made for the event. There were beautiful arches spanning the street at the Triangle and Willis Avenue. An arch was placed across Second Street at the crossing of Lucinda. Fred Knell also had an arch erected across from his place of business.

The city placed arches at the northwest and northeast corners of the Triangle. The merchants on the west side placed a very handsome one across the street on their side of the Triangle.

An arch 60 feet wide, from the center of which an immense horseshoe was suspended, was erected by Messrs. Steele, Worth, Shotwell and Davis across Willis Avenue. The next arch was put up by Messrs. Durges, West, Henness and Edquist. It consisted of a hook and ladder on either side of the street (worked in evergreen) and in the center was an immense floral bell. At the crossing of Fifth was a large double arch erected by Messrs. Rude, Condon, Roddan, Diddy, Spaulding and Longshore.

The procession marking the official welcome was formed at the engine house and was led in the line of march by the Knights of Columbus Band of Perry. After the procession broke rank at the Triangle, Norris Brown was introduced and gave a speech.

Judging the band competition of the event brought a sour note, which played loud and long. There was only one other band entered, besides the Perry band, but because the judges they appointed scored the Perry band high and the Perry judges tried to be fair, the Perry band lost.

Perry hosted another tournament in 1899, this one in conjunction with the two-day Fourth of July festivities. Burning eloquence greeted the visitors as attorney W.H. Fahey made the welcome address on behalf of Mayor Allen Breed. The celebration included a baseball game, concerts by the Perry band, and a re-

Perry Hosts Firemen's Tournament

Firemen's Tournaments were major spectator events around the turn of the century. Perry hosted this one in 1913.

ception and dance given by the firemen in the new Elliott block.

The glorious Fourth was ushered in with plenty of noise. A parade was formed at the engine house and made a circle of the town, coming to a halt at the amphitheater built for the occasion. There were also races of various kinds and a large crowd was on hand to see the conclusion of the firemen's program.

When the City Council met that winter, a petition bearing the signatures of the businessmen around the Triangle was presented, urging that the Rock Island crossing at the depot be repaired. It had been torn out for the tournament in July. Fire Chief Fred Knell promised to attend to the repairs.

Enthusiasm was high at the 1912 tournament at Sioux City. Not only did the Perry Fire Department earn many first places, they also won the right to host the state meet in 1913.

The people at home were jubilant. Hundreds of citizens were at the Milwaukee Depot when the team returned home on No. 6. A line was formed, led by the band, and the march was made to the fire house. Everyone was stepping proud.

In preparation for the 1913 meet, the department added a number of the fastest high school trackmen to the organization

Skills Competition

Hand drawn hose carts were once standard equipment in fire departments. Sturdy firemen tugged and pulled them thorugh the dirt streets of Perry and other small towns. Team racing pulling a cart was part of the firemen's tournaments.

that spring. There was really nothing underhanded about this procedure, the rules of the tournament only stated that the runners be members of the department.

Work began early in July for the event, which was to be held at the driving park. A bunk house was built for the bunk hitching of the fire horses and for men to make their slide down the brass pole into the wagon.

The bleachers and circus seats, which were secured in Chicago to enlarge the seating capacity of the grandstand, arrived July 13 over the Interurban. The shipment was a fast one being two days en route.

Scenes in the park were lively. Teams were on hand participating and visiting firemen came early to get used to the track. On any given day leading up to the event, a great number of people were at the park watching the trial runs.

The tournament opened with a grand parade, that included the drill team from Marion, which was famous from coast to coast. Marion won first in the competition, Newton second. Atlantic, with sixty members present, won the prize for the company having the most men in the parade.

It was estimated that 3,000 witnessed the event. Rude Auto Company reported that one man was kept busy all week filling the tanks of visiting autos. This tournament was the last event to be held at the driving park.

These state tournaments diminished in interest because so many towns were getting motor trucks. Consequently, in 1915, the racing cart, pipe, couplings, harnesses, and shoes which had been worn by the members of the track team were disposed of by Chief Timeon. They were used that year by members of the volunteer department of Grand Mound, a small town in the eastern part of the state.

Melick Fires

About 1 a.m. on a Sunday in September 1893, Perry residents were awakened by cries of fire and the ringing of bells.

The basement of G.R. Melick's Grocery in the Triangle block was filled with smoke. The fire had gained such headway that an entrance could not be made into either the basement or the storeroom.

Despite the efforts of firemen and volunteers, the flames spread rapidly to the adjoining rooms as there was no firewall. The double block, two buildings on the south and two on the north were destroyed.

The greater part of the furniture of F.F. Frush was carried out. So, too, was the hardware stock of E.M. Jones, the jewelry stock of M.H. Overholser, Miss Gordon's Millinery, A.T. Parker's restaurant, H.H. Annis and Company, G.W. Worth, the Express Company, and Frazier and French.

All of Melick's grocery stock was destroyed. R.H. Culbertson lost everything, including his stocks of tobacco, cigars, and household goods. The aggregate loss was about $30,000.

The fire department worked faithfully, took desperate chances and "for a company that received no salary and was untrained they were deserving of unlimited praise," *The Chief* said.

Early on the morning of January 26, 1907, fire again broke out in the Melick block on the west side of the Triangle, destroying much of the grocery stock of the Perry Co-op Company. All of the stock of the Candy Kitchen was also destroyed.

Melick Block Burns Again

*The Melick block burned a second time on January 26, 1906. The Candy Kitchen
also burned. The building was rebuilt during the summer.*

The fire was discovered in the Candy Kitchen, but gained good headway. The alarm was sounded by the power plant and the waterworks. The fire department and citizens responded promptly. People flocked downtown in great numbers.

There was a bright moon and hardly a breath of wind. The flames illuminated the sky so that people from a distance could tell Perry was having another fire.

On the north was the Frush building into which the Bulkley brothers stock had been moved from a fire a month earlier in the Clements building. They had just received new goods valued at $5,000.

On the south was the Capen Harness and Hardware Store and Capen's stock was removed as was most of the Bulkleys'. Nothing could be saved from the Candy Kitchen and not much of the grocery stock. The rooms over these stores were vacant.

Melick had some insurance on his stock and building. Van

Epps of Moreland owned the building in which the Candy Kitchen was located.

Howard Moody fell while working on the roof, but was able to resume work.

Walter Bolt was given the contract to rebuild in December 1908.

Fire: Determined to Destroy

John Clement was born in Ireland. Shortly after attaining his majority, he married. At the age of twenty-six he came to America, landing in New York with his wife and just one dollar. Not having funds to proceed farther, he went to work there.

He had Western fever and gradually succumbed to it. He spent time in New Jersey and then went to Ohio. He came to Iowa, settling in Marengo in August 1854. In 1862, Clement enlisted as a member of the 28th Iowa Volunteer Infantry. He served under Phillip Sheridan until he was discharged due to wounds he received in Cedar Creek, Virginia.

In 1881, Clement came to Perry and started a lumber business which he conducted for ten years. He built the Clement block on Second Street and also owned five nice residences in the city.

About 8:30 on a Thursday evening in November 1899, the fire alarm brought hundreds of people to the Clement block where a fire had secured quite a dangerous headway. The Fire Department arrived promptly and soon stopped the spread of the flames. The damage was confined to that part of the building used by *The Advertiser* newspaper.

The heat was so intense that the type in the cases melted and ran together even though the fire had not reached into the room in which they were kept. The fire had eaten through the floor and ceiling and the joists and rafters were afire before the firemen had things under control.

The Advertiser's loss was about $600, which was covered by insurance. Damage to the building was about $200, but was also covered by insurance.

On a Saturday evening in January 1904, Dr. Frush of the firm Miller and Frush (dentists), was working by the light of a coal oil lamp in his lab in the Clement building. The lamp ex-

Determined to Destroy
The Clement Block burned on December 26, 1907.

ploded and burning oil was sprayed all over the small room. The furnishings immediately caught fire and the fire quickly spread to the walls and ceilings.

The flames burst from the front window and the bellow of the fire alarm was heard. To the immense crowd which gathered quickly, the building seemed doomed. The fire was soon contained, but the dentists' office was in shambles.

Across the hall, the office of Henry Nash and the dressmaking rooms of the Smith sisters were filled with smoke. In J.K. Olds' real estate office, books, papers and furniture received water damage. The stock of the Bulkley Brothers Dry Goods Store (located under the dentists' office) was also damaged by water.

Fire seemed determined to destroy this building. At 5:40 a.m. on Christmas day 1906, three of the best stores were in ruins and professional men suffered heavy losses in yet another fire at the building. The estimated loss due to this fire was put at $50,000.

Bulkley Bros. Dry Goods Store, John Daw's Drug store (which he had purchased one year before), and the Golden Rule were all losers. Stoops Photograph Gallery was a total loss. Dr. R.E. Doidge saved only his books and medical case. Dr. C.W. Harter, a dentist, lost everything and Orl Howell's books and cu-

Up From the Ashes — For a While

The Wimmer and Williams buildling was erected on the site of the Clement block. This building was also destroyed by fire in 1945.

rios burned.

The origin of the fire was a mystery. It started under a stairway to the second floor. Before the fire department arrived, volumes of smoke were rolling from the building. Many of the firemen had just returned home from a dance a few hours earlier, but none was late for the fire and all worked valiantly.

By 6:30 a.m. all that remained of the Clement block was a tottering wall on the south side and a shapeless mass of rubbish reaching to the wall on the north. The old fire wall in the center of the ruins was still standing, but it collapsed about 10 a.m. It fell on the nozzlemen; W.J. Doss received a flesh wound on his thigh. Tim Dooley was unhurt, but Don Flannagan injured his legs.

Water pressure was weak at first. The standpipe was cut off so as to work direct pressure. The light plant pumped enough water from their well into the mains to supply one hose. The roundhouse brought their hose and helped. Luckily, there was no wind and it was not cold enough to freeze the hoses.

George Clement, son of the owner, notified his father (now in California) of the fire. It was expected that the buildings would be rebuilt and occupied by the late tenants.

In March 1907, Charles Timeon was working on plans for the new block when he was ordered to stop. The Clements' lots were sold to Wimmer and Williams.

The contract for the new building was let to A.A. Roberts in July 1907. Plans called for three store rooms on the first floor, but with a different arrangement. The corner room on Willis and Second was the smallest and the other two were "L"-shaped. The building was completed in 1907, with the Bulkley brothers installed in the north room in January 1908. Total cost for the new building was more than $35,000.

Ed Carter bought the Wimmer and Williams building for about $60,000 on January 14, 1913. The name was changed to the Carter block. Carter sold the block to W.C. Harbach of Des Moines in September 1935. Harbach died on December 10, 1939.

The three-story building was again destroyed by fire on February 12, 1945. This fire started at 12:45 p.m. in the waste paper room in the basement of the J.J. Newberry Variety Store.

Local firemen were aided by firefighters from Bouton and Woodward, as well as farmers and citizens. The Des Moines fire chief came bringing several hundred feet of hose. Besides Newberry's and Woolworth's, Fisher's Barber Shop, Dr. Ross' office building, and Cox Plumbing Company, which was located in the basement, were also destroyed by this fire.

Professional men who lost offices due to the fire were: Dr. E.C. Wittee, dentist; Dr. P.W. Beckman, physician; J.B. Coakley, realtor; George Sackett, attorney; Charles Joy, attorney; B.C. Dilenbeck, realtor; Robert Wheelwright, gas and oil agent; Ray McManus, attorney; Leslie Burrell, realtor; and Dr. J.H. Worrell, dentist.

Leo Davidson of J.C. White Contractors of Des Moines operated the crane which dug out the debris that was then hauled to a central point for salvage.

The first two days of January 1946, saw the rapid rise of steel for the new Harbach building. The contractor was Kucharo Construction of Des Moines. The new structure was one story and fire proof. F.W. Woolworth was to be the new tenant.

An Ice House Burns (1905)

When Josiah Petty and his son put up ice in January 1905, they hired eighteen to twenty haulers to fill their two big ice houses.

All the crop was harvested from the river, back of Dr. Mowrer's place where there was a deep channel with a sandy bottom.

The following year, besides his own supply, Petty put up ice for H.M. Shively for his pop factory and for the Milwaukee Railroad. A force of men and a dozen teams were used. They still used the same old method and the Raccoon River was the best ice field, but it was expensive to harvest.

The harvest was so small in 1908 that by August, for the first time, artificial ice was used in Perry.

Petty had about fifteen men and sixteen teams putting up ice during the winter of 1909-1910. The eleven-inch blocks were crystal clear, but many people were hesitant about using the ice. The old ice dam was near the mouth of the sewer on the river. This was claimed a needless worry as the ice came from ponds and bayous which lined the river, entirely removed from the dam and in no way contaminated.

Worry about ice then came from another quarter. At 3:30 p.m. on March 29, 1910, a fire thought to have been started by a spark falling on the roof of the ice house from a passing train, totally destroyed the ice house, barns (including three horses) and the office of the company, as well as the Shotwell building.

W.A. Petty personally turned in the alarm and then rushed from his office to fight the flames. Although Petty was gone but an instant, the fire had spread all over the ice house as Petty and Jack Stockburger ran into the barn to free the horses. The men had to flee to save their own lives. A blind mare which Will tried to save, came to the door, became frightened and jerked away, running back into the burning structure.

Hundreds of volunteers worked to confine the blaze to the ice house buildings and the Shotwell building. The Ammerman Feed House with its flammable contents was guarded most thoroughly, saving not only that business, but likely the entire business section which would have burned had the feed house ignited.

Back of the firefighters stood city workers. Engineer Joe Hager and night pumper Kirk Hiney were both on duty. Although as high as six and eight leads of hose were laid, and all were taking water, the pressure stayed up to the limit and the standpipe was running over at the time. The wells held out exceptionally well; there never was the slightest danger that the water would run out.

That August Petty filed a damage suit against the M. & St.

L. Railroad in District Court, seeking damages totaling $7,219.50. The case went to the jury in November and the railroad was exonerated.

A motion for a new trial was filed. Shotwell had suffered a heavier loss in the same fire and filed a claim on the grounds that a spark had set the fire. The railroad promptly settled for $2,850 without delay. Petty filed a claim at the same time, but the company refused to settle.

The Day of Reckoning

Imagine the surprise the people of Perry must have felt when they read in *The Chief* on December 3, 1909, that the city had been sued for failure to pay notes on the hook and ladder truck the town purchased in 1900.

The city had used the truck for almost ten years and not paid one cent to the dealer they bought it from — the Seagraves Company of Columbus, Ohio. The bill amounted to $620 plus interest and would have been outlawed if allowed to run a few days longer.

The city had been granted deferred payments on the truck for three years after the purchase. After that, it must have fallen through the cracks. A banker in the state came into possession of the note and sent it to the First Natioanl Bank for collection. Other than correspondence, nothing had ever been done about it.

Faced with the prospect of a lawsuit, the city allowed the bill of $989.90 (the price plus interest) on April 5, 1910.

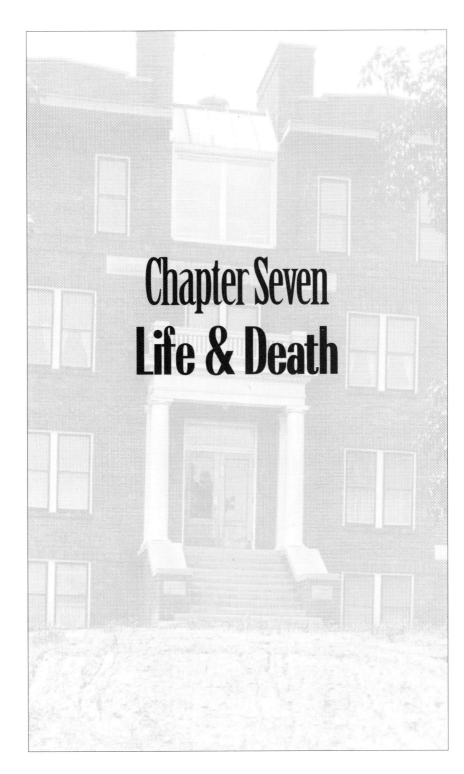

Chapter Seven
Life & Death

Dr. P.A. and Margaret Mowrer

Dr. Peter Mowrer donated land for the Spring Valley School which was built in 1861. Mary Roberts, a school girl, died of burns after her dress caught fire when polishing a stove. Before her death she requested to be buried in the school yard. Dr. Mowrer consented and the cemetary became known as Mowrer Cemetary.

Dr. P. A. Mowrer (1854)

Dr. P.A. Mowrer came to Dallas County in October 1855, and was the town's only physician at the time.

The doctor was born in Chester County, Pennsylvania, on October 31, 1830. His father was a farmer and, in 1856, accompanied by his family came to Buffalo Grove in Boone County where he farmed until his death. The doctor was the oldest of eight children: five boys and three girls. Those who lived in Perry were: Sarah, wife of Andrew Rhodes; Nathan, who married Laura Vernon; and Ella, wife of Albert Miller.

Mowrer was educated in an academy in Chester County, Pennsylvania, and took up the study of medicine in the office of Dr. Dickenshad. He also attended the old University of Pennsylvania in 1849 and graduated from that institution on the completion of a course in the medical department in 1851.

Soon after graduation, Dr. Mowrer located in East Vincent, Pennsylvania, where he remained for three years. In 1854, after a brief residence in Keokuk, Iowa, he came to Dallas County and settled near Perry. His nearest fellow practioners were in Adel, Boone and Jefferson. However, by 1884 there were nine doctors in Perry.

Dr. Mowrer married Margaret L. Fagen on December 20, 1863; they had seven children: Lettie (Mrs. Archibald Newport); Kate (Mrs. George Donahue), Mona (Mrs. M. Andrews), Edna (Mrs. Ed Mullen), Dr. William P., and Hezekiah (who died in 1892), and Genie Braman.

Perry people were shocked to hear the report in October 1892, that Dr. Mowrer's youngest son had been killed near old Xenia. On a Friday, Ray Heaton, Lock Aiken, and Hezzie Mowrer went in a wagon to the Des Moines River to camp and hunt. The boys were all about sixteen years of age, and had been warned by Mr.

Macy, who drove them, to be careful with firearms. The boys were boon companions and had a very pleasant time.

About 1:30 they started home, Mr. Macy driving, Ray and Hezzie occupying the second seat and Lock riding on the tent behind. A crow flew over and Lock picked up one of the guns to shoot it. As he did so, one of the hammers caught in the ropes of the tent, discharging the gun. The muzzle was right against Hezzie and the charge entered his body in the small of the back, making a terrible hole. He was at once conveyed to a nearby house, and Ray mounted a horse and was off for Woodward to summon a doctor. As he rode to Woodward, he was able to send two messages: one to Dr. Mowrer and one to Dr. E.R. Aiken. Not until he returned did he know his friend had died.

The body was brought to Perry on Sunday evening; funeral services were conducted by Reverend S. Jones and Reverend Wright on Tuesday at the residence. The remains were followed to the cemetery by a large circle of friends; one report indicated that more than 100 buggies were involved in the procession.

To no one did the shock fall heavier than poor Lock Aiken, yet he was blameless; even the bereaved parents did not feel he was at fault. His grief was so great that for several days he was unable to rise without help; he was still weak and showed in a painful manner the sadness he felt. Lock was not aware that a shell was in the gun, as both he and Ray said they did not load it. It was possible that the deceased had thoughtlessly left the gun loaded.

Dr. Mowrer maintained his office on his farm which was just outside the city limits. In 1899 he moved his practice into Perry, where he shared an office with his son, Dr. William P. Mowrer.

Dr. P.A. Mowrer died at his home southwest of the city on September 14, 1909, at age seventy-nine; he was preceeded in death by his wife on June 1, 1909. Services were held at his home, officiated by Rev. W.W. McDade of Red Oak, formerly of the Perry Methodist Church.

Dr. Samuel Pangburn (1874)

Dr. Samuel Pangburn was born on September 19, 1841, near Red Oak, Union Township, Brown County, Ohio. His early edu-

Dr. Pangburn

Dr. Samuel Pangburn was a physician and surgeon who not only figured prominently in the organization of the town, but was also the first W.M. of the Otley Masonic Lodge, which was organized in 1871.

cation was obtained in the public schools of Ripley, Ohio. Later he attended the Ohio Wesleyan University at Delaware, Ohio, and Miami College, Oxford, Ohio, leaving there a junior.

After leaving college in 1859, Pangburn commenced the study of medicine under Dr. A.N. Wylie. When the Civil War commenced, he temporarily gave up his studies and enrolled as a member of Co. H.O.V.L. He served three years, three months, and ably assisted in winning laurels that encircle the history of "the Gallant 12th."

The war having been fought to a successful issue, he resumed the study of medicine and graduated from the Medical College of Ohio in 1866. Pangburn also attended and graduated from Bellevue Hospital Medical College in New York in 1868.

Pangburn married Elma J. Keep of Mexico, Missouri, in 1870 during the time that his medical practice was based in Monmouth, Illinois. His next move was to Perry. He was practicing here as early as 1874, and his office-residence was at the corner of Fourth and Willis. For nine years he was surgeon for the Milwaukee and St. Paul Railroad. During his 20 some years of residence in Perry, he gained a wide reputation as a skillful physician and surgeon. He moved to Denver, Colorado, in 1889, and from there to Maysville, Kentucky in 1890.

Doctor Pangburn died on October 4, 1900, in Maysville. His illness was only of a few hours duration and consciousness remained with him until within a few minutes of his death. Funeral services were held at the Mitchell Chapel, Maysville, with interment in Maysville Cemetery conducted by the Grand Army of the Republic Post and by the Masonic order of which he was a knight. He was survived by his wife and two of the four children they brought into this world: Elbert, of Maysville, Kentucky, and Harry, who was a student at Rush Medical College in Chicago.

Perry's Lady Doctor (1895)

In the days when it was difficult for women to enter the field of medicine, Perry was proud to include a "lady doctor" in the professional circle.

Dr. Eloise Grosenbaugh was twenty-nine years old when she came to Perry in 1895. Within a few months she had established a growing practice.

A native of Iowa, she had studied at three universities with graduate diplomas from two. She had first considered becoming a teacher but decided she was better suited for the art of healing.

She graduated from the Bennett School of Medicine in Chicago, one of two women in a class of thirty and had practiced medicine for two years before coming to Perry. Her specialty was diseases of women and children, and she had been thoroughly prepared for this field of medicine.

One reason Grosenbaugh was so well accepted in Perry was because she did not match the public perception of lady doctors. The general impression of a woman doctor of that day was that of a short-haired, loud-voiced, mannish type of person; Doctor Grosenbaugh, on the other hand, had a gentle voice, an attractive face, and a refined manner. Her office was in the Breed block. There was a parlor with a half-dozen or so diplomas adorning the walls and an inner room for examinations.

Shortly before Doctor Grosenbugh's arrival in Perry, a young man by the name of Homer Alonzo Foltz came to town. He was an engineer on the Milwaukee Railroad. Sometime before the big fire of November 1898, these two were married. Their home was in that burned-out block.

It was reported that the first thing they tried to save from the fire was their piano. It was saved, but got some rough treatment

The Lady Doctor

Dr. Eloise Grosenbaugh-Foltz came to Perry in 1895 and was one of Perry's thirteen practicing physicians in 1928.

in the process. They managed to get it to the head of the stairs. Foltz said, "Let her slide," and the piano did for a few bumps before becoming wedged crosswise on the stairs.

Not relishing the prospect of being trapped in a burning building, with great effort, Foltz managed to dislodge the piano. It completed its descent of the stairs end-over-end. At the landing it took out the door casing and came to rest on the sidewalk. Even after such a fall, it was said the piano still produced good music.

In 1902, Homer Foltz decided to become a dentist and finished the course at the Dental School of the University of Nebraska at Omaha. In April 1905, Dr. Barnard, who had built up an excellent dental practice, decided to leave Perry. Foltz, who wanted to locate here, took advantage of the opportunity and bought Barnard's practice.

As a matter of convenience, Dr. Foltz the dentist moved from the bank building where Dr. Barnard was located and opened his dental office next to his wife's office in the Breed block. They used the same reception room and had living quarters on the same floor.

Foltz the dentist went into partnership with Dr. A.L. Brown in 1907, and moved into the Myrtle block with him. The following January, Dr. Grosenbaugh announced that she was moving her office from the Breed block into their residence at the northeast corner of Third and Warford. When Foltz's partnership of 11 years with Doctor Brown ended in 1917 with Brown's retirement, he moved his dental practice to his home. He maintained his office there until his death on April 21, 1933.

Mrs. Foltz continued to practice medicine until 1945 when

she sold her house and property at 1222 Warford to the Fareway chain. The Fareway store was built on this lot. The house was sold to Dr. Harrison Jewell, who moved it to a site just south of the old clinic building which was on the southeast corner of Third and Willis. The house was subdivided into apartments. Both buildings have since been torn down to make room for a parking lot for the new Fareway.

Dr. Foltz then went to Denver to make her home, but returned to Perry in 1947. She died on May 13, 1948, at her home on Fourth Street where she had been living with Mrs. Austin Robinson, who cared for her. There were unusual circumstances surrounding their deaths. Both women were found in separate rooms by the authorities several days after their deaths, both died of heart attacks.

It was as though Mrs. Robinson, age sixty-six, had gotten up for her glasses, which were in her hand when she suffered her attack and fell to the floor. Mrs. Foltz, age eighty-two, had apparently heard the fall and had one foot off the bed as though trying to go to her assistance.

Both funerals were held in the Methodist Church on the same afternoon, Mrs. Robinson's at 2 p.m. and Mrs. Foltz's at 4 p.m.

Hello World

This is how some birth announcements appeared in the newspaper in 1882:

"J. Ross found a good sized baby boy at A.A. Trunicks at Angus.

"Dr. Mowrer wants credit for a nine pound boy at Peters, southwest of Perry.

"Dr. Pangburn reports a new boy at Mammay's since Tuesday morning."

Death in a Melon Patch (1886)

Perry people were startled on Sunday morning, August 29, 1886, to hear the report that Thomas Council had shot and killed a man in his melon patch.

Council lived two and a half miles directly west of Perry and made a specialty of raising garden truck of all kinds. He also had a large melon patch. Council had had a melon patch in 1885, but before the melons were ripe the "boys" made a raid on it, pulling up the vines and stacking them. Council resolved to keep watch during the night the next season and, for that reason, lanterns were placed on poles in different parts of the patch and he and his help kept watch with a loaded shotgun.

About midnight that Saturday, eight young men decided to go after Council's melons. A cornfield was on the north side of the patch, so they entered the patch from there. Council saw them and made a rush. The last one to go was Frank Marsh and when Council was within thirty steps of him, he fired. Marsh yelled "Murder!" Council called a halt and fired again. Marsh fell after going a few steps.

All left except for George Marsh, the victim's brother. Council called J.B. Wilcox for help. Marsh was carried into Council's house where he died about twenty-five minutes later. Doctor Mowrer was sent for but did not arrive in time.

Squire Chappelear summoned a coroner's jury and Drs. Aiken, Leonard and Mowrer made a post mortem examination which showed sixty-three shots had penetrated his body, mostly through the back.

An injunction was sworn out charging Council with murder. Constable Dave Willis made the arrest. Squire Chappelear, knowing the circumstances, placed bond at $1,000 and set September 11 for the preliminary hearing.

Council secured bond and was at liberty until Thursday night, September 2, when word was received from the county attorney that the first information was worthless as it failed to specify a crime. A new information was filed and Council was arrested again by Constable Thornburg.

Public sentiment was divided over the shooting. Council was said to be a good neighbor and an industrious man. Rumors were thick Wednesday night September 1, that Marsh's friends were going to take matters into their own hands, so Council came to town and put himself under the care of Constable Willis.

Council was indicted by the Grand Jury for manslaughter on October 29, 1886. Council was defended by Henry Cardell and John Shortley. The address to the jury by prosecutor Williams was said to have been one of the best heard in the court room, but he could not claim laurels against the addresses made by Cordell and Shortley.

The trial occupied nearly the whole week. On the 30th, after being out for about twenty-four hours, the jury returned a verdict of not guilty.

Thomas Council died on May 17, 1909 at age seventy-one after taking ill in January. He was buried in Crocker Cemetery.

Death in a Corn Field (1889)

Will Kessler was a well-known, genial clerk in West and Weast's Hardware store and seemed to be an exemplary young man without fault and without an enemy in the world.

So, Perry citizens were stunned one Wednesday in September 1889, to hear that Kessler had suddenly disappeared. As the day passed, the mystery became more alarming.

He had not been in the store since Monday, reportedly because he was not feeling well. On Tuesday evening he was at supper with the H.P. Lods, where he was considered almost as one of the family. In the evening the Lods attended a party at Chandlers and, when they returned, were surprised Kessler was not home. His absence did not alarm them until morning.

Inquiry was made of everyone, but no clue to his whereabouts could be discovered. Wednesday evening, a large posse started out and remained all night searching for Kessler. Then hundreds of men and boys began to scour the country west of town to the river — all in vain. In the afternoon, all the business houses closed and the country was searched in all directions.

Kessler's nearest friends were puzzled over the affair. He had nothing to leave for and he had a good job and lots of friends. He was not one to create a sensation and he never left Perry without leaving word.

Friends thought that during the evening he had been taken with a fever, become delirious and walked off and laid down in some secluded spot. Others felt he had been foully dealt with and his body covered, still others that he had jumped into the river and committed suicide. The mysterious affair cast a gloom over the entire town.

Kessler was about twenty-nine years old; five feet, seven inches tall; rather heavy set, with a light sandy mustache and blue eyes. When last seen he wore a stiff black hat, light scotch coat and black vest and pants.

His father arrived from Illinois and the search continued. A week went by with no trace of young Kessler. His brother also came from Illinois. Every effort was made to discover his whereabouts. Search parties were organized and thoroughly scoured the countryside for three or four miles in every direction.

Then, some time later, just as *The Chief* went to press, it was learned that Kessler's body had been found in a corn field known as Mace's Farm about six miles east of town. He had with him about $65, a few papers and a revolver. He had a bullet through his head and, as one of the chambers was empty, the presumption was that he had committed suicide. Nothing remained of his body but a skeleton which was identified by his pocketbook and the papers therein.

The inquest was held by H.A. Chappelear. The jury consisted of H.P. Lods, H.W. Weast, and A.E. Willis. Their verdict was that the deceased came to his death by way of a pistol shot from his own hand while laboring under a temporary fit of insanity. His remains and clothing were sent to his parents in Illinois.

His body was found by Brown McDuffie who, in the company of Evans, was husking corn. The field was about forty acres and well traveled roads were along the south and west sides; the railroad ran on the north and west to Little Beaver. The land was not improved.

The parties had husked corn to almost that spot before they noticed anything unusual. The clothes were found lying near the remains. The revolver was found lying under the clothes and the two gaping holes in the skull told how the unfortunate man had ended his life. The hogs had torn the body to pieces and scattered bones all over the field. Only some of them were found. Thus a deep mystery had been solved?

It was later heard that Evans and McDuffie put in their claim for the reward money. Several of Perry's better citizens expressed their views most decisively as to what they thought of the claimants asking for the reward.

John Pattee's Midnight Funeral (1894)

John Pattee was a younger brother of D.J. Pattee and was a carpenter and contractor. He married Estelle Willis in May 1884, with the Reverend Simons officiating. In 1887, he and C.W. Dixon worked at Fort Dodge, building and repairing bridges.

He enlisted in Company E on July 21, 1888, and transferred to Company B on April 30, 1892. He was a marksman and went to the World's Fair in Chicago in 1892 as a member of the National Guard Rifle Team. He was elected Captain of Company B in Perry on March 29, 1893, succeeding Captain Kenworthy; McKean became Second Lieutenant, Pattee's former position.

John died at his home on March 18, 1894, of the dreaded disease "black diphtheria."

A week before, he was working as usual in the bank. It was known during the week that he was very ill, but because of the precaution necessary about the disease, friends could not call to learn of his condition. In appearance he looked to be strong and well, but he had been troubled by throat problems and, consequently, was susceptible to diphtheria.

During the week, he continually was up and about, he could not sleep. He was unable to lie down and was not put to bed until the afternoon of his death. He was delirious at times, but passed away quietly. Dr. Johnson was in attendance, consulting with other physicians.

At 9:30 Sunday night, the members of Company B of which the deceased was captain, passed slowly up Otley Avenue with silent step and passed in single file in front of the large north window inside of which was rested the coffin covered with flowers. A few intimate friends were gathered at that hour to show their sympathy.

At 10 p.m., the march to the cemetery was begun. Company B, keeping at the head of the procession, marched north on Sixth Street while the various carriages kept an even pace on the street. The AUWW and Odd Fellows were also in attendance. Every precaution was taken to prevent exposure to the dread disease.

At the grave the wind was weird and mournful. The moonlight just made it possible to see faintly while a few lanterns made the site more pathetic. The militia stood in line just north of the grave while the pall bearers brought the coffin and lowered it into the grave.

Scarcely a word was spoken. David Pattee tried to thank the company and all the friends, but was barely able to control his emotions. Following this, a few words were spoken by Rev. H.D. Stevens, recalling the unusual occasion. A prayer closed the services. Three volleys were fired over the grave by the militia; then, the mourners returned to the city. It was nearly midnight.

John's six-year-old daughter also contracted the disease and died ten days later. His widow later married Walter Shotwell in Des Moines. She died in Minneapolis in 1951, but was buried at Violet Hill.

A City Prepared (1897)

Perry was well prepared to withstand the ravages of any epidemic in the winter of 1897. There were in the city, fourteen practicing physicians and five drug stores. If all of these failed there were two undertakers and two tombstone manufacturers.

Druggists' Dilemma (1900-1910)

To be a druggist in the first ten years of the Twentieth Century was to live under the threat of court proceedings.

In the days of prohibition, the drug store was the only place to legally secure liquor and, to do that, a permit to dispense it had to be secured. This liquor could be used for medicinal purposes only and anyone could assert that a certain sale was illegal. The doctors wrote prescriptions and there was a surprising amount of sickness in the town.

The pharmacy laws of Iowa were so written that the burden of proof was put on the druggist; the statement made by the purchaser on the request form cut no ice at all. Innocent until proven guilty did not apply to the pharmacist; in Iowa, they were considered guilty until proven innocent.

In 1906, temperance workers interested in enforcement of the law were determined to keep Perry a clean town. After cleaning out the saloons, beer parlors, and closing out the slot machines, these virtuous citizens turned their attention to the drug stores. So relentless were they in their attack that very shortly five druggists were reeling.

Five druggists were taken to court. Some saw discretion as the better form of valor — rather than to fight against a stacked deck, some pled guilty, surrendered the permit, paid the fine and had injunctions slapped on them. Others chose to fight but met with the same fate. As a result, there were five retired druggists in town in 1910.

The zealousness of this campaign attracted statewide notice. A Perry man, former Mayor C. Durant Jones, was made state superintendent of the Law and Order League.

Before the year was out, the five druggists were back in business in different locations and under different names. Still, it was risky and dangerous to violate an injunction, so none of the five was selling a certain type of "prescription."

Because doctors did write prescriptions for wine and liquor, one druggist who had purchased the stock and equipment of one of the retired men applied for a permit. It was then that a curious fact came to light.

When the numerous cases were begun, injunctions were sought, secured, and later made permanent and part of the record. Lawyers and judges alike thought the injunctions were against the operators. When that druggist (who had not been involved in the earlier cases) applied for that permit, it was discovered that the injunction stood against the entire Clement Building, enjoining the sale of liquor in the building perpetually. Through due process of law, this injunction was finally lifted and a permit was later granted.

About this time, the mayor also joined the clean-up crew, setting out to improve the moral atmosphere of the town. In addition to closing the gambling rooms, he ordered all card playing stopped in all public places.

There were a number of licensed places in the city where it had become a practice to play cards for amusement. This was deemed contrary to the terms of the license and ordered stopped.

The lid was on in Perry in 1906 and on very tight.

The Smallpox Scourge (1901-1913)

While unheard of today, smallpox was a serious problem in the early days. The very mention of the word brought fear to the brave.

Perry encountered this scourge several times, the winter of 1901-1902 being one of the worst.

The first mention of smallpox was in a wedding story. The bridegroom, a Milwaukee Railroad man, secured the license on a Saturday afternoon in late October and went to see his bride at the Murrie House where she was employed. While he was there, a quarantine was placed on the hotel, and he and 24 others were shut in. He called the mayor and stated his problem. So, Monday evening about 8 p.m. Mayor E.J. Wilson donned a long-tailed coat and went downtown to perform his first wedding ceremony.

The couple stood in the open window on the north side of the hotel, while the mayor and the two witnesses stood in the middle of the street. At the close of the ceremony the window was closed and no one was released until the first part of December. It was a double quarantine, for on the last day someone came down with the disease, was removed to the pest house, and the quarantine extended.

Local newspapers never admitted there was an epidemic in Perry. The Boone paper reported there were 200 cases in Perry, but this was considered a form of getting even as a Chicago paper had listed Boone among the Iowa cities having smallpox and Perry was not mentioned.

Epidemic or not, a campaign for compulsory vaccination was begun, and officials canvassed the city demanding to see proof of vaccination and that all others were. But people would not be vaccinated and they broke quarantine. Not all who had the disease were confined to their homes. Many went to the pest house north of the cemetery.

Food and medical care for those in the pest house cost the county dearly. The Board of Health decided not to give medical attention unless absolutely necessary. Some on the board felt the pest house patients should not be fed so well. And, since the disease had been light, it was predicted that people would feel more ill when they had to pay their taxes.

Summer came and the smallpox siege was over for that year.

Another smallpox outbreak came in the winter of 1912-1913. Once again, the first mention of the outbreak dealt more with an unusual event than with the disease itself. In this case, an Austrian hobo, not a worker in the company was discovered in a bunk car near the new Milwaukee roundhouse where he had crawled for shelter. The workman who found him became alarmed and summoned a doctor. A hurried diagnosis indicated the man had some form of variloid. The word smallpox was not used.

The men in the camp went to work throwing up a slight grade, laying ties, carrying steel; by morning the sick man rested in the car some 300 yards out in a corn field, isolated from the rest of the company. Harry Hull, who was immune from the disease, acted as nurse and caretaker for the patient. Thus, a complete quarantine of the encampment was avoided and work on the new roundhouse could be rushed to completion.

While it was admitted that there were two cases of smallpox (the hobo and Dr. H.B. Wilkinson, the city physician who cared for him), others became ill but were not quarantined. Doctors differed in their diagnosis; some called it English chickenpox or swinepox. A state Board of Health official was called in, who declared the disease smallpox. In all, eighty-six homes were quarantined that season.

It Used to Be the City Cemetery (1905)

It used to be called the City Cemetery, that ten-acre plot north of the city. Perry citizens often wondered why something was not done about it.

Finally in 1905, the City Council asked for all those interested to send the name of their choice to either C.D. Oldham (owner of the marble works) or to *The Chief* before the first of April. The council would then choose the name they considered the most desirable.

Among the names offered: Linwood; Greenwood; Mount Hill; Pleasant Hill; Hillside; Greentown; Silverleaf; Rose Hill; Rose Lawn; Zion; Glenwood; Mount Hope; Crown Hill; Silent Mound; Lawn Hill; Birch Knoll; Fairview; and Fairmont.

The Council chose the name of Silent Mound which had been submitted by W.E. Brown. It was adopted on April 3, 1905,

Violet Hill Cemetery

The cemetery was called Violet Hill by children because of the blue looking carpet of flowers which covered its gentle slopes. It became the official name of the cemetery in 1905.

and signed by Mayor B.F. Edmondson.

The name was not a popular one. Instead of usage softening the dislike for it, antagonism grew. Even people of surrounding towns sent in letters asking why the council didn't change the name.

Many felt it far better to go back to the name the children had so appropriately called the sacred place so long before. Because of the blue carpet which covered the gentle slopes, they had given it the name Violet Hill.

One Saturday afternoon that year, at an adjourned meeting of the Federation of Women's Clubs, the matter of changing the name was talked over. A petition to be sent to the council asking the name be changed to Violet Hill was left at Dr. B.Roy Emms' office for signatures.

The petition was presented to the council that same month and they voted a tie. The mayor broke the tie with his vote to change the name.

The Pest House Burns (1910)

The dilapidated, unsightly old frame building which served as the pest house for so many years burned down at about 2 a.m. on a Sunday in late November 1910.

Located on a hill north of the cemetery, it was outside the fire limit and beyond the reach of the water mains. So, the firemen, tired from the long run of pulling the hose cart, sat comfortably within the radius of the heat and watched the dancing flames consume the place.

It had become the hangout of the tough element of the city for their poker and crap games and drinking bouts.

Vote for a Hospital (1911)

March 27, 1911, was a big day in Perry. Not only were city officials to be elected, but voters were also being asked to decide whether or not Perry would have a hospital.

The election was a "turn 'em out" campaign. In every ward in the city the people rallied to the cry; voting was fast and furious against the men on the Citizens' Ticket, with the single exception of W.T. Powers in the Third Ward, who weathered the gale. With this exception, the entire People's Ticket headed by C. Durant Jones was chosen.

So great was the heat of the campaign and interest in the election of the officials that there seemed no mention of the hospital's fate. However, shortly after the election, it was announced that receipts on opening night of the new Majestic Theater would be given to the King's Daughters for the hospital fund.

Through the Thomas Agency, the site for the proposed King's Daughters Hospital was purchased. The tract was a gift to them from B.C. Dilenbeck. When the plans for the founding of this much-needed hospital were first talked over, Dilenbeck told some of the ladies that he would purchase and then donate a site for the building.

Dilenback commissioned a real estate firm to make the purchase. The agent settled on land in the Highview addition because of its many excellent points in the matter of location and

King's Daughters Hospital
The balcony on the second floor was just below the operating room

surroundings.

With a magnificent donation of $12,265 made by the audience at the hospital rally at the Grand Opera House on September 29, 1912, the building of a fine hospital on Willis Avenue was assured. The campaign was waged by a band of twenty young women.

The bid of Jacobsen and Stombeck was $17,850. Braman Electric won the wiring bid at $500; Henry Miller the heating at $2,050; and Miller Brothers got the plumbing contract with a bid of $1,700.

Just one year later, the members of the Perry Circle of King's Daughters took part in the ground breaking ceremony for the hospital, each digging a shovelful of dirt and carrying it beyond the line made by contractors Jacobsen and Stombeck. The ceremonial laying of the cornerstone was held on October 19, 1913, and in one month's time, the brick work was completed and the building entirely enclosed.

The dedication was held on April 29, 1914. Judge W.H. Fahey

was the speaker. An open house was held from 1 p.m. to 9 p.m. This was also parcel day and all visitors were asked to bring a parcel containing articles which would be useful in the new hospital.

The first surgery was performed on May 7, 1914, on the daughter of Mr. and Mrs. J. Morton, owners of the Wolfe place. Drs. Ross and Mowrer were in charge and Dr. McCarthy of Des Moines did the surgery. It wasn't until July that the first baby saw the light of the world through the windows of the new hospital.

There were accommodations for twenty-eight when all rooms were occupied. Superintendent Victoria Carlson had a force of five nurses working days, one on night duty and two student nurses taking training.

The hospital nurses lived in a house in the Dilenbeck addition, but in September 1915, they moved to a house nearer the corner of Tenth and Warford. The house was large enough to accommodate the entire corps of graduate and student nurses. Superintendent Carlson, who had always had a personal room at the hospital, also moved into the house.

The Farmers' Auxiliary to the King's Daughters, the only organization of its kind in the world, was made a permanent organization on January 13, 1917, at a meeting in the Perry National Bank. The men who had so generously aided the Alpha Circle had gone on record that their support would be forthcoming at any time.

It was in 1950 that the ax fell, this one wielded by the state fire marshal. The hospital was sold to the Lutheran Association and became a home for the elderly.

By March 1978, the old four-story building was gone and the last of the brick and plaster trucked away. The building had served the community as a hospital for about forty-two years and for twenty-two years as part of the Lutheran Home.

An Unwanted Patient (1913)

It took Mayor C. Durant Jones to take a case of smallpox and give it a new twist. Madrid officials were up in arms on March 15, 1913, because Perry officials had allegedly dumped a smallpox patient onto that town and, in so doing, exposed the passengers on the Milwaukee train to the disease. The matter was reported by the Madrid officials to the Milwaukee Railroad. Madrid

Mayor Cedarquist intimated the matter would be taken up with the state Board of Health.

The young man at the center of the episode was Shorty Bowman, son of Mr. and Mrs. C.H. Bowman of Perry. He was an engine watchman employed at Madrid.

The Madrid mayor claimed that Bowman had gone to Dr. A.M. Rogers of Madrid complaining of a cold and fever, having all the symptoms of pneumonia. When the doctor informed Bowman of his diagnosis, the sick man said he wanted to go to Perry. The claim was made that the early symptoms of pneumonia and smallpox were similar and it was not known that he had a contagious disease. At any rate, Dr. Rogers was not the city physician of Madrid, so the case had no official recognition.

The morning of March 15, Bowman came to Perry. He was sick and Drs. Trout, Paul and Wilkinson examined him and said he had smallpox. Doctor Wilkinson called Mayor Jones who talked to the young man. Since Bowman worked in Madrid and considered it his home, Mayor Jones told him to get to Madrid on the next train.

The Madrid mayor further claimed that Dr. Wilkinson had called the Madrid telephone operator asking her to tell the doctor who waited upon Bowman that the young man had smallpox, and for him to take care of his own patients.

This angered Madrid officials. When Bowman arrived back in Madrid at 9:30 that night, town officials took Bowman in charge and, for want of a better place, put him in the town jail. They tried to make arrangements to place him in a shanty down on the river which a contract firm had put up for smallpox patients that winter, but were refused. This meant they would have to erect a building for him, but they would see that Dallas County stood the expense.

Perry's side of the story was a bit different. It was claimed that Bowman came over, saying he had been in the care of Dr. Rogers, that he was just breaking out when he arrived and was in that condition when he left Madrid. While the rash was showing, the doctors claimed there was no danger of contracting the disease until the postules formed, so he was ordered back. The feeling in Perry was strong that Madrid was trying to unload the case, so for that reason, he was ordered back to Madrid before that course would be impossible.

What was indicative of things to come, the Madrid mayor

said he was going to Des Moines and lay the matter before the state Board of Health to ask that the state investigate the case.

The Milwaukee Railroad, as soon as it was discovered that a man suffering from smallpox had been riding in a car on their train, ordered that the car be set out. It was not to be put back in service until thoroughly fumigated.

The second chapter of this case opened later that same month with Mayor Jones being served with papers for "knowingly sending a person affected with a contagious disease out of the city." The information was signed by Mayor Cedarquist of Madrid. The papers were served by a Boone County constable. Mayor Jones immediately gave bond for his appearance, waiving the preliminary hearing and allowing the matter to go before the Grand Jury at the next term of the Boone District Court.

The Grand Jury met at Boone on May 5, and returned an indictment against now former Mayor Jones (there was a city election in Perry during the interim), charging him with the shipping of a smallpox patient into Boone County, thus violating state quarantine laws.

Attorney H.G. Giddings was in Boone and made an appearance for his client and furnished bonds for his trial appearance. Jones was in Kansas at the time.

The case was assigned for December. It had been on the docket for a number of times and each time continued. When Jones and Giddings arrived for trial in Boone on December 9, they found that, without saying a word to anyone, the Boone attorney had dismissed the case.

Mysterious Death (1966)

Six weeks after he was last seen, police were alerted to the disappearance of Harry Vernon Ramsey, age eighty-three. Floyd Taylor, who was a second floor roomer in the Ramsey home, made the report.

Ramsey was born on August 3, 1882, in Boone and came to Perry in 1922. He was often seen pulling a wagon down the streets or carrying a canvas bag with pens, pencils and greeting cards or other merchandise to sell.

Taylor said he had shaved Ramsey and cut his hair on January 15, 1966, the last date he'd been at his house. Taylor told police that Ramsey was planning to make a visit but hadn't indicated where he was going.

Marion Ramsey, a brother in Phoenix, Arizona, had no knowledge of Harry's whereabouts. A pension check which had arrived at the mail on February 1 was unclaimed.

By April Dallas County Sheriff John Wright reported that his office was starting an investigation into the disappearance. Police could find no evidence in a search of the home. It had been completely gone over, including the furnace room where all sizes of wood and leaves for burning had been placed. A search of a large vacant house next door produced no evidence.

C.M. Brooks, Perry's funeral director, reported Ramsey often came to him for advice but that he had not seen Ramsey since January 7, when they spoke in downtown Perry. Brooks also talked with the brother in Tucson and obtained a picture in April 1966 of the man who by this time had been missing for three months.

After a year, Dallas County and Perry authorities still had no leads in the mystery.

Things began to happen after the house was sold at auction on order of the Dallas County District Court. Claude Altig was the high bidder.

A few days later, Mrs. Altig and her children visited the house and started what she described as a treasure hunt. They found at least 200 boxes of greeting cards and small novelties before they came to a small pantry on the northeast corner of the house. They opened the door and became alarmed by the unmistakable odor of death and left. As soon as Mr. Altig come home from work, he immediately called the police.

Sergeant Harold Wicks and Officer Doug Clark searched the room. They carried out armfuls of paper then Wicks, using a pitchfork to probe the debris, discovered the body.

The sheriff, county attorney, and coroner were called and a further search of the house was conducted. Reed said the officers gathered up possible clues including a stained and slashed pillow and a knife found in an oatmeal box.

An autopsy was performed on February 6, 1967, to determine the cause of death. Officers from the Iowa Bureau of Criminal Investigations came to Perry to assist. They found no conclusive evidence of foul play.

The mystery of the pillow and the knife taken from the house was solved, however. After the body was found, three freshmen boys went to Leo Pedersen, boys' advisor at school and admitted that they had entered the house during the summer. As a prank, they slashed a pillow on Ramsey's disheveled bed and smeared it with ketchup. The boys were questioned at length by Sheriff Wright, Dallas County Attorney James Van Werden, and Warren Stamp of Des Moines. No charges were filed against them.

Several explanations were given as to why police had not discovered the body earlier. That no odor was detected during the early search could be explained by the fact that the house was unheated and the body very likely froze. Then, as Wright and Reed both explained, just because a body is missing, a house is not torn apart to search.

The junk and debris in the house had to be seen to be believed. Clutter completely filled the basement and hallways on the first floor. The unmade bed on which Ramsey apparently slept was covered with four or more heavy quilts and dirty sheet blankets. Traces of rats or mice were everywhere. Investigators speculated that most of the flesh on the body had been consumed by rodents.

Rumors persisted connecting Floyd Taylor to the case, the last person known to have seen Ramsey alive. Taylor was then living in Yuma, Arizona. He requested a lie detector test and two were administered by Robert Voss of the Bureau of Criminal Investigations. These tests completely vindicated Taylor of any connection with the case. Taylor had requested this test shortly after Ramsey's disappearance, but it was not given as the only person qualified to administer the test was hospitalized at the time.

Taylor accompanied the officers on a tour of the house where the body was found, but was unable to throw any further light on the case.

Dr. Chapler of Dexter, the medical examiner, said on February 15, 1967, that the case was definitely not closed. Exhaustive tests conducted by Dr. Helen Dawson, an Iowa City anthropologist, failed to determine a cause of death. The death certificate was signed "Under investigation."

Services for Harry Vernon Ramsey were held in February 1967, over a year after his death.

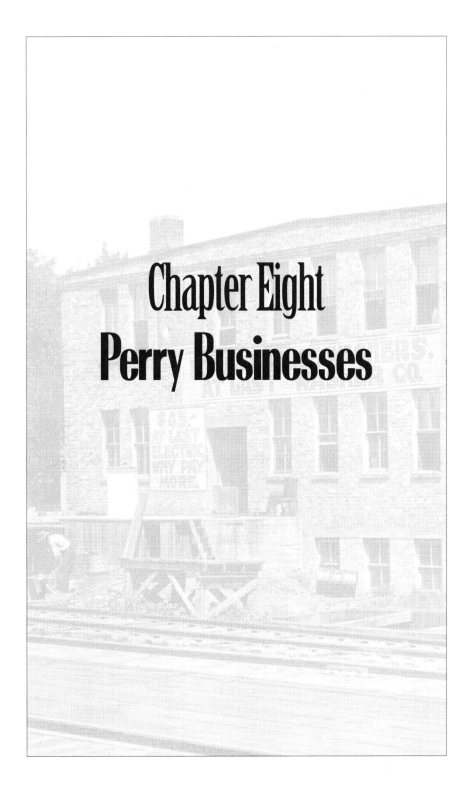

Chapter Eight
Perry Businesses

Chinese Store

AR SHONG & CO.,

DEALERS IN

STAPLE AND FANCY

GROCERIES,

Tea, Coffee, Notions,

Tobacco, Cigars, &c.

PERRY · · IOWA.

Ar Shong

An advertisement for Perry merchant Ar Shong that appeared in the February 22, 1877 edition of the Perry Chief, left, and his Americanized spelling of his name as it appears on his tombstone.

Ar Shong — The Chinese Merchant (1875)

Ar Shong was a Chinaman who came to Perry in 1875 and became one of the town's earliest merchants. He purchased George Usury's building in the northwest corner of the intersection of First and Willis. The space had previously been occupied by Frank Swan's store.

He joined the Presbyterian Church when he first came to Perry. Lizzie Pierce, who was his Sunday School teacher, took an interest in him and gave many an afternoon teaching him reading and writing. It was about this time that he changed his name to William Arshong.

Arshong was a genial soul doing well in business in Perry. Shortly after he opened for general store, break-ins were reported at his store. A few months later, the store was robbed again of both goods and money. Still he prospered. Arshong bought the J.D. Miller property on First Street adjoining Robert Ginn's in 1883 and five years later made an addition to his store.

As a naturalized citizen, Arshong refused to comply with a federal law enacted by the Congress in 1892 requiring all Chinese to register. The law was called off the following year until a test case was tried. For many years Arshong had been a property holder and voter.

Then he fell victim to real trouble. Stolen goods began to show up in his store. Many felt Arshong was not guilty, but was being set up by those who had committed the thievery. It was generally known that Arshong would buy anything from a muskrat hide to a span of mules.

For some time his store was shadowed by detectives and, finally, officers armed with a search warrant succeeded in finding a large amount of clothes which had been stolen from the Rock Island depot. Arshong's store was looked upon as a fence for stolen goods. In fact, merchants from neighboring towns found large portions of their stolen goods in Arshong's possession.

The merchant insisted the articles were brought to his store by men who were strangers to him, He told what he thought was the truth of how they had come by them. He further claimed that he never saw the men before and had not bought goods from the same man twice. In every case, the articles found by the officers had the original mark. This led many to believe Arshong was not in league with any organized band of thieves, but simply had been spotted as an unsuspecting person who would believe any probable story and buy the goods for cash.

The year 1894 was a fateful year for Arshong.

In January, another lot of stolen goods was found in Arshong's store. It had begun to seem that everything stolen within a 100-mile radius of Perry was making its way to Arshong's headquarters. Someone even started the rumor that he had stolen the pile of wood which occupied a prominent place on his First Street property. About a week later he was indicted on the charge of larceny and held on bond of $800, which was furnished.

In September the case was dismissed as the principal prosecuting witness could not be found. Arshong never went to trial.

Still, the year went into a downward spiral from there for Arshong. It started in November when he had a serious run-away. The horse was standing at the back of Billy Howe's residence where Arshong had taken a load of wood. The horse became frightened by a piece of paper and started to run, scattering wood along the way. In turning a corner, the wagon upset and was shattered. He had to hire a man and a wagon to gather up the wood.

On December 2, 1894, it was reported that Arshong was very ill, presumably of typhoid fever. Two days later he was dead.

There was a strangeness in the circumstances of his death. Arshong was a man born in a distant land, dying as a Christian of a rather mysterious death in the midst of a civilized nation, ignorant of his age and whereabouts of relatives.

Arshong's estate was valued at $2,500. He had no will or heirs, so the amount left after the claims were paid went to the state, then to the school fund.

Arshong was buried on December 5. His funeral was in the Presbyterian Church and it was well filled by local citizens who came to pay their respects. The Reverend E.M. Jones officiated.

By December 10, the sale of his stock of goods had begun

and closed out way below wholesale prices. All through the opening day the store was crowded with people, some of whom went out of curiosity, but all invariably bought something before leaving. By the 14th, the stock of goods was closed out.

The assignee's sale of the real estate took place on February 22, 1895. The old buildings owned by Arshong were torn down, leaving little to remind anyone that he had ever existed.

At the sale of the property at the county seat, the lots on Willis Avenue were sold for about $1,100. The property was divided into three separate lots and were purchased by J.B. Swearingen, Charles F. Dana, and J.B. White.

Almost twenty years passed before Perry had another Chinese resident.

St. James Hotel (1876)

Small as the little village of Perry was, there was a surprising number of hotels and boarding houses. One of the longest in existence was the St. James, though it was called by another name when it opened, and a different name by the time it was torn down.

The first version of it was a wooden structure which had stood on the site of the old Fort Dodge Railroad depot, but was moved to Second and Otley when the railroad was built. William McLuen owned it then, and opened a harness shop in it.

In 1876, J.F. Perry purchased the property from McLuen and fitted it out to be a hotel. McLuen moved his harness shop to another location. The hotel opened in April and was called the Commercial House.

Later, the hotel was called the City Hotel, perhaps in the same way Violet Hill Cemetery was called the City Cemetery for so many years. The building of the Fort Dodge Railway meant the coming of more salesmen, prospective businessmen and visitors, and the hotel was ideally located to host them.

The foundation for an addition to the City Hotel was laid in August 1882. It was a veneered building ninety feet by thirty fee and three stories high.

A reporter was shown through the building in July 1883 and he described it through the columns of *The Chief*. The new part had thirty rooms for guests, many of which were suites with a

The St. James Hotel

An article in the Des Moines News about the St. James Hotel in 1889 declared it to be one of the best in the country. The accommodations were considered first class in every way.

closet for each. Behind the main office were the baggage and wash rooms, a gentleman's waiting room and a large sample room and a laundry. The entire building (new addition and original frame part) had rooms for fifty-five guests.

In June 1884, Professor W.D. Lummis was arrested for maintaining a nuisance on his hotel premises in the way of manure and offal. The trial was held and the professor was discharged on the grounds that the city had no right to make a criminal action of the matter.

Lummis, the landlord, further improved the facilities later in 1884 by putting in pipes so water could be forced to the bathrooms on the third floor. In the washroom on the first floor, there was a tank so arranged as to supply water for a number of washbowls by means of a faucet. The fame of this hotel was widely noted, bringing praise from the *Des Moines News* in 1889.

The wooden section of this hotel seemed a favorite target of the fire fiend. In 1891, just after the waterworks system was completed, and on the day the City Council was to meet to accept it, the hotel caught fire. Thus it furnished the first test of the efficiency of the water supply.

Mayor Allen Breed, who at some previous time had become the owner, decided to make some changes in 1897. A new and spacious dining room was made in the brick part back of the office and the kitchen and sample rooms were moved into the old dining room.

Fire broke out twice in the same week of May in 1898. The first fire was put out without making a fire call and was caused by the careless dropping of a cigar stub on the hallway carpet. Night watch Pryor had seen the smoke and went to investigate.

Fire broke out again in the frame portion a couple of days later. Soon three lines of hose were at work, but the water didn't seem to reach the spot. Holes were cut in the roof — getting a hose up there was another problem as the city had no ladders.

A rope was tied to the hose, just below the nozzle and one end thrown to a man on the roof, who pulled it up. Just as the nozzle went over the edge of the roof, the stream shot up the fellow's pant leg. He held on and slid over the cone of the roof, remaining there until someone shut off the water. By this time the fellows at work on the north side of the building had the fire out.

After this fire, Mayor Breed announced that the wooden structure was to be torn down. But it wasn't. Another announcement appeared in *The Chief* in May 1901, again stating that the building would be torn down, but, again, it wasn't.

The fire company was called out at 11:30 a.m. one day in July 1901, to fight yet another fire at the hotel. This one was on the roof of the wooden structure and was started by sparks from the chimney falling onto dry shingles. The fire burned a hole in the roof five or six feet square.

The roof of the south wing of the St. James caught fire on July 23, 1906, furnishing excitement and a run for the fire department. As usual, the blaze was out before they arrived. Soot from a burning chimney fell upon the roof and set the shingles afire. The fire was put out with a couple of buckets of water.

Again the story was put out that Breed was going to rebuild and again the plans seemed to go awry.

The hotel management splurged in January 1901 by putting a beautiful new coach in service. The running boards were yellow and the body black, while the sides had beveled plate glass. There was a seating capacity of eleven inside with a tallyho seat on top for four more. Under the driver's seat was a cabinet for a storage battery which supplied electric lights consisting of three Keystone brass trimmed lights.

The batteries also heated a large steel plate inside the vehicle making it comfortable in even the coldest of weather. The coach cost $785 and, with the addition of a matched team of horses, represented an investment of more than $1,000. The coach met all trains; Harry Foster was the driver.

Fire continued to plague the hotel. By this time fires at the hotel had become a standing joke among the firemen. Every time a call sounded, someone asked if it was the St. James. Every member of the fire department had been through the old part of the hotel so many times that they had no trouble finding their way through the rooms and halls, even in thick smoke.

After at least ten fires in the old wing, an ad in *The Chief* gave the information that the old eyesore was to be torn down and the lumber sold. Before this was done, however, Mayor Breed closed a deal in 1909 with C.W. Council of the Perry Auto Company for the sale of the hotel property. Council promised the old part would be torn down and it was.

Council let the contract on August 2, 1910 for the construction of a one story brick storeroom between the Odd Fellows Building and the hotel. A new cement block sample room was built at the rear.

Council traded the St. James Hotel, the small storeroom occupied by the Barker Dairy and other property to J.H. McCaskey in July 1923. This started a period when the hotel changed hands frequently. In 1934, the parlors were opened as a public amusement parlor. A dance floor was installed and a beer permit secured.

A new front was added in 1947 after John Williams of Fort Dodge purchased the hotel from Mr. and Mrs. Norman Miller. The name was changed to Hotel Rainbow. New baths were installed and new furniture was purchased for what was then a 23-room hotel.

A $17,000 remodeling project was underway in 1964. The main improvement was the adding of eight rooms on the first floor where the taproom was formerly located. The name was changed again to the Snell Hotel.

Sometime between 1960 and 1963, the name was changed to the Rogers Hotel and when it was demolished in 1982, it was called the Triangle Apartments.

Heaton Opens "Chicago" Store (1879)

William H. Heaton was born in Brighton, Iowa, on October 8, 1845. His early years were spent in that town. When the Civil War broke out, he enlisted in the 30th Iowa Infantry and served three years.

Heaton came to Perry in May 1879, attracted by reports of the growing business of the little village. He was actually on his way to Belle Plaine to investigate opening a store there when someone on the train asked him why he did not go to Perry.

Arriving in Perry he found a little storeroom on the north side of the square owned by D.J. Pattee, which was vacant. Later this became the site of the Pattee Hotel. Mr. Pattee was in Adel on business which could keep him there for several days. Rather than miss the opportunity to obtain the place, Heaton secured the services of Matt Bibbins' Livery and was driven to the county seat, closing the deal to rent the building from Pattee.

The Chicago Store, a dry goods store, opened in Perry on

The Chicago Store

Heaton's Chicago Store in the Breed building at the northeast corner of Second and Warford. The proprietor, William H. Heaton is on the right, the woman in the center is Mattie Ebner. The identity of man on the left is not known.

May 10, 1879. The original firm was Friend and Heaton, although the senior member, Friend, never lived in Perry and visited the store for just a few days each year. The stock held in the store when it opened on that beautiful spring morning was immense. It had been arriving for many days.

The depot was filled to overflowing and Billie Jennings, the agent for the Fort Dodge Railroad, was overwhelmed with the goods. The room wasn't ready and the depot was full. Billy Clark, the drayman, was the only source of news for the people and he was besieged with questions concerning the stock and where all the mammoth dray loads were being stored.

The only advertising done was the posting of the name of the store and its opening date on walls, posts, and what few fences could be found in the country.

The doors were not opened until everything was in readiness. Then the $25,000 stock was given over to the public's selection and praises.

From morning until midnight, one of the largest crowds, heaviest buyers and most delighted public the town ever saw reveled in the lines offered. It was general stock including everything one would want or need.

Heaton married Naomi Smith, the daughter of Mr. and Mrs. Barton Smith on November 3, 1881.

In subsequent years, the store was moved several times. In November 1898, it was located in the Breed building at the northeast corner of Second and Warford. The big fire that struck that building was "a disastrous one for Heaton for with all the salvage of the stock and the insurance, he was still a loser by about $5,000." After Breed rebuilt his block, Heaton was back in business in the Breed building.

Heaton died in April 1920. His only son Harry took over his father's business, closing it around 1939.

If Walls Could Talk (1889)

If only the walls of the old Stewart Hotel building could talk. What a story they could tell.

The three-story double front structure was built in 1889 by John Stewart. O.T. Fuller of Manilla was engaged by Stewart to take charge of his new hotel. Fuller had been manager of the Depot Hotel at Manilla and it had the reputation of having the finest restaurant on the Milwaukee Railroad line. The newspaper reported Fuller was a "live Republican and a working Sunday School man."

Fuller came to Perry in September 1889, to attend to purchasing the antique oak furniture, stoves and carpets for about $4,000. On a Sunday in October before the hotel was fully completed, a number of Perry citizens called and took dinner with the landlord.

The dining room and office faced the street, with the stairway to the double parlor on the second floor between the two. The windows on the front were of plate glass and colored glass, making the rooms light and cheerful. At the rear of the offices were the wash rooms, writing room and two sample rooms to accommodate traveling salesmen. The private rooms of the proprietor were on the ground floor, as were several guest rooms. The third floor was devoted entirely to guests.

The main stairway, hall and all rooms on the second and third floors were carpeted, nearly all in a different pattern. Every room was connected to the office by an enunciator so that calls could be made to and from each other. At the rear of the brick building was another two-story frame structure used for laundry work. Sleeping rooms for the help were on the second floor.

Hard luck came early to the hotel. There were changes in ownership and managers until, finally, the furniture was bid off to satisfy a mortgage holder. Harry Wooders took charge in March 1895, and began to clean the neglected hotel. By this time the owner of the building was James Harvey, father of Allen and R.M. Harvey, who at one time owned *The Chief*.

The wooden building at the rear of the hotel caught fire three times within ten days in August 1899. There was little left of that structure. For some time, extra rooms had been needed and the burning of the frame building hastened the plans. A two-story brick fifty feet by fifty-feet addition, valued at $2,000, was begun immediately.

During the transfer from one management to another in 1900, the house was temporarily closed while new furnishings were put and considerable papering and painting done. Hot water heat was installed. That summer, Sunday dinners were served for thirty-five cents.

The Stewart Hotel

The three-story building on the right is the Stewart Hotel as shown in this 1908 postcard view looking south down Second Street in Perry.

Sometime after the turn of the century, Fred Ling became the landlord. It was reported in 1909 how he complied with the state law requiring fire escapes in every room. The bedrooms were fitted with rope escapes which worked with a pulley arrangement fastened to the frame of the window. They were said to be strong enough to bear an extremely heavy weight, but no one would test them.

Ling was in charge until May 24, 1913, when he sold the furniture and fixtures to a Boone man. The hotel remained a $2 a day house. E.D. Carter bought the building in March 1920. That was the year Ben Mon, a Chinaman, and two others took over the management.

Ben Mon had been in the laundry business in Perry for a number of years. He was born in China on April 15, 1888, and came to America about age eleven. He had been a resident of Iowa since 1911.

Then it was reported that he, along with George Fong and George Chang were together in the operation of the Stewart House. The two Georges remodeled the south room (formerly the office) into an up-to-date eating place in March 1921, while Ben Mon retained control of the two upper floors. The cafe was named the Royal; Chinese food was its specialty. It seems that there were other specialties at the hotel.

This hotel was raided in the spring of 1921. Officers Frase, Carter and A.B. Needham raided the place in April and arrested two men. Ben Mon, the manager, was bound over to the Grand Jury under $1,000 bond. Bill Chung was charged with being in a disorderly room. He was find $50 and costs after pleading guilty.

The raid was pulled off about 11:30 p.m. after officers had been watching the place for several hours, during which time several men were seen entering by the back door. Chung was found in a room with a woman. County Attorney Harry Wifvat conducted a hearing before Mayor Adrian Cross. The woman was ordered out of town after her evidence was taken.

On November 28, Ben Mon, owner of the furniture, moved out and the building ceased to be a hotel. Ben Mon, age forty-five, died of cancer in the Kings Daughters Hospital. He is buried in Violet Hill Cemetery.

The remodeling of the old Stewart in December 1921, into a modern apartment building with two store rooms on the ground floor, marked the passing of one of the most famous of the early day hotels. The building itself had not only been changed, but also the name. It became the Arcadia Apartments.

The thirty-eight rooms on the second and third floors were remodeled into eight modern apartments from three to four rooms each. City heat was installed in all the rooms, and the apartments were equipped with a gas range. Most had a private bath. All the old decorations were removed and the interior refinished in mahogany.

T.W. Jackson, who had charge of the decorating for National Wood Works, said that he removed from some of the walls thirty-three layers of wall paper to the thickness of nearly one half inch.

As a hotel, the Stewart had been a big factor in the civic and commercial development of the city. It was here that the old Perry Commercial Club held its meetings. It was here that transient visitors received their first impression of Perry's hospitality.

George and Addison Birdsall bought the building in November 1928, and completely refinished and remodeled the interior, fumigating, papering, and painting all apartments and laying hardwood floors in some of the second floor rooms.

Since then there have been different owners and many tenants but the building is still standing, though minus its third floor.

It was removed and the roof lowered making it a two-story structure.

The Creamery (1882-1912)

Perry's first creamery was located at the south edge of town, near the Fort Dodge Railroad. In 1882, a new creamery was built just west of Frog Creek on the south side of Willis at a cost of $3,000. The egg room was large enough to hold over a million eggs when cased and these were shipped to New York, Boston, Oregon, the British possessions, and Alaska. In the winter, the firm handled poultry.

By 1888 the creamery was churning up to 300 pounds of butter daily and their goal was to have a dozen teams gathering cream from all sections around Perry. Mrs. Selma Green told how she had seen the huge churns when she went there with a tin pail to get the buttermilk which was always given away.

Of course, the plant was not without troubles. Fire broke out in the cold storage and ice house in the spring of 1893. Because no hydrants were near, the steamer was ordered out, but it was not in working condition and the entire structure was destroyed. A workman had been burning grass around the building and had left the fire to go to dinner. While he was gone, the wind changed and the building caught fire.

Citizens living on West Willis complained about the odor arising from Frog Creek, which they said was caused by the offal the creamery emptied into the stream; the current was not sufficient to carry the waste away.

At eleven o'clock on a November night in 1898, the creamery caught fire again. It was necessary this time to lay a long line of hose from the waterworks station and, because of the length, it was difficult to keep the hose from bursting. The fire burned so fiercely that all the adjoining buildings were destroyed. The plant was rebuilt and made better than ever.

Henry Moody, owner of the creamery had bad news for Perry on October 28, 1909. He announced he was leaving Perry to go to Oregon. The plant would be closed.

W.W. Winegar purchased the Moody Creamery tract in November 1912 from Moody estate of Salem, Oregon. He platted it, had it accepted as Winegar's addition to Perry and placed the lots on the market. Most of the lots faced Willis and West Seventh, and were considered among the best in that part of the city.

Culbertson Makes Cigars (1889)

R.H. Culbertson, who began the manufacture of cigars in Perry in 1885, moved his plant, the Eureka factory, to rooms over Melick's grocery in February 1889. *The Chief* noted it had printed 5,000 labels for boxed cigars for the factory and that was the second order of the year.

When the Melick grocery burned in September 1893, Culbertson lost everything. He moved to rooms in the Gamble block formerly occupied by the business college, and was back in business again in October.

He moved back in December 1894, to the rooms he had before the fire. The firm occupied the entire second floor for the factory and drying room. He was making 4,000 cigars a day, but was still several weeks behind in orders. Popular brands were Bullfrog, Monkey, Owl and Seal Skin. In seventeen years he had

Enjoying Their Culbertsons
Engineer Billie Howe, Engineer Billie Bloomfield and Conductor A.C. Hann enjoying the Bob Culbertson's "Bullfrongs" after a meal at Welch's lunch room.

made over 3,000,000 Bullfrogs, a large portion of which were sold in Perry.

In April 1902, he sold a half interest in his factory to Dell McCollough, a young Perry man who had been employed by Culbertson in the factory for eight years.

The public was greatly surprised in March 1904, to hear a rumor that the firm had failed and their factory closed. The factory was then located on Warford in rooms formerly occupied by the Star Restaurant.

The Big Fire (1898)

The big fire of November 20, 1898, was the most destructive fire in Perry's history, as both sides of Second Street from Lucinda to Warford burned. Twenty-two business houses were destroyed and the estimated damage was about $300,000.

It was about 9:30 on a Sunday evening while citizens were sitting by their fireside or preparing for bed that the fire alarm was heard.

The fire was found in the out building of the Oxford Restaurant, which was opposite the post office. The flames were soon put out and those who had gone out to see the blaze returned to their homes. They were aroused by a second alarm at about 10:30.

The fire had a better start this time and played havoc with much valuable property. The flames were breaking out from the back of John Mitchell's Livery Stable and, being a frame structure, it burned like tinder.

The roof of Mitchell's barn collapsed and fell upon 15 horses, that could not be removed because of the intense heat and rapid spread of the fire. Twelve of the horses belong to Mitchell and one was valued at $1,000.

The adjacent buildings were also frame and quickly caught fire. Cal Miller's large barn was soon one massive blaze and it was not possible to save all the vehicles and animals. A strong northwest wind saved Miller's residence, that of L.D. King, and the old Town Hall.

The Sani Restaurant went next, followed by Leonard's Meat Market. Dr. E.R. Aiken's office was ignited but by some mysterious circumstance escaped destruction. However, Gough's Tailoring and Miss Oliver's Millinery shop did not escape.

Trouth and Miller's agricultural store and the Armory and Chandler's block soon caught fire. It became apparent that both sides of the street were going to be destroyed when the Grand Leader department store on the east side was seen to be ablaze.

The flames on each side seemed to be racing to see which could destroy the most property in the least time. The fire on the east side reached Warford Street first. On the west, Mrs. Walker's restaurant and the Philbrick building were soon things of the past. With so many streams of water going, it was a severe test of the waterworks.

The heat from the west side broke the large plate glass window in the store opposite and it became certain that the Masonic Temple, the Opera House, and their contents were doomed.

Fenner and Johnson's Shoe Store, Miss Pierce's Millinery, and Ringheim's Dry Goods, Gilbert's Hardware, and Heaton's Dry Goods — all with valuable stock of merchandise — were consumed by the flames. Brick walls seemed to melt.

Fire continued on the west side. The Wild and Rall Shoe Store, Bailey and Robinson Clothing, Roland and Dowling Grocery and Gamble's Furniture store soon disappeared.

Firefighters struggled against the odds. The crucial battle was at Gamble's store; if the flames were not stopped there, they could jumping across the street, south to Reed's Jewelry store or across the alley to *The Chief Reporter* office. It was a victory when the walls of Gamble's store fell in and the fire was under control.

It was thought that this had been the work of a fire bug. During the early part of the fire, before the east side was torched, someone kindled a fire in the outbuilding back of McCamman's Clothing Store and next to the oil room back of Gilbert's Hardware. This was discovered and put out.

Another attempt was made during the time when every effort was being made to save the Citizen's Bank. Men on the roof of the frame building east of the bank saw a man start a fire in the outbuilding back of Ammerman's Grocery. As soon as he realized he was discovered he fled down the alley and was soon out of sight. The handsome bank survived.

The Perry Advertiser, another newspaper located on the second floor in the heart of the fire, was destroyed. Only the subscription list and account books were saved.

The Chief Reporter's office, exposed on both the north and east sides, was in the path of the raging flames and it was feared that the narrow alley was not wide enough to serve as a fire break. When the solid brick wall of Gamble's did not fall, the escape of *The Chief* office was assured.

The Madrid fire department responded to the call for help. When the fire had gained such headway, the second section of Train No. 63 was at Maxwell. Chief Dispatcher Pat O'Connor ordered the train sidetracked and sent the engine and crew to Madrid to bring the fire department to Perry. The fire boys were ready and waiting to load, and they had the fastest ride of their lives, reaching Perry in twenty minutes.

The chief of the Des Moines department accompanied by scores of men and hose carts made the thirty-five-mile run to Perry in forty minutes, arriving just as the fire was brought under control.

The stiff wind scattered sparks. W.B. Taylor's residence, three-fourths of a mile away, caught fire three times.

There was much looting during the fire. Thousands of dollars of property were carried or hauled away by thieves. Not being satisfied with what they could carry, some used wagons to transport large quantities of goods.

After the fire had been burning for some time, people coming in from the north of town passed a load of goods being hauled away and, as it was Sunday and no merchants were open for business, believed it had to be wholesale robbery.

A buggy full of merchandise was found a few miles east of town where it had broken down. Citizens coming in from that part of town on their way to the fire passed several persons carrying armfuls of loot.

Wilson and Ferguson kept their horse and buggy in back of their furniture store in the Triangle. When they went to get the horse on the following morning, they found the halter strap cut and the horse covered with foam and sweat. Someone had used it to help in the plundering.

Russ Phillips had run Gamble's wagon out of the barn, but that was the last he saw of it that night. The Revend Rosenberger found the wagon the next morning in front of his home with one roll of carpet in it.

S.C. Gough, the tailor, reported his loss by robbers as greater than his loss to fire. Being one of the first places to catch fire and a frame structure, all of his goods were removed. What was not stolen was considerably damaged. It would have been better had his goods not been touched as his storeroom did not burn.

Monday morning another wagon was found near Bouton where it had broken down. Some of the goods were still in it.

As Elmer Millard was coming to the fire, he saw someone running down the street with some blankets. He called to the man and the fellow dropped the blankets in the ditch and disappeared.

It was a bleak sight which met the eye of morning after the fire. Both sides of the block devastated by the fire, now had a light blanket of snow partially covering the ruins and the bodies of dead horses in their stalls.

Council Extends Fire District (1898)

One aftermath of the Great Fire of 1898 was an awareness of the need for preventive action. The city fathers held a special council meeting and suspended the rules so an ordinance extending the fire district could be passed at once. The ordinance also included a requirement that all new buildings had to be built of non-combustible materials.

At the first regular city council meeting following this action, a trustee of the Methodist Church was present and asked permission for the church to erect a barn at the rear of the parsonage on condition that it be veneered in brick. He further stated that the church wanted to abide by the council's decision.

Now the council had enacted ordinance after ordinance that had never been enforced because of the penchant of the councilmen for granting favors. But, this time they were determined that the fire limit was going to be enforced.

Councilman P.H. O'Connor made a forceful speech to the effect that it was time to begin earnest enforcement and that a precedent should be established so that all petitions of a like nature would be refused. All the councilmen made speeches along the same line except Councilman David Blue.

It seemed the council was of the opinion that the Methodist Church could afford to put up a respectable building without imposing any hardship on the congregation. The petition was refused by a unanimous vote.

Wash Bennett purchased the framework of the new barn on

the Methodist parsonage lot and moved it to his place in the northeast part of town.

At the council meeting, the usual bills were allowed, with one exception. The bill of the Perry Telephone Company for $20 maintaining the fire alarm system for two months was rejected. It was the opinion of the council that an alarm turned in over the system in the present condition would go nowhere.

Prisoner Escapes (1898)

In mid-December 1898, one Fred Laird was a prisoner in the Angus jail. Some of the goods purloined on the night of the big fire had been found in his possession.

Laird had been among the last to offer his services to Mr. Rall in removing goods from his store. Rall paid cash to all who helped, but this man was not anxious to receive any pay and almost had to be forced to accept a little money.

Soon it developed that this fellow had in his possession a number of tools corresponding to those discovered missing the next day by workers on the Christian Church. A revolver which was the property of Fred Ling was also missing. No definite information was received until a friend of the man, either because he was angry at him or too confidential with another fellow, informed him as to who had some of his missing goods.

In the meantime, Laird had moved his household to Angus and it was there that he was apprehended. He was brought to Perry where he was interrogated by Rall but refused to admit any guilt.

Laird was asked to remove his shoes and an examination showed they were originally a tan shoe but had been stained and the manufacturer's name removed. The shoe was identified and Laird was jailed by county officials.

But by January 1899, Sheriff Payne had lost his prisoner. Laird picked the lock on the jail door and made good his escape. The "hash hole" in the door had been left open and it was by this means that he reached the lock. It was about 10 p.m. when Laird escaped. Sheriff Payne discovered the escape a few minutes later, but Laird was not found.

East Side of Second Street Rebuilt

This is the look of the east side of Second Street in the Breed block after it was rebuilt following the Great Fire of 1898.

Block Rebuilt (1899-1902)

Perry was fortunate that the businessmen who were victims of the fire of 1898 did not give up, but immediately began the task of rebuilding. By the middle of the following January, the rubbish and rubble had been almost cleared away.

Allan Breed had plans for his new block prepared by C.C. Cross and Son of Des Moines who were the architects of the new Christian Church.

In April, the weather for which the contractors had been waiting arrived and work on the Breed block went forward rapidly. The room on the corner of Second and Warford streets was fitted out for a bank with two office rentals in the rear having an opening onto Warford.

The next office was fitted expressly for W.H. McCammon and Company, the clothiers. The others planned for Thomas J. Gilbert Hardware, H. and E. Ringheim Dry Goods, W.H. Heaton Dry Goods, and Fenner and Edmondson Boots and Shoes. The second and third floors of the latter two were for the Masonic Fraternity.

West Side of Second Street Rebuilt

This is a view of the west side of Second Street after that block was rebuilt following the Great Fire of 1898.

The seventh and eighth storerooms were added in 1902, when Breed covered the remaining fifty feet between his building and the Elliott block, making the Breed block complete and uniform.

New buildings on the west side were the L.D. Gamble double storeroom on the Warford corner; then Wild and Rall Shoes. Bailey and Robinson put up two rooms for them and one for Pierce the Milliner and upstairs rooms for the AOUW and other lodges.

John Shortley's building was occupied by Dooley Drug and upstairs was the law firm of Shortley and Harpel.

W.T. Philbrick had the next lot. Chandler's double building was to house Auspitz Grand Leader Department Store, with the upstairs for the Armory. George Leonard's double building was for him and a renter.

Orvis Thornburg was next, with room for him and one for the Chicago Bakery. John Mitchell's building was on the Lucinda corner, with a large livery barn just back of it for himself.

The Elks purchased the Philbrick lot between the Shortley and Chandler buildings for $2,500 in January 1899. Building began in the summer. Joe Courtney had charge of the brick work and Veach was foreman of the carpenter gang. It was rented to Edmondson and Graney Shoe Company.

In January 1902, John and George O'Malley Furniture, which

was headquartered on the Triangle, purchased the lot on Second Street north of the Grand Leader of George Paul. Paul planned to build on his remaining lot at the same time.

In May, some bricks which had been unloaded ready for use in the O'Malley block became wet from rain and were slacked like lime. They had the appearance of very hard and durable bricks, but the moisture got to them and they had to be scooped up with shovels. The bricks came from Fort Dodge and it was fortunate that they experienced their problem with water before they were put into the building.

The first kiln of bricks at the new Perry Brick and Tile Factory was opened. These bricks were fine and withstood a thorough test. C. Modlin said they were as good a brick as would ever be seen in Perry. The first lot of bricks was used in the O'Malley building.

This block of buildings has had many different tenants and owners over the years. There has also been much remodeling of buildings in the block but, with the exception of the Perry State Bank Building, they have remained basically the same.

Shortley Building (1899)

The building which for years housed the Holcomb Drug Store was erected by Attorney John Shortley in 1899. He and attorney Harpel had an office on the second floor and Dooley Drug Store was located on the ground floor. Shortley included a swimming pool in the basement for his own entertainment and that of this friends.

The pool was very elaborate for its day, measuring about fifteen feet by twenty-five feet and had city heat system pipes installed to heat the water. Shortley also put in athletic equipment for his private gymnasium.

Shortley died in 1913 at the age of sixty-two, but for some years before that the pool had not been used.

At about 2 a.m. on June 16, 1915, fire broke out in the Shortley Building. It was first seen the Glenn Woods' studio located upstairs at the back where he and James Harvey were sleeping.

When this blaze was brought under control, another fire was discovered in the basement in the rear room where the swimming pool had been built. For years it had been used as a dumping place and filled with rubbish, which the fire consumed. The flames finally ate into the joists which supported the floor of the Dooley Drug Store.

It was difficult to get at this fire as the west wall of the pool stopped the water. As soon as the firemen could penetrate the clouds of smoke to shoot the water over the barrier, the work of extinguishing the blaze proceeded rapidly.

The day before the fire workmen had gone over the wiring, putting everything in conduits. It was believed that a voltage overload due to lightning might have been the cause of the fire, because it had started in two places.

At the time of the fire, Fred Tolbert's Barber Shop was located in the front basement room and attorney Harry Wifvat and Judge W.W. Cardell had offices upstairs.

Attorney George Sackett, owner of the building in 1945, decided to put the unused space in the basement to use for storage. Getting rid of the pool's four and a half foot tall, six-inch thick brick and concrete walls was a problem. This was solved by dynamite.

John McCarthy and Earl White blasted down the walls, placing charges so that brick and mortar fell in to fill the hole made by the pool.

Workers in nearby buildings were apprehensive while blasting was going on, but there was only a series of dull muffled explosions and the walls came tumbling down and the pool was filled in.

Remains of Two Industries (1907)

In Forest Park Museum there are two Perry-made washing machines: an At Last Washer; and a double-tub Quicker Yet machine. These were the last products from what were once two thriving manufacturing companies based in Perry, the Globe Manufacturing Company and the At Last Washer Company. A.S. Kibby was an important member of each.

Born in Davenport, Kibby moved with his family to Audubon. There he became highly interested in a washing machine which an old man had produced.

Globe Manufacturing

A.S. Kibby was the inventor behind the Globe Manufacturing Company's Quicker Yet washing machines. Financing was provided by a group of Perry businessmen.

Kibby enrolled in college at Ames and went on to form a company to manufacture bed springs. Then, he and O.H. Watkens invented a mechanized washing machine. Watkins became Kibby's partner, but he did not want to manufacture them, so the company dissolved.

Perry Commercial Club members H.C. Modlin, J.C. Bryan and J.P. O'Malley heard of the washing machine invention and thought it might be a good thing for Perry. They went to Ames to see the machine. As a result, Globe Manufacturing Company was organized in 1906, with Kibby as a stockholder. The company was incorporated in January 1907, with O'Malley, Bryan, C.D. Oldham, Josiah Petty, Watkins and Kibby as directors.

A lease was signed with Shotwell and Davis for the building which had been their butter and egg house for many years. It was located along the Milwaukee Railroad on West Second Street. The former tenants, the Perry Concrete and Stone Company, had moved to another location.

Kibby moved his family to Perry, also bringing his machinery for the factory. A sample washer was exhibited at a gathering of retail hardware merchants in Des Moines in February 1907. It was handsomely finished and had the name "Quicker Yet" inscribed over a globe background.

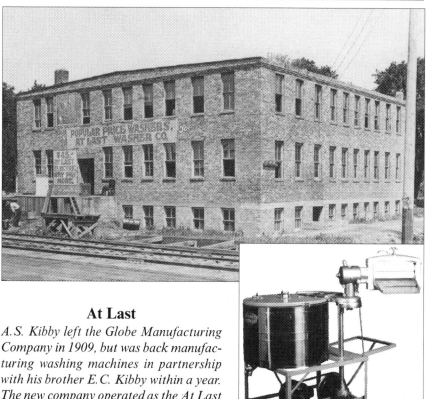

At Last

A.S. Kibby left the Globe Manufacturing Company in 1909, but was back manufacturing washing machines in partnership with his brother E.C. Kibby within a year. The new company operated as the At Last Washer Company. The At Last plant is shown above. At right, is one of At Last's electric washers.

In December of that first year, the factory building caught fire. P.H. O'Connor and Harry Steltzer were going home about 5:30 p.m. when they noticed a small blaze on the roof. The fire department was immediately called and the alarm was sounded by the waterworks whistle, but for some reason the electric whistle was not sounded. As a result the majority of people did know there was a fire.

In the factory 600 tubs were just being finished for the market, and Kibby was looking after the varnishing process in place of the regular man. At nearly closing time and without warning, the entire varnish room was ablaze. Kibby received burns on his arm which required a doctor's care.

Business was so good that the directors decided in 1908 to erect a new three-story building. Lots were secured along the

Milwaukee tracks on Fourth Street. By October 1908, they were running full blast in their new quarters with 20 men on the payroll and 50 machines being completed each day.

In September 1909, Kibby resigned from Globe to open his own machine shop and pressed steel novelty works. He rented the first and second floors of the Shotwell Building on West Second where the Globe Manufacturing Company had begun business. His brother, E.C. Kibby, joined him in the new venture. Kibby, the inventor, was a genius when it came to mechanical work. While with Globe, he often secured the machinery he needed for projects by building it himself.

Kibby's new concern made one of the first electric washers ever built and business increased steadily until the Grinnel Washing Machine Company started a fight on invention royalties in 1912. The battle took over four years and cost about $30,000, but Kibby prevailed.

In May 1912, the At Last Washer Company purchased lots on the east side of First Avenue, just north of the Milwaukee tracks and a new building was erected. In 1916 work commenced north of the Milwaukee depot on a new factory to make castings for the washing machine factory.

The Globe Manufacturing Company building was again destroyed by fire and another three-story building was put up in 1916. This building had a room on the third floor for employees and a complete kitchen and dining room were established. Meals were served at cost. A clubroom adjoined with a library, newspapers and magazines so the men could spend their noon hours in relaxation.

Finally, the time came when sales fell and the plants in Perry followed in the footsteps of nearly every washing machine factory in the country — they closed down.

At the request of several banks, a receiver was appointed for the Globe Manufacturing Company in 1922. The building, after being purchased by the Des Moines Valley Produce Company in 1930, was destroyed by fire yet again.

The At Last Foundry was sold in 1919 and opened again as the Perry Foundry. For a time Kibby continued to make washing machines for a Chicago firm at the At Last Foundry. He died in 1929 and Mrs. Kibby sold the factory building in 1931 to J.M Smith for his Disintone Manufacturing Plant.

James H. Stanley of Perry had a push mower which had the

name of Globe Manufacturing Company, Perry, Iowa, stamped on the wheel. There seemed no record of when or why the company made this product.

Dignan's Double Header (1907)

In May 1882, just two days after his marriage, John Dignan and his bride went west to seek their fortune, intending to stop in Omaha. On the train their plans were changed by stories of how great the town of Perry had become, so they stopped here. Dignan went to work on the section (the Milwaukee Railroad) and soon managed to save enough money to start in business for himself.

Almost two years after settling in Perry, Dignan went to Des Moines to purchase his first bill of groceries. It was also his first trip to that city. He bought out Blodgett who had been conducting a grocery store in a wooden building in the 1300 block of Second Street. This grocery was the only business house between Chandler's block and the Milwaukee depot, excepting the Stewart Hotel.

In July 1898, Dignan traded an eighty-acre farm near Dawson for the R.E. Fitzgerald building north of the Stewart House. The building was occupied by a meat market and the Star Grocery. He had a new glass front installed and painted and papered the interior. It was a striking room. Four 600-candlepowered gasoline lights were secured which made his store as light as day.

When he first began, the firm's name was simply John Dignan's Groceries. About the turn of the century, the Milwaukee Railroad adopted a policy of hauling heavier trains and of double-heading the engine in order to save one train crew. Since he was in a double storeroom, he thought it would be a good idea to call the store "Dignan's Double-Header." For years his ads carried a cut of a double-header pulling a train.

A new branch was added to the store in February 1905, when Dignan purchased Shield's Bakery. He had the front part to rent as the baked goods were sold at his store. Grocery men on their rounds had numerous calls for bread, pies, and cake and it always meant they had to go out and buy it if they wanted to accommodate the customer. With Dignan's new deal, people could have baked goods delivered at the same time as their groceries.

Dignan's Store

John Dignan's store building prior to it burning to the ground in May 1907.

Dignan used spring gatherings of farmers in Perry to conduct a rudimentary survey of farm activity in the area. In 1896, he hired six boys and stationed them at every entrance into Perry with the instruction to count every team that entered the city.

The boys hired to conduct that first survey were: Eddie Baldwin, Frank Brown, Harry Wychoff, Fred Hemming, Ray Courtney, and John Pendy. They were stationed at the corner of First and Park, West Willis, near the Milwaukee stockyards, South First, and the road to the cemetery. Their total count that year was 482.

Dignan repeated the exercise on April 1, 1905. This time his sentinels came up with a count of 494 teams entering Perry.

But, Dignan's run of good fortuned ended in 1907 when fire, the persistent nemesis of businesses in Perry, struck his operation.

It was noon on a Sunday in May that a fire started in the rear of the store. Within a few minutes the entire building was in flames. A strong south wind made it impossible to check the fire before it reached the north end of the block. Four other buildings were destroyed, a barber shop, bakery, and two empty buildings.

Before the alarm bell sounded, several of the firemen on their way home from church had seen the blaze and went to the engine house after the cart and ladder trucks. The city water supply was not sufficient, but Bert White, water supply man for the Milwaukee Railroad, cut into their connection. This helped put out several small fires which started in the block north and at the elevator. J.D. Hall's building was damaged.

As a result of Dignan's blaze, fires also started at the Washington School, Wolfe Elevator, Dr. Johnson's office, the Hunter residence on Dewey, and the Rice residence on First. A determined effort was made to keep the Modlin Lumber building from igniting. Many garden hoses and ladders were pressed into service.

Dignan reported that he would soon put up a new building. In the meantime, he bought the Fred Alex Bakery and ran the business in the Kerns building.

The contract for his new building was let in September 1907 to John Oleson. This was a fifty feet by ninety feet building with a seven-foot basement with cement floor for a bakery.

Just nine months after the fire, the handsome new brick building valued at $15,000 was ready. It was said 2,625 people called on opening day. Thirty clerks were kept busy all day long. The restroom for the ladies was a thing of beauty, and many took advantage of its presence on the first day. One of the main attractions was the refreshment booth, where hot biscuits and coffee were sold.

Dignan discontinued his practice of making morning house-to-house calls for orders. Those who had phones were requested to call in their orders and delivery loads left the store four times a day.

In 1919 he installed a system of delivery that assured the housewife getting groceries in the shortest time possible. Auto trucks were put into use and orders left the store almost immediately after being received. All goods were sold Collect on Delivery unless paid for at the store. This would be in keeping with his motto "Pay Cash and Pay Less."

John Dignan retired from business after forty-one years in January 1926, selling his stock to C.J. Swartz of New Sharon. Dignan died on May 16, 1926, at the age of seventy-two at his home on First Avenue.

Stop the Fires — Mayor's Orders (1907)

After the fire at Dignan's store, Mayor Modlin made a ten-minute speech to the City Council in October 1907, in which he issued an ultimatum — Perry had to stop the fires. To do so meant all old buildings and sheds in alleys had to be done away with. The constant report of fires was hurting Perry's image all across Iowa.

The mayor suggested that property owners be notified that all wooden buildings were not to be allowed within the fire limits even if they were only a foot high, and that all then under construction would have to come down.

The mayor proposed that the fire committee be instructed to inspect the buildings and report to the council with recommendations. Mr. Carmody seconded the motion. The fire committee, composed of Wildman, Miller and Thomas, was not disposed to accept such a responsibility for work that might create adverse comment. Wildman moved that the entire council make the tour of inspection. Diddy objected to this because he said it would not be fair to make the city mad at all the councilmen.

After much discussion, it was decided that the entire council and the mayor would make the tour. Dilapidated sheds and trash were found everywhere. Almost every property owner and businessman in the fire district received a communication from the mayor.

The six brave councilmen, true to their pledge to each other, did make the trip, following Mayor Modlin and City Clerk Cross. They prowled around the alleys and sheds, closets and rubbish piles, attracting much attention.

Everything on the tour was going along nicely when suddenly the entire group found themselves inspecting the jail. They condemned the jail and ordered it removed to the waterworks, since all of the crowd was on the water wagon anyway.

Welcome to the Shorthill Plant (1912-1919)

Not since Perry had secured the Milwaukee division point in 1881 had such a single piece of news been so welcome as was the securing of the Shorthill Iron and Steel company in 1912.

The plant had begun as a blacksmith shop in Marshalltown in 1860. Over the years it had grown to the point that its original site could not accommodate the factory any longer. Management let it be known that a new site was being sought.

James A. Shorthill, the founder, had died in 1901, and C.H. Spears, who had joined the company in 1898, took over active management. It was he who sent word on February 20, 1912, to H.C. Giddings, vice president of the Perry Town Lot and Improvement Company, that the contract submitted by Perry was satisfactory and was signed.

Perry had promised the company ten acres of land to be donated for a factory site, free water and taxes for seven years, assurance of adequate side track, electric power furnished at three cents per kilowatt or less, up to $50,000 in bonds to be sold to finance construction of the factory, and $75,000 worth of stock in the company to be sold.

B.C. Dilenbeck announced on April 4, that the sale of stock for the Shorthill plant was completed and the entire $250,000 needed for that organization was raised.

Because there was no such building going on in Perry in 1912, there was a dearth of laborers. So a crew of twenty-five black workers was brought to town to work on the steel plant on 18th Street, north of the Milwaukee tracks.

A complex called "Camp Lincoln" was set up at the construction site, bunks installed and a cook hired for the men. This camp was the scene of some excitement on July 23, when, during a quarrel, camp cook Jeff Herks shot Charles Cooley, one of the workers.

According to stories told by a number of witnesses in Justice Haskin's courtroom, Cooley took a seat in the center of the table which was assigned to him when he arrived on the job. The cook told him to take another seat and he refused. A quarrel followed and after supper, while Cooley was seated under a tree near the camp, Herks ordered him off the place. He refused to go until Herks started shooting. One of the bullets struck Cooley in the arm, inflicting a minor flesh wound.

Officers Hines and Hart were summoned. They arrested Herks east of the camp where he had gone after the shooting.

Thirty Marshalltown men, all employees of the Shorthill plant arrived in Perry on the Milwaukee Train No. 3 on September 18, to inspect the new plant and to attend the Red Tag lot sale in the Dilenbeck addition near the factory site.

The men were met at the depot by 15 automobiles and the Madrid band, which was in Perry to play for the big lot sale. The visitors were welcomed by the city and shown the business blocks and the residential district.

After a delay of several weeks, the carload of tools and machinery which Superintendent Garrigan had been waiting for arrived and unloaded at the site on July 8, 1912.

The first commercial work done by this factory was delivered to the Elks Lodge in June 1913, in the form of some iron beams to be used in the reconstruction of their building. Most of the plant's work had been in the fabrication of steel to be used in their own building east of the city.

The first shipment of steel completed at the Perry plant consisted of seven steel bridges, which were placed in the vicinity of Alexandria, South Dakota, in July 1913.

At last the Shorthill plant was officially installed in Perry. The plant at Marshalltown was closed down and workmen commenced taking down the machinery there on September 2, 1913.

The Perry plant was unusual in that there was eleven miles of putty strips used. The glass for the factory windows, which made up the walls of the mammoth building, arrived in November 1913. It was thought to be the largest glass setting job ever tackled in Iowa.

Work was really picking up in 1914 and a force of twenty men was employed at the plant. So, it came as a complete surprise when, on September 21, 1914, a petition for the receivership of the plant was granted by Judge Henry. The move was taken in an attempt to save the plant and protect the shareholders.

The company re-opened for a short time, but closed again in November. Evidence of "frenzied finance" and juggling of the assets and resources was shown in the receiver's report to the District Court in January 1915. The company was hopelessly bankrupt.

The big plant was sold at a referee's sale at the courthouse in Des Moines in May to Clyde Brenton of Dallas Center for $18,250. There were only two other bidders: B.C. Dilenbeck of Perry and one other whose name could not be learned.

The judge refused to approve the sale and it was put up again on November 10. This time it was sold to the Chicago House Wrecking Company for $21,500. They turned around and sold it to A. Harris of Chicago in December 1915. Harris made a business of buying machine shops and closing them.

Mr. O'Connell of the wrecking company arrived in Perry on January 19, 1917, to oversee the tearing down of the plant. He was experienced in the work, having performed his first labor of this kind when the Ferris Wheel was torn down after the Chicago World's Fair.

About fifteen local men were employed and a steam derrick and crane were used. Every part of the building was saved, loaded on cars, and shipped to Chicago.

It could be said that this site went from pig iron to just plain pigs, for in 1919, Charles Hausserman began erecting a packing plant on this land.

Chapter Nine
Trains

First Milwaukee Railroad Yard
The C., M. & St. P. Railroad roundhouse was between Seventh and Eighth streets.

Perils of Railroading (1869-1924)

The first train on the Fort Dodge line entered Perry on July 5, 1869. The first ticket office was in a boxcar. A depot was built in November 1883, it was remodeled by adding a new passenger room and a bay window.

One of the fastest running trains in Iowa was put on in 1883. It was called the Cannonball and covered the distance from Perry to Des Moines, thirty-five miles and seven stops, in one hour.

Due to a dense fog, a combination freight and passenger train ran into some coal cars which were standing on the main line in January 1884. The engine was destroyed; the tender, the boxcar, and four coal cars were smashed. The noise of the crash startled Perry people and hundreds visited the scene and gained a faint idea of the perils of railroading.

The engineer, Jack Daugherty, and the fireman jumped and were not injured. The engine and tender left the tracks, struck the coal cars, and rolled into a ditch — a complete wreck. Passengers on the train were shaken up and frightened. The damage to the company was heavy as the engine was a new one and considered one of the best on the road.

As early as December 1886, it was rumored that the Rock Island would take formal possession of the Des Moines Fort Dodge Railroad. This extended from Perry to Ruthven, a distance of 138 miles. The Rock Island had formally operated the line on a fifty-year lease. They took control in April 1887.

The Minneapolis & St. Louis (M. & St. L.) had its terminal in Angus and the line went to Des Moines over the Rock Island. The Fort Dodge-Ruthven property was really needed so they quietly secured a controlling interest in it. When the Rock Island lease was up in 1905, they were unable to negotiate another lease, so they were forced to withdraw.

In January 1914, the M & St. L. purchased the line. A few years prior to that time, some of the stations had been rebuilt, old rails replaced with eighty-pound steel and other improvements made on the property.

The road also gave the Minneapolis line the coveted terminals and entrance which it needed in Perry. The old terminal at Angus put the line at a disadvantage to the successful operation of its freight and passenger service.

The Chicago, Rock Island, and Pacific bought the Des Moines Valley Railroad, the oldest system in Iowa, on August 19, 1924 for a cash consideration of $1.2 million.

It is ironic that the first train to Perry is the only one of the three to still have tracks. Occasionally a train makes its way up from Des Moines by way of Dallas Center and Minburn and from Perry goes to Herndon, then south to Yale.

And occasionally, the mournful whistle of the engine is heard, bringing a feeling of nostalgia for the times when Perry was such a busy railroad center.

Storm Blows Train from Tracks (1881)

One of the stormiest days ever known hit this section in 1881. A little after 5 o'clock in the afternoon the storm swept across the country between Perry and Grand Junction from southwest to northeast. Wrack and ruin were the results.

At Coaltown, the west wing of Shaft No. 2 of the Climax Coal Company was completely demolished.

At Rippey great damage was done. The northbound passenger train on the Des Moines-Fort Dodge line, which left Perry at 4:25 p.m., was blown from the tracks at a point two miles this side of Rippey.

The coaches were well filled with passengers, all of whom were more or less injured. Among the employees who were the most injured were Conductor Eugene Weston, who was "hurt in the legs," and U.S. Express messenger F.M. Hoeye, who was badly bruised "across the bowels and on the face."

The cars were carried several feet from the track, which was torn up for several rods. The inside of the cars was a sad mixture — window glass, coal, seat cushions, etc., being thrown around "promiscuously."

After the wreck, the rain came down in torrents.

Milwaukee Railroad Established (1881)

In December 1880 a party of surveyors had run three lines through the town — one through the northwest part, one through the southeast corner, and one through the town. They were very reticent about their business, but it was supposed that they were employed by the Chicago, Milwaukee & St. Paul (C.M. & St. P.) Railroad. The surveyors were very reckless and slashed through shrubbery and orchards that stood in their way, nearly ruining a number of fine fruit trees belonging to D.J. Pattee.

Iron had been laid almost to Xenia by 1881. In September a number of the iron gangs struck and came in from their work. They were very clamorous until they received their pay.

The railroad bridge across the Des Moines River was completed in March 1882, and the first train from Marian to Coon Rapids went through Perry. It consisted of a baggage car, a passenger car, and a sleeping car; on board were General Manager Merrill and other railroad dignitaries who were inspecting the road.

The Perry depot was occupied in June 1882. It was a two-story structure with a one-story freight house on the east side. A lunch counter was added in 1883 and proved very satisfactory financially to the proprietor, Mr. Beeber.

All the depots between Cambridge and Council Bluffs were framed in Perry. The Milwaukee Company had a huge supply of lumber piled in the yards. Tracks were laid all over the yards in every direction to move material around; a turntable was placed at every junction. A car loaded with lumber could be pushed wherever needed.

A new telegraph office was built at the roundhouse in December 1882.

Chief dispatcher J.M. Bunker had a telegraph line built from the depot to his home on First Street so he could be with his family and at the same time give advice to his subordinates.

When the Milwaukee was first built through Perry, the roundhouse was located north of the tracks, in the vicinity of Seventh and Eighth streets. Until it was completed, a temporary engine

Popular Engine Type

Engines such as No. 923, shown with Engineer Henry Nichols and Fireman John F. Lutze, were a popular type of engine on the Milwaukee line around the turn of the century.

house was built west of the depot on First Street, north of the tracks.

Word came down on February 3, 1882, that the company would locate the division in Perry if suitable ground would be donated for a machine shop and engine house. This cost was in the neighborhood of $8,000.

It was announced on February 10, through the columns of *The Perry Chief,* that all the money needed to build the shops had been raised. The committee had worked diligently and to them went the credit.

Those who contributed $50 or more were: J. Clement, I.F. Langford, C.H. Ainley, A.Y. Rawson, W.H. Chandler, G.B. Paul, J.F. Ford, Thomas Scott, Waldo and Thornley, George Harlan, W.L. Campbell, W.D. Lummis, B.B. Campbell, Goss and Carrough, J.R. Stewart and Company, T.C. Norris, W.S. Russell, and D.J. Pattee. J.A. Waldo contributed both personally, as well as through his company.

The Waldo land, forty acres northeast of the city, was contracted for the shops. By the last of July all trains were made up in Perry instead of at Coon Rapids. Only half of the round house was ready for use, but the other half was almost completed. It had sixteen stalls, with shops built of stone with a slate roof. The coal shed was completed and the big well finished. An ice house was also built, so the company could fill the refrigerator cars at the Perry division.

The company wanted to build cattle yards, but they could not find the land for which they could justify a price. Those were eventually completed through the help of local citizens. When the company contacted Perry people about the project, W.H. Chandler and W.W. Cardell met with some businessmen on the subject and, in about three hours, they had raised the needed $350.

Work on the yards began the last week of June 1883. Ground was surveyed and staked out. Twenty-four loads of lumber were unloaded showing the backers just how extensive the yards would be. The Milwaukee Company began grading down south of the roundhouse, making ready for an additional twelve stalls and other buildings. A house track at the depot was extended clear to the yards.

By 1884 the Milwaukee Railroad was well established in Perry and points west.

Two railroads, the Minneapolis and the Milwaukee played havoc with Dick Correy's land in Dallas Township. The Milwaukee ran across two forty-acre places and the Minneapolis managed to strike the same tract diagonally, and cut a good-sized corner from another forty acres. This cut up the best land he had and the damage to him was considerable.

By December 1884, the Milwaukee had put in a side track about six miles west of Perry on W.E. Tolle's farm. A grain house was built there. They also put in a switch, built a platform, and made a waiting room out of the grain house. Quite a number of persons got on and off the trains at Dawson.

Life on the rails in those days was perilous. On the lines of the Milwaukee Railroad during the year 1884: one passenger was killed; six were injured; twenty-two employees were killed and thirty injured; twenty-two other persons were killed and twenty-six injured; 316 beasts were killed during the year, for which $3,245 in damages were paid.

In 1900, it became necessary to extend the front walls of the roundhouse eight feet in order to accommodate the monster engines being put into freight service. Sixteen engines replaced a large number of small engines which were sent to the smaller lines operated by the company.

One night in March 1904, the people of Perry were awakened by the shrill piping of the roundhouse whistle and the hoarse alarm of the power house. The weather was "blizzardly" and the long haul of the hose carts and paraphernalia was a rigorous trial of the nerves for the fire department members.

The Milwaukee ice house, east of the machine shops and roundhouse near the north end of Eighth Street was on fire. A hard two-hour fight raged before the fire was under control. By then, only the side walls of the building were left standing.

The two houses contained about 1,000 tons of newly harvested ice. It was a spectacular site as the flames caught the sawdust protecting the ice and fierce winds swirled it high in the air.

The cattle yards were destroyed by fire during June of 1910. It was impossible to save the buildings and fences as the nearest hydrant was at the yard office and there was not enough hose in town to reach the distance.

Three Drapers, One Wreck (1890)

A wreck occurred in the Perry yards on the Milwaukee Railroad early on the morning of December 6, 1890.

There were three Drapers involved in the accident: Moss "Daddy" Draper, engineer of the switch engine; Frank Draper, conductor of the passenger train; and Posey Draper, conductor of the caboose which was hit.

The night of the wreck the passenger train was about five minutes late. The yardmaster, Al Swim, thinking it had passed, ordered the switch engine, with the caboose of Moss Draper's train (which had just come in) out on the main line.

Frank Liddle was engineer on the passenger, which came thundering into Perry at forty miles per hour. When he saw the caboose carrying Posey Draper and brakeman Barney O'Brien, Liddle reversed his engine and applied the air brake, but the distance was too short.

The pilot crashed into the rear of the caboose, which was crushed to kindling between the two engines. Brakeman O'Brien, who was in the caboose washing, received a severe cut on the head and several body bruises. His escape from death seemed a miracle. No other trainman was injured, except Engineer Draper, who was hurt when he jumped onto the frozen ground.

The mail car was badly wrecked and had to be left in the yards. The mail was transferred to other trains. A similar wreck in the same place happened in July 1911.

Daddy Draper, the engineer of the switch engine, walked home and never went back to work — never even called for his time. O'Brien also left the railroad and became the owner of a popular blacksmith shop on First Avenue.

The Interurban (1901)

Once there was the Interurban, an electric line connecting Perry with Des Moines. Cars made the trip each way several times a day. There are still those who can remember the bumpy ride with the swaying cars of shoppers going to Des Moines or students from Moran coming to Perry to attend school.

For ten days in November 1903, a party of surveyors headed by F.S. Cummins (the nephew of Governor A.B. Cummins) was in the field investigating a proposed route for an electric railway from Des Moines to Perry.

It had been announced that the line would reach Perry in the summer of 1905. Some grading had been done on the other side of Gardiner. All curves were made to permit greater speeds — 60 miles per hour was the target.

A crew of surveyors arrived in Perry in March 1905, to run the lines inside the city limits. The route was not the same as previously announced. It was changed so that the line would pass north of the John Moore home instead of south of it and it would also run north of the Thomas Brady home instead of through it.

The company decided not to try to meet the summer 1905 deadline, accusing some property owners of "extortion" when the company tried to purchase needed rights of way. In July word was out that a gang of graders assigned to work on the Interurban had been transferred to the Woodward line, raising fears that the Perry line might be abandoned.

Fortunately, the right-of-way agent still had faith and made every effort to close with the high-priced land owners. He got along so well that there were only four tracts of ground not contracted. The Perry line would not have been built had some public-spirited citizens not assisted in the changing of conditions.

Interurban Car and Depot

Passengers disembark from a car of the Interurban Railroad at the Perry depot.

The building of this line brought about the opening of two new towns in Dallas County. One was Moran at the junction of the Perry and Woodward lines; it was named for William Moran, one of the wealthy land owners in that section. He had been very interested in the project from the beginning and did much to put the road through.

The other new town was Gardiner, located just east of Perry on land belonging to T.H. Gardiner. The railroad platted the town, graded the streets, and then claimed every other lot in the little town. The railroad also wanted Gardiner to donate 10 acres of land for a depot, siding, stockyards, and an elevator, which he refused to do.

The grader gang arrived in Perry in September 1905 and pitched tents on the Interurban grounds on West Warford Street. There were twenty-five teams and a corresponding number of men. In November, ground was broken for the depot on the corner of Willis Avenue and West Third Street; workmen immediately began excavating the foundation and basement.

Ware and Riley moved their camps out of Perry in May 1906 to the Brady farm, three miles to the northeast. Grading work on the Perry end was done; they were ready for ties and steel.

The tracks were laid across Willis Avenue up to the new depot at 4 o'clock on a Saturday afternoon in September 1906. A large crowd witnessed the event. A month later, trolleys wires reached Perry. At quitting time there was still about a mile and a half remaining and the men returned after supper, working until 2:30 a.m. to finish the project and connect the terminals. Passenger service began on November 5, 1906.

Before the new service officially began, a crowd of more than 100 Perry people went to Des Moines on the new line. John P. O'Malley and other enthusiastic Democrats arranged to have a car leave the city at about 4 p.m. so as to reach Des Moines in plenty of time to attend a rally featuring a speech by William Jennings Bryan. A larger-than-anticipated crowd showed up at the depot and a number of disappointed souls chose to remain home rather than stand for the entire trip.

There were a number of ladies in the party and everyone was cheerful — even the Republicans who went just for the novelty of the ride. Roadmaster R.S. Eberhart accompanied them to see that everything ran smoothly. The return trip was made after midnight.

The cars were stuck for the first time in March 1907. A bad storm with raging wind, rain and sleet had covered the wires and tracks when the last car left Perry with about thirty passengers. They reached Moran, but could go no farther. While the people were wondering what to do, the car from the Woodward line came into sight. It, too, could go no farther.

Each time an effort was made to move, the trolley would burn out. Ice was a half-inch thick on the rails. A car with extra trolleys was sent out from Des Moines but burned out before it could get very far.

It was impossible to get accommodations in Moran, so the company ordered livery rigs from Woodward and took the passengers there, a distance of three or four miles. They were given a breakfast and some of them departed on the Milwaukee while others remained in Woodward until the line opened again.

The first serious accident on the Interurban occurred in February 1908 at 10:10 a.m. The Woodward car ran into the Perry car standing on the main line at Moran junction, waiting for passengers en route to Des Moines.

A mile out of Woodward, motorman George Richards lost control of the power. He tried air brakes, but they would not work. He reversed the current and completely lost power. The car slid

The Turn Around

An Interurban rail car making the turn around as it prepared to head back to Des Moines.

into the Perry car at nearly thirty miles per hour.

Six people on the Woodward car were injured. Richards suffered a broken finger and an injured arm when the stove wedged him in and he could not free himself. George Sixberry, a motorman living in Woodward but on his way to Des Moines to take out a run, was standing on the rear platform. He was thrown through the door, cutting him severely on the face and hands.

Three Woodward women, Mrs. Walter Smith, Mrs. Will Todd, and Mrs. James Nolan were thrown into the backs of the seat in front of them, all had teeth knocked out. Mrs. Smith's year-old baby was cut by flying glass.

Drs. T.S. Rogers, Brookings, Fields and Eugene Carmichael of Woodward were rushed to the scene where the injured were treated, then taken back to their homes.

The Interurban line served Perry and community for may years before falling victim to "progress." The line was bought by Polk County for $63,000 in back taxes at a public tax auction in 1943.

In 1949, a notice was posted on the door of the depot in Perry stating the company's intention to abandon passenger service. A hearing was set for September 7 . Several letters of protest were sent, but the abandonment was authorized and passenger service discontinued after September 28, 1949.

The old bumpy electric car had some new guests for its final trip — a delegation of civic leaders rode from Des Moines to Perry. Those from Perry invited by the railroad to make the trip were Mayor Leslie Wright, Councilman Herb Taylor, John Burnett (president of the Commercial Club), and Harley Wilcox whose Perry Milk Products was one of the largest users of the line.

The last official run began at 4:30 p.m. and the final run back was completed at 7:52. Generally, this car stopped overnight in Perry, but this time it returned immediately to Des Moines, never to be seen in Perry again.

Passenger No. 1 Strikes Again (1911)

A wreck occurred on the Milwaukee Railroad in the Perry yards early in the morning on the last Sunday in July 1911.

No. 1 was just coming in and was running at a speed of at least twenty to twenty-five miles per hour when the switch engine was run out onto the main line. H.E. Nichols was the engineer of passenger engine 917 and Tom Wilcox was the fireman. Lathan Walton was in charge of the yard engine 1122, and Frank Schloe was on the left side.

Fireman Wilcox saw the danger and called to Engineer Nichols who gave three or four sharp blasts of the whistle, threw the emergency air brake, and both men jumped. Nichols landed hard on the ground then rolled. Wilcox was less fortunate. He waited until the engine shot past some stock cars and then jumped, lit on his feet. He bruised ligaments, slid on his knee and leg, rubbing all the skin from them. He tried to break his fall with one hand, bruised it, and ground it full of cinders, finally falling on his shoulder and face.

How the two men escaped without more serious injuries was a miracle. Nichols believed he was not much hurt, but an examination revealed that he had fractured a rib, in addition to getting a pretty good jolt and jar.

All that saved the crew of the switch engine was the warning whistle Nichols had given. None of the switch crew knew of the rapidly closing danger. They had run through a lead switch which let them out onto the main track. Fireman Schloe called out to

Wrecked Again

Passenger train No. 1 (engine 917) struck a switch engine on the main line in Perry in July 1911. No. 1 was involved in a similar accident on the same track in Perry in December 1890.

his engineer (who was an extra and was working the yard for the first time that night), both men jumped just in time to avoid being injured.

When the 917 hit the switch engine, it toppled over onto its side. The noise of the impact was heard for several blocks and brought people out in a hurry.

The right side cylinder on the passenger train broke off but the connecting rod still held the piston. The rod and piston swung to the ground, and the force of the impact helped send the mass of iron reeling onto its side. The main rod was twisted like a corkscrew. The front trucks of the baggage car went off the rails. One of these rails, torn from its ties, the spikes ripped out as though they were common pins, was found run through the fire box of the 917.

Nichols had applied the air about eighty or ninety feet east of where the trains struck. The passengers in the coaches did not know what had happened or that a wreck had occurred. Back in the sleepers, they were told that the engine had broken down.

Two lady passengers bound for California from New York walked out to get some air and arrived at the scene of the wreck without the slightest idea of what to expect. They rushed back to the sleeper for their Kodaks and took pictures of the wreck. Though both had traveled the continent a number of times, neither of them had ever seen a train wreck before, much less had ever been in one.

The coaches of the passenger train were switched around over the passing tracks and the train, pulled by another engine, went west a couple of hours later. Hundreds of Perry people were at the wreck site during the day, watching the workmen clear the debris.

Late in the evening the wrecker arrived and the engines were righted. They were tied onto a train and headed for the Dubuque shops on their own wheels, there to receive thorough and badly needed overhauls.

The New Perry Yards (1912)

Secretary E.W. Adams of the Milwaukee Company signed a check for $51,650 for the land west of the M. & St. L. crossing and east of the Raccoon River in July 1912.

New Milwaukee Roundhouse and Yards

The Milwaukee Railroad bought the land west of the M. & St. L. crossing and east of the Raccoon River in July 1912 for use as a new roundhouse and yards.

As the story was told by a veteran railroader, a "hick" had come to Perry dressed in scrubby overalls with the line that he wanted to buy a farm. It was considered quite a coup when these sandy acres were unloaded on the unsuspecting buyer; it became a joke enjoyed by the local citizenry. The smiles soon faded when the deal was closed and the site of the new Milwaukee yards made known.

There was so much building going on in Perry that year that workers were difficult to hire. A gang of brick masons was brought in to work on the new roundhouse. Soon these terminal yards became a mecca for pedestrian and autoist sight-seers. One mild Sunday in October it was reported that there were 200 autos at the site and that an estimated 1,500 had walked out from the city to see the progress.

In January 1913, before the boilers were set and fired up, thirty stoves were set up in the east half for use in heating the building and to provide heat for the cement gang. The round-house had been completed to the point where passenger engines could be housed there.

Engineer John Leaf, the man in charge of switch engine 1120, ran the first engine into and out of the new roundhouse. The 1120 had serviced the Perry yards for years and had shunted carloads of materials to the roundhouse construction site all summer.

Leaf felt he and the engine were entitled to the honor. He was right on both counts. Thirty-two years earlier, Leaf had run the first engine into the first roundhouse in the eastern part of Perry. Another coincidence was that the superintendent of construction, David Grant, was the builder of both roundhouses.

A Popular Place for Boxcar Tourists (1912)

The loafers who congregated at the Milwaukee Depot every night had anything but a pleasant time on December 10, 1912. That night they were lined up along the wall at gun point and forced to accept the business card of an itinerant sign painter.

It was a late hour when the painter, who had been in Perry for several days, blew into the waiting room. He made too much noise to please the sleeping throng of loafers and they decided that he had to be quiet. They talked to him a little rough and then things began to happen.

He whipped a young cannon out of his pocket and lined the gang up against the wall. Then with a suave smile he presented each with one of his business cards, then walked out the door.

The company looked for the fellow. He was the kind of man they needed for night policeman during the time the depot was so popular a place for a lot of boxcar tourists.

Park Street Underpass (1921)

A.D. Haskins, a prominent Perry citizen, first came to town in 1870, buying a farm from the father of T.R. Phillips. In 1872, Haskins sold the farm and moved into town.

Park Street Tracks

The underpass was built after A.D. Haskins died in an accident here.

Haskins was born in Chautauqua County, New York. His mother died when he was a small boy and most of the time he lived with an uncle in Wisconsin. When the Civil War broke out, he was one of the first to enlist in May 1861. He later received a commission as a captain. He was with Sherman on that famous march to the sea. After the war, Haskins returned to Wisconsin and on January 28, 1865, married Harriett Mott.

It was the result of his death in January 1921, from injuries received in an automobile wreck on the M. & St. L. crossing that eventually brought about the Park Street underpass.

The crossing had long been considered a dangerous one and for years efforts had been made to force the company to raise their tracks and construct an underneath crossing. Several accidents and many narrow escapes had occurred there.

Drivers coming from the west could not get a clear view of

the tracks until they were within 50 feet of the rails; the fact that the grade was high and narrow increased the danger.

On January 17, 1921, Haskins was returning to the city after taking his granddaughter, Celia Covey, to her school west of Perry where she taught when he was fatally injured.

The locomotive struck the rear end of the Ford sedan, pushing it along for a few feet and then threw it to the right side of the road, into a ditch.

Webb Burrell, a farmer living northwest of the city, and his two passengers were a short distance behind the Haskins car. They, along with the train crew, and train passengers, rushed to the aid of the injured man. Haskins was unconscious when pulled from the wreck and died at King's Daughters Hospital without regaining consciousness.

The day after Haskins' death a petition was circulated urging the railroad commission to take immediate action on this long-delayed improvement.

Again, the railroad company procrastinated. The Perry committee, becoming tired of the delaying tactics of the M. & St. L., turned over to the Commercial Council of Iowa all correspondence and proceedings.

Finally, the welcome news came and the underpass was ordered. The crossing was closed to traffic on August 3, 1921, and opened again on October 13. Because so many railroad men used this road to go to the roundhouse, they later succeeded in getting it paved.

While the railroad no longer exists, the road is still well traveled. Most of the motorists never give the underpass a thought, but the drivers of so many of today's huge trucks do. Because of the low clearance, they still have to take the one and one-half mile detour around it.

Chapter Ten
The Auto Craze

A Popular Team

The REO auto and the Rude Auto Company were a very successful combination in Perry. The Rude Auto Company was Perry's most successful auto shop in the early years of the auto craze.

Pavement Didn't Come Easy (1901-1910)

Pavement for Perry didn't come easy. The issue was long discussed, several times ordered, and almost as often canceled. Even
after the matter seemed settled, the discussion as to the kind of
paving to be used threatened to wipe out the whole project.

In April 1901, when Perry's streets were very bad, a petition
was circulated asking for brick on Second Street from the Triangle to the Milwaukee depot. Summer has a way of drying spring
mud, so the project was dropped.

While often talked about during the following years, people
only began agitating for paving in earnest in the summer of 1908.
That was the time the automobile craze hit Perry and the newspapers were listing names of car owners and the makes of their
cars. This, no doubt, was a factor in the revival of the paving
question.

At its July 1908 meeting, the Perry City Council passed a
resolution creating an improvement fund, levying a two-mill tax
for street intersections and paving around the library if and when
the day might come.

Many property owners wanted to wait until the following
year. Others wanted to start paving at once. So, a committee was
appointed to complete a canvass to see which plan was more practical.

Later, at an adjourned council meeting, Councilmen J.W.
Diddy and J.C. Byron were named to go to Des Moines to investigate the new oil roads being built there.

In spite of all efforts, the paving issue was killed in a council
meeting in December 1908 when a hearing was called for the purpose of hearing objections.

The audience portion of the superior courtroom in the library basement was filled to overflowing with property owners

Slogging Through

A wagon team crosses a muddy intersection on Second Street. The wagon is heading east on Warford. The pedestrians are walking on a boarded path across Warford.

and other citizens. The meeting was one of protest, though said to be very orderly and free from bickering and accusations.

Mayor H.C. Modlin reported council members repeatedly had been taken to task because nothing had been done. Yet a number of men who said they wanted pavement were among those who signed the list of objectors. As a result, all consideration of the project was discontinued and all proceedings up to that time were annulled and held for naught.

The issue continued to smolder. Before an audience of one, a couple of newspapermen and the city clerk and solicitor, the council clashed on the question of paving and graveling the roads for an hour or more. The audience learned a great deal about pavement and found out just where the council members stood. As usual, no progress was made.

The result was depressing. Perhaps one of the newspapermen at the meeting was responsible for an editorial which appeared shortly afterwards. In it the writer said something seemed to be wrong in Perry, that the enthusiasm which united the work of the city was gone and had been replaced by selfishness.

The decline was evident. It had been hard work to swing the Chautauqua program and the enthusiasm over the horse show was just a dream. The lighting of Second Street dragged and the paving discussion had become a dividing theme. All tended to stop the wheels of progress.

Still the pavement question was not mentioned at the October meeting nor was it touched upon at the November meeting. By this time the roads were bad. More accurately, they were awful. Perry's five rural mail carriers were compelled to give up the morning of November 3.

In Perry at this time, streets were about as bad as they could get. It was felt if the citizens could have their way, paving would begin at once on all the main streets.

Thus a citizens' meeting was called on December 4, 1909, in the Superior Courtroom to discuss the question and devise some means of settling the question. If they expected the matter to come up before the December 9 meeting of the city council, they were doomed for disappointment.

After routine business was completed, O'Malley began to talk about Perry's great need. The majority thought the hour too late and a motion to adjourn carried.

The next night, property owners on Willis called a meeting in the courtroom and petitioned the council asking that pavement be ordered for Willis from Third Street to Eleventh when the business district was paved.

Property owners on Warford were not about to be outdone and they went their Willis neighbors one better by starting a petition for pavement on Warford from Third to Eleventh, asking it be laid at once. First Avenue residents who claimed to have the finest street in the city joined the boosters and circulated a petition calling for pavement on First Avenue to Park Street.

The paving issue had been kept alive by those who wanted it now, those who wanted it next year, and those who didn't want it at all. When the matter of road improvement seemed certain, another problem arose. What should it be? Brick, creosote blocks, asphalt, or just plain gravel?

The trustees of the Methodist Church called a special meeting in which the questions were discussed. Seven of the nine members were present and all were in favor of paving of some sort, but were concerned about what constituted the best kind. They finally decided in favor of the creosoted blocks, believing this would be comparatively noiseless and the broken pavement on Third Street many years later indicated that was what was put down.

History was made at a special meeting of the council on December 20, 1909, when the largest municipal improvement the city had ever attempted was under way. Paving was ordered to cover three miles, costing property owners and the city between $175,000 and $200,000.

Past Peeks Through

Original creosote blocks used in Perry's first paving project shows through a worn section of asphalt at the corner of Third and Warford.

Though the council had passed the resolution ordering paving, the councilmen could not get together on the material to be used. Despite the fact that most felt the question settled, it was still the most engrossing subject discussed on the streets. It was feared agitation between those favoring asphalt and those favoring creosote blocks would delay the matter yet another year.

In April 1910, council members compromised and contracts were let. Asphalt was to be put down on Second Street as soon as the grading and curbing was completed.

The first creosote blocks were laid July 13, 1910, on First Avenue at the junction of Willis. The work was witnessed by a large crowd of interested and curious citizens. Three carloads of blocks came in on the Interurban from the mill in Mobile, Alabama, and two more followed the next day. After that, blocks were shipped in as they were needed. Each car contained enough blocks to pave 500 square yards.

The work was finished in the afternoon of November 14, 1910. Since early summer the streets had been torn up and a great deal of inconvenience suffered. The real beauty of the new pavement was not evident until the following spring when the sand and shale were removed.

It was clearly stated in the newspapers that First Avenue was paved with creosote blocks, Second Street with asphalt and the intersection of Third Street with creosote blocks. What was used on the rest of the original three mile job was not indicated.

Newspaperman Rides in an Auto (1901)

C.E. Wintrode of Huntingen, Indiana, came to Perry in 1901. He manufactured and sold his own invention — a machine that made the Practical Wire Fence.

A brand new auto was unloaded here for Wintrode's private use. He could afford to ride around in it because his patent had made him independently rich. His auto cost $800 and was to go next to Emmettsburg. Over ordinary roads it could make thirty miles per hour.

One afternoon he stopped by *The Chief-Reporter* office and took the editor for a ride. It was an offer which couldn't be refused, though there were all sorts of rumors around about autos running away or blowing up.

Wintrode pushed the lever "over in the corner," pulled the throttle, and away they went. The newspaper man was apprehensive but he was convinced that autos were here to stay and soon would be as common as the bicycle.

Wintrode's driving on Perry streets during his short stay in town was not without effect. On First Avenue, near Mr. Robert Ginn's place, he met two women out driving — Mrs. Charles Case of Mason City and Mrs. James Bradley. Wintrode saw their horse become frightened by the auto, so he stopped. The horse came on until abreast of the auto, then gave a snort and a lunge and went up the avenue at breakneck speed.

The ladies couldn't control the horse and, when it turned east at Brumfield's corner, the buggy was thrown against a telephone pole, smashing the buggy and throwing the women out. Mrs. Case was found in the ditch with the buggy piled upon her, while Mrs. Bradley was tangled in the wreckage. Drs. A.W. Trout and E.R. Aiken were called and found both to be badly bruised, cut, and generally shaken.

This prompted the newspaper to print an editorial giving suggestions as to driving on thoroughfares to prevent further accidents. Willis, Otley, and First were wide enough and graded so as to be a double road and teams were asked to keep well to the right side of the road.

Auto Factory (1902)

Almost before the automobile was seen in Perry, a factory to manufacture them was erected in the city.

W.B. Brown, president of the Improvement Association, called a meeting of the citizens early in September 1902 to consider a proposition from the DeLoura Manufacturing Company. H.E. DeLoura had offered to move his $20,000 plant from Fort Madison to Perry, buy a lot, put up a building and hire thirty to fifty men — if a consideration of $1,500 in cash was made to him after he moved his property. His company manufactured automobiles, gas engines, launches, etc.

Allen Breed and S.E. Carrell went to Fort Madison on September 11 to look over the plant and to check if everything was as represented in the proposal. They returned highly pleased. A message was sent to DeLoura informing him that the money had been raised and Perry doffed her hat to the new enterprise.

DeLoura arrived in October and began work at once on the new building, which was located on the north side of the Milwaukee tracks between Third and Fourth street.

In January 1903, DeLoura appeared before the city council with two requests. First, he wanted the privilege of tapping the water main which ran under his building to the roundhouse so as to avoid laying a pipe for 100 feet. Also, he asked that the automobile factory be exempt from paying any water tax for five years, explaining that the amount of water used would be small.

The factory steamed up for the first time a few days after this meeting and blew the whistle promptly at 6 a.m. The machinery and engines were yet to be tested, so it wasn't until March 4 that work was begun on some new $650 gas automobiles.

DeLoura had been delayed in the construction of his building, but he was doing some work on some machinery for the Perry Lily Laundry and on a steam auto which was soon to be turned over to the paint shop.

All his buildings were painted red with white lettering.

Considerable delay had been experienced in construction of the building. Besides the machine shop and the paint shop, plans called for two other buildings. His help had begun to arrive from Burlington and elsewhere. DeLoura said he would prefer to hire local help but the work was such that expert machinists were required.

DeLoura also announced he would sell to the first Perry buyer a $650 machine or a $700 steam carriage for $600, but only one would go at that price. There was no record of any DeLouras being sold in Perry.

A number of businessmen took a tour of the factory one afternoon and were surprised at the amount of work going on, and the lack of noise for such a busy place. S.R. Emms had been pressed into service in the blacksmith department. On the shop floor, they saw two automobiles rapidly taking form.

In May 1903, the DeLoura Company placed a new gasoline burner under *The Chief*'s linotype machine. The design was the same as the car company used to furnish their steam carriages and was one of the simplest yet most perfect mechanical piece.

By considerable effort Perry had secured the factory, and by June 1903 the town ran the risk of losing it. Fort Dodge businessmen visited the plant. On return to their city, the men enlisted citizens in an effort to raise $15,000 and furnish a location to move the plant there. DeLoura had offered to sell stock to a company of Perry men for $7,500, but the whole amount could not be raised — only $2,000 was offered. Fort Dodge acted quickly, raised $20,000, bought three-fourths interest in the plant, and began the campaign to move it to their city.

DeLoura reported it had cost him $416 to move the plant to Perry and that he had lost money coming here. His machinery was mortgaged then and still was. He said he had become embarrassed and either had to lose his plant and cause his creditors to lose or to sell an interest and pay all honest debts.

This brought about a closer look at the contract Perry had with the company and it was a clever one. The Perry citizens who had contributed $1,500 to the DeLoura Company could be the happy owners of some frame buildings. The auto company held a lease on these lots from Pattee good for ten years. The buildings were on these lots and some lumber liens were on the buildings. If the company moved, the liens would be paid off and the lease turned over to the contributors, so they could begin paying the rent. Most were not happy with this contract.

In the contract, the factory promised nothing and faithfully performed what it had promised. The dissatisfied contributors could only blame themselves. The company had promised to move to Perry and accept $1,500, which agreement it perfectly performed. It was further to operate in good faith, but the number of days was not mentioned. That was also performed.

The company was to give a mortgage on one building and to give each contributor credit for his contribution in case he bought $500 worth of products from the company. That was all the company had promised and the lawyers, bankers, merchants, and others accepted that as a contract. This was not DeLoura's fault. He had offered to make a better, more perfect contract, but having such a gem of an agreement in hand, the Perry investors declined his offer to improve the contract.

The company's first product in Perry was a handsome single seated automobile and was driven through the streets on its test trip. It was valued at $750 and was shipped to St. Paul where it was sold. The other machine was completed and shipped east.

In July 1903, at the request of DeLoura, W.A. Winegar called a meeting of the executive committee of the businessman's association in his office. DeLoura gave notice that he would vacate the building occupied by his factory in the first part of August. He packed his traveling automobile trunk on August 5 and shipped it to Fort Dodge. By September reports were that the buildings for his new plant there were going up rapidly.

Perry's First Car Owner (1904)

One of the first automobile trips to be reported in a newspaper was in September 1903, when the J.H. Bowman family of Decatur, Illinois, came to Perry to visit relatives.

They drove an Oldsmobile and were two weeks on the road, having been held up for four days by rain. The road was rough and the driver remarked that he never knew there were so many hills in Iowa.

Perry finally had a local car owner in 1904, when Will and George O'Malley and Lawrence Tiernan purchased a beauty (the newspaper didn't tell which make). The important news was that the men made the trip to Adel and back in one morning with no trouble at all.

They soon discovered what popular fellows they were after they learned to operate their new machine. They found that First Avenue was about the best street in the city on which to drive, as the road was good for a long distance.

Auto Craze (1907-1909)

The winter of 1907-08 had been ideal for car owners as there had been but a few days when the cars could not be driven, especially Fred Kennison's Ford. In fact, cars were becoming so numerous laws were being made as to what must be done on meeting horse-and-buggies. If necessary, the driver had to get out and help control the unruly beasts.

It was predicted that there would be no fewer than 100 cars in the city and immediate vicinity come summer.

Some makes of cars mentioned in *The Chief* were: REO, Mason, Maxwell, Mitchell, Queen, Winston, Buick, Ford, White, Steamer, Chalmar, Velie, Carter and Firestone.

The auto craze struck Perry in earnest in 1908. The newspapers printed a list, a rather short one it is true, of those who owned and enjoyed automobiles.

Liveries were being converted into garages and new garages were being built. Also, with selling the car, the salesman must also teach the new owners the rudiments of driving. Such lessons were short and the drivers were often caught in minor difficulties.

Iowa Plates

A truck with an Iowa license plate in 1919

By 1911 autos were getting so numerous that the city council passed an ordinance regulating the speed of all cars, except motor trucks, ambulances, etc. The fine ranged from $5 to $100, and a jail sentence if cash was not forthcoming.

There were two speeds permitted within the city. Between the Milwaukee depot and Otley Avenue and a block each way between these two points, the maximum speed was twelve miles per hour. In all other parts of the city, city drivers could speed up to fifteen miles per hour — if they were cautious.

The first arrest for speeding was made in May 1911, when W.H. Pattee was taken before Justice A.D. Haskins. He pleaded guilty, but believed himself justified in driving faster than the speed limit. The information against him was filed by Mayor C.D. Jones.

Returning home, Pattee was caught in a rainstorm on West Willis. His sister and another lady were in the car, both without wraps. As there was no one on the streets, he speeded up to escape a drenching. The justice felt no exemption should be made, so Pattee paid the fine of $5 and costs.

First Accident Victim (1908)

Dr. R.E. Doidge was the first real Perry victim of an auto accident. In September 1908, he was going to see a patient near Dawson and had taken Allie Powell along for the ride and to show him how the car worked.

While passing the Frank Alborn place traveling along at ten miles per hour, the rod connecting the steering apparatus broke. The car turned over, throwing Powell out but pinning the doctor beneath it.

Powell succeeded in lifting the car, allowing the doctor to crawl out. A horse and buggy took the two injured men to Perry, where the doctor's fractured collar bone and ligaments were treated. The car was a wreck; the damage estimate came in between $300 and $400.

Dr. Doidge bought a new Ford roadster in October 1912, to use some of the time to give his old touring car a rest. He had then had the old car equipped with a limousine body for cold weather and when the roads were bad, keeping the new car for summer and winter. In two years time, the old car had been driven 25,000 miles, an unusual record to which all Ford owners pointed with pride.

Advertising Mason Car (1908)

In 1908, Council Garage was located west of the Library and C.W. Council, the owner, created quite a sensation with his advertising stunt for the Mason car.

The Mason Company staunchly advertised their car as the

The Mason Platform

The Mason was said to be the best hill-climbing car of its day. To demonstrate its prowess, the Mason Company and car dealer C. W. Council erected this platform with a fifty percent grade on Willis Avenue near First Avenue.

best hill climbing car made. It was being proven in Perry by means of an incline, built 16 feet high with a 32-foot runway making it a 50 percent road grade. A platform large enough to hold the machine was erected at the top.

The Mason took the climb without a start of any kind. In fact, Fred Carver, who did the driving, occasionally stopped half way up then completed the climb. A number of other makes of cars tried to make it to the top, but none was successful.

Firemen Welcome Autos (1909)

In October 1909, it was reported that the coming of automobiles to Perry was welcomed by members of the fire department because of the assistance they gave. Time was when the boys had to pull the heavy hose carts and the hook and ladder truck to the scene of a fire and when they arrived, they were so tired they were almost unfit to fight the fire.

A few years before, the city council agreed to pay the drayman, bus driver, or anyone else who arrived first with a team, and the troubles of the fire boys were eased to a certain point. The rivalry between the drivers to get to the station first was intense, but the autos generally beat them and hauled the carts to the fire.

Rude Auto Company (1909)

P.C. Rude was a Southerner by birth, born January 22, 1831, in Virginia. His parents left that state at the beginning of the Civil War to reside in Syracuse, New York. In 1864 he went to Des Moines and came to Perry from there in 1872. He was first in the real estate and loan business.

P.C. Rude died at his home on Willis Avenue on October 7, 1902. His sons Perry and John became involved in the auto business before their father's death.

In May 1909, Jacobs-Rude Garage began on a large scale in rooms in the former Model Laundry building on Willis. A large door had been made in the rear of the building with plans for an elevator so the basement and upper story could be used.

The company kept three makes of cars in stock, with four models to choose from: Ford touring, REO runabout; REO touring; and Mitchell touring. They also expected to get the agency

Rude Autos
P.C. Rude's sons Perry and John in front of their new dealership circa 1911.

for the Thomas Flyer, Stoddard, Dayton, and Oldsmobile.

In 1911, L.B. Morgan of the Gamble Furniture Company, constructed a new building for the Rude Garage on the northeast corner of First and Warford. Austin Howard purchased the house which stood on the lot and moved it to another location for remodeling. The house had been built by John H. Shively in 1869 and was the second house built in Perry. In the days when the Fort Dodge Railroad was being built, it was a boarding house for the men employed in the work.

The new building had a display room, office, repair room, and storage room for twenty-five cars. Entrances were on First Avenue and Warford. Rude Auto Company moved into the new building July 28, 1911. One of the most appreciated things was the new method of filling the gas tanks. Instead of the old way with a bucket and funnel, the gas now ran through a hose from a measuring machine directly into the car's tank.

In October, the company sold the first six-cylinder car in the vicinity to Henry Schnoor. It was a Mitchell five-passenger, forty horse power vehicle, selling for $1,750. It was gray with black trim, instead of brass.

The first auto delivery vehicle in Perry was sold by Rude Auto Company on May 14, 1914, to Charles Hausserman to be used by the local meat man. This truck's capacity was 1,000 pounds. That year, Rude sold eighty-seven new cars by July 1.

For a time, the Rude brothers were selling so many cars that factories limited the number they would ship to Perry. The Rudes turned to selling cars on a first come, first serve basis.

The Rude Auto Company was sold to Lecocq Motor Company in July 1926.

Through Wet Cement (1910)

One evening in June 1910, the residents on the north end of First Avenue were startled to see coming up the avenue a buggy which was hitched to a team. The buggy was occupied by a single man.

The street was closed while the concrete for paving was being put in. The man drove the full length of the avenue from the railroad tracks, over the piles of sand and gravel which had been

First Avenue Before Paving

It was up this street that a man and his team tracked right through a stretch of wet cement.

hauled for the paving work, around the mixer and machinery and piles of cement. The driver then splashed through the fresh concrete which had been laid during the afternoon, and left hoof marks of his team and the wheel marks of the buggy over the entire job until he reached the firmer concrete which had been in for several days.

One of the horses was shod, the other was not. The wheels of the rig tore through the mixture and left a broad and desolate waste behind. At the north end the man had to remove the barricade which closed the street in order to get out again upon the open highway.

Workmen repaired the damage as best they could the following morning.

Horses Meet the Automobile (1914)

With so many new cars sold and so many inexperienced drivers behind the steering wheel, accidents were bound to happen. Fortunately, there was not the danger to life and limb which came later with the faster, more complex machines.

William George, Dave Kelley, Carl Moody, and Virgil Everett, went to Coon Rapids with Charles Council to attend a baseball tournament. On returning home, while driving up the hill between Dawson and Jamaica, the engine failed. The brakes didn't hold and the machine started to back down hill. All jumped except Council and Everett who were shaken up when it went into a ditch and turned over. Two wheels were broken and all had to walk to Dawson where they boarded a train to Perry. Then next morning, new wheels were taken out to the car, changed and the car driven back into town.

Herman Tingwald of Bouton had a narrow escape from death at about 6 p.m. on March 22, 1914, when his Cartercar turned over on the grade a mile and a half west of Bouton. He was pinned underneath the car but escaped with slight bruises and scratches though the machine was considerably damaged.

Tingwald had tried to pass James Graney who was driving alone in his new Studebaker. Tingwald ran too close to the edge of the high embankment and rolled to the bottom of the ditch. A man named Benshoff was walking along the road and helped free Tingwald while Graney drove to Bouton for help in getting the car upright and on the road. As for the car, the top, windshield, lamps, and radiator were damaged, but it was driven back to Bouton under its own power.

Another accident occurred in July 1914 in which three young men were involved. Ben Workman and his horse-drawn rig and Ed Benz and Fred Hager in their Overland car were the victims. The young men in the car were returning from Bouton when they saw Workman approaching. They honked the horn, slowed down, and Workman pulled his rig to the side of the road.

Just as they were abreast of each other, No. 6, the passenger train came along and whistled for the station. That frightened the horse. He reared up and came down on the hood of the car, his hoofs struck the windshield and hurled broken glass into the front seat.

The boys received a number of cuts and gashes, but were able to drive to Perry. They went to the home of Dr. U.G. Grigsby, who patched their wounds, a number of stitches being required to close some of them.

Horses seemed bent on getting even with the horseless carriage which threatened to replace them. Graham's delivery horse in June 1916 is a case in point.

This horse which was being driven by Gilbert Thornley was left standing at the corner of 12th and Warford streets while the young man delivered some groceries. The wind suddenly blew the umbrella off the wagon, startling the horse, and causing him to start running. As he came down Willis, he managed to run into Dr. Pond's car standing in front of his office and, in the next block, to sideswipe Dr. McPherson's car, the wagon knocking it into the sidewalk in front of Coakley's Drug Store. While the horse was thrown down and the wagon overturned, he had managed to badly dent the fenders of both cars.

A Bad Day for Driving

Perhaps the most unusual chain of crashes occurred on Sunday morning, December 2, 1923. A dozen cars were damaged, some badly, in half as many accidents. No one was seriously hurt, but a few received cuts and bruises.

It began at Third and Otley, when cars driven by N.J. Buckles, F.L. Taylor, and Jess Saunders tried to cross the intersection at the same time. The Buckles car, a new Maxwell sedan, was going east on Otley; the Taylor car, a Buick, was coming west. Saunders, in a Ford, was driving north on Third Street, when he struck the rear of the Maxwell with sufficient force to throw it up on the opposite side of the street. All the cars were badly damaged. The rear end of the Maxwell was a wreck while the front ends of the other two cars were considerably bent and twisted.

Ray Ellett, who lived on North First Avenue, driving an Essex roadster and Mr. Bartlet in a Hudson coach, met at the corner of Second and Warford. The Essex lost a fender and the Hudson a bumper.

A few minutes later, the McCarthy wrecker going to the scene of the Ellett-Bartlet mix-up was hit at the corner of Second and Willis by a Buick driven by James Hood. The service car was not damaged but the Buick came out with bent fenders and hood, and a damaged frame.

A Ford touring car driven by Clyde Harper of Madrid was squarely struck by a Ford roadster driven by Walter Booth at the corner of Fourth and Warford. The Harper car lost a running board, fender and windshield together with a couple of blow-outs. The Booth car received a badly smashed front end and lost two headlights as well as otherwise damaging the fenders, steering apparatus, radiator and hood.

Frank Landis, in a Ford, smashed into a milk truck driven by Henry McLellan near the Washington School. Both cars received considerable damage.

Only slight damage was done to the Edwin Kuhl sedan when T.R. Phillips struck the rear end of the car on his way to the Freestone fire.

As an anti-climax, the next morning Edwin Halley's Ford lost a rear wheel just before crossing the M. & St. L. tracks on Willis Avenue. When the car came to a stop it was across the rail. Bystanders assisted Halley in pushing the car clear of the tracks a few minutes before the 9 o'clock passenger train was due.

Chapter Eleven
Flying Fever

Expecting to Fly

Ralph McMillen in a plane at the Glenn Curtiss School of Aviation in San Diego prior to take off in March 1912. (Right) A detail showing McMillen in same photo.

Perry's Daredevil (1889-1917)

Perry's young daredevil Ralph McMillen first gained attention for his escapades behind the steering wheel of an automobile, before moving onto feats in the flying machine.

Ralph McMillen was born in Perry on April 28, 1889. His father Chris was a conductor on the Milwaukee Railroad who later bought the Peel farm north of Perry and turned it into a fruit farm. Ralph's mother Mary taught in the Perry schools.

After graduating from high school in 1906, Ralph went into the auto repair business and later became the head of that department for the Rude Auto Company.

Derring-do was his forte. A number of Perry people were interested in the car races at Boone, but only one entered — Ralph McMillen. In what could be seen as a preview of what life held for him, an accident put McMillen's car out of the race.

In making one of the short turns on the course, a front tire blew, startling spectators who saw the wheel go to pieces with spokes flying through the air. The car plunged over the side of the track, down an embankment about 60 feet before coming to a stop. McMillen was uninjured, which was more than could be said for his car.

Ralph didn't always confine his racing to the track. He had a bout with the courts in 1911 when he was charged with speeding on Willis Avenue.

According to witnesses, McMillen and Fred Kennison were driving to the Perry Gun Club grounds for a shooting tournament; they were going about 15 to 18 miles per hour. Kennison passed McMillen just before he came to a buggy driven by Mrs. Cummins. As Kennison went around her, McMillen also passed the lady on the opposite side. The horse pulling the buggy was not frightened but the lady was.

Marshal Hart was crossing the bridge over Frog Creek at the time and Mrs. Cummins made complaint a to him. The marshal swore out a bill of information against the pair. Judge Shortley found them guilty, not of speeding or driving recklessly, but of violating a statute on the use of public highways. McMillen and Kennison were fined $5 each, plus court costs.

In early February 1912, McMillen, who had been studying aviation, went to San Diego and entered the Glenn H. Curtiss School of Aviation near there. He progressed so rapidly that he drew the attention of the head of the school and was given special training. On March 22 McMillen passed the final examination, was licensed to fly a biplane and was then eligible for exhibition work.

He returned to his parents' home in Perry. He purchased a Curtiss two-passenger, eight-cylinder biplane. McMillen asked the officers of the Perry Racing Association for permission to place the hangar for his machine on their grounds west of the city.

The last of April 1912, McMillen received a message from Hammondsport, New York, requesting him to report there to try out his new plane. The machine was then shipped to Perry in large packing cases. With the help of friends, McMillen assembled the plane in Perry.

McMillen gave an evening exhibition once the plane was ready. At 7 p.m. the evening of the exhibition, the plane was run out of the hangar, across the track, and onto the turf in the center of the driving park. With the young aviator seated and fastened in with shoulder straps (which held him steady, but allowed him the shoulder movements needed to steer) the plane roared across the speedway as it gathered speed and became airborne.

Fifteen minutes later the plane made a long, graceful glide to earth. As the wheels gently touched the sod, a burst of applause came from the crowd.

A day or so after McMillen's first exhibition in Perry, Fred Harvey, foreman for *The Advertiser*, and Joe Wells, an employee of *The Chief*, were on the road near Harvey's home when they saw the plane leave the ground. The two remarked on how low the plane was flying. The pilot, it seemed, had trouble getting altitude and turned as if to return to the landing strip. Some of the supports on a wing snapped and there was the sound of a heavy backfire explosion before the plane fell.

Harvey and Wells ran to the machine which had hit a creek

bed and fallen over on the two crewmen. They found Harry Williams (son of Mr. and Mrs. Frank Williams of Willis Avenue) with his feet sticking up in the air and his face pressed against them with a mass of tangled wires and sticks between them. McMillen was found almost buried in the mud and would have suffocated had Harvey and Wells not been there.

Telephone messages for help were dispatched and Dr. U.G. Grigsby came in H.I. Steltzer's auto. Both flyboys were taken to the doctor's office, where Grigsby worked on McMillen. Dr. H.B. Wilkinson stitched up Williams' wounds.

The next day McMillen lay in his parents' home on Third Street with both legs and his right shoulder broken and possible internal injuries. Harry Williams, son of Mr. and Mrs. Frank Williams of Willis Avenue, had twelve stitches in his chin and lip plus bruises about the head.

McMillen was taken by train to Mercy Hospital in Des Moines in order to have skilled care during the critical time of his recovery. He was accompanied by his parents and Dr. Grigsby. The wrecked machine was boxed and sent by express back to the factory in New York to be rebuilt.

Six weeks later, McMillen left the hospital accompanied by Dr. Grigsby and was taken by ambulance to the M. & St. L. station. There he was transferred to a cot and placed on the train. Arriving in Perry, Claude McMahon was at the depot with his auto. The cot bearing McMillen was placed over the tonneau and the trip home was safely accomplished.

By September, McMillen was back in the air in his rebuilt plane. He gave an exhibition on the fifth of that month at Grinnell. After his highly successful flight, his assistant Oscar Johnson, dismantled the plane and prepared it for shipment to Nebraska, the site of the next scheduled exhibition.

In November, the big biplane in which McMillen had nearly met his death was being set up again in the Perry driving park. A huge crowd was on the grounds and hundreds outside to watch the Perry birdman make three exhibition flights. The entire program was not carried out, but those who paid admission got their money's worth.

A violently strong wind gave McMillen trouble in take off and made it necessary to come in at much greater speed than desired on landing. The plane came down all right, and McMillen dropped the drag he used as a brake. The plane was going so fast when it hit the sod that the wires snapped on the drag — there was no way to hold the machine. He called to the people to grab the plane, but only one of his friends was able to get hold of it and he could not stop it. The plane struck the board fence at the west end of the park and stopped. The damage put it out of commission. The plane was repaired the next day and placed in boxes for winter storage.

In 1915, McMillen was selected as the pilot of one of the largest airplanes built to that time. It was a high honor. This plane was 250 horsepower of sufficient size to carry five passengers and enough gasoline to remain aloft for up to twenty hours. It was built for the transcontinental flight from New York to San Francisco.

McMillen was killed in a plane accident at Saint Francis, Kansas, on September 2, 1916. His body was shipped to Perry over the Milwaukee Railroad and taken to Phillips, Tiernan, and Sherman Funeral Parlor. The services were held at the Christian Church, conducted by Rev. William Knotts. Burial was at Violet Hill Cemetery, where the Masonic Lodge had charge.

After his early death, McMillen's fame and notoriety seemed to pass, his name just an inscription on a tombstone in Violet Hill Cemetery. That changed some in 1975, when *The Chief* received a call from Nebraska asking about McMillen.

A book was being compiled on Nebraska history which included a section of the 1915-1917 Aviation Corps of the Nebraska National Guard. It had been discovered that McMillen had been commissioned a captain in this small group in 1915. His many flights had brought him recognition. Researchers had discovered that McMillen was from Perry.

The Chief provided the Nebraska researchers a picture of McMillen in his Curtiss Model D airplane which became the front piece of their book.

Flying Fever (1920)

Interest in the airplane and flying began to grow in Perry again in 1920 after Burd White and pilot J.M. Watson dropped in on August 9 after an eighteen minute flight from Des Moines.

White was the owner of White Aircrafts, a company engaged in flying and airplane repairs. The trip to Perry was to make arrangements to operate here during the round-up.

Some people in Perry were fascinated by flying even if it didn't seem all that safe. Even two forced landings in the vicinity could not dampen locals' enthusiasm for flying.

Alfred Jewett was pilot of a big DeHavilland, one of the planes on the new mail routes. He left Chicago on June 20 with ten pouches of mail, expecting to deliver them in Omaha four hours later. The mail reached its destination at about 9 a.m the next day, but the pilot did not.

After leaving Chicago, Jewett encountered all kinds of bad weather. In spite of this, he managed to get to the Omaha vicinity, but the fog was so thick that he couldn't find a landing place. He circled around for a time, but became hopelessly lost. Hours later, with fuel running low, Jewett took a chance, came down through the mist and landed in a stubble field near the Taylor farm between Perry and Dawson.

As soon as he could get to a phone, Jewett put in a call for aid. Howard Hall brought him to Perry and the manager of a filling station sent out gasoline and oil. The ten sacks of mail were loaded into a car, turned over to Harry Smith at the post office, and sent to Omaha on train No. 11 on the Milwaukee. The ground was so soft that the pilot could not get away until late afternoon the following day.

Just about a month later another mail plane based in Chicago made an unscheduled landing in Perry. The pilot had left Iowa City in a storm and the weather became worse the farther west he flew. He had to give up landing on a field near the Frank Slaniger farm in Washington Township. The cargo was turned over to the Perry post office and his 13 pouches of mail went to Omaha on No. 11. The pilot was able to leave the next morning.

Despite all of these incidents, W.O. Keller bought a plane, which was delivered on December 30, 1920. This was the first plane owned by a Perry man since Ralph McMillen had his. This machine was a two-passenger Dougherty, with a Kirkham 6 motor. It had been purchased from the Chicago Aero Works Company.

Keller had had the bug for some time and had started to build his own plane but thought better of it. John Watkins, a Des Moines pilot, agreed to teach Keller to fly.

The Parker Aircraft Company (1921)

In August 1921, Fred Parker of the Parker Aircraft Company flew in from Fairfield and, after a conference, announced he would open an office and warehouse in Perry. He had operated airplane supply houses at Ottumwa and Des Moines but had decided to move the Ottumwa stock to Perry.

Parker carried all parts for standard Canadian and American planes. He also announced plans to purchase twenty-six Canadian planes to be assembled in Perry to open an aviation school and an airfield. In fact, if all his plans materialized, Perry would become the center for flying in Iowa.

However, bad luck befell Parker before the Perry operation was even launched: he was involved in an accident.

Parker had a machine in Perry owned by two men from Blakesburg and was taking up passengers on Saturday and Sunday for 10-minute rides over the city. George Fenner, a Perry machinist on the Milwaukee Railroad, was a passenger on the fateful flight.

Ascent was made at about 6:30 in the evening, and when the plane reached about 2,000 feet, the motor backfired and the gasoline in the carburetor caught fire. In an instant the machine was enveloped in flames. Hundreds of people on the ground watched in horror.

When the trouble started, Parker headed for the ground. Fenner, riding in the front seat, was caught by the flames first; he unbuckled his seat belt and started to climb out. Parker thought Fenner was going to jump and grabbed him with one hand while handling the levers which controlled the plane with the other. After a struggle, Fenner was dragged into the rear seat. Parker managed to land the plane in an oat field on the Johnson farm north of the city.

Men sped to the scene soon had the fire out. Fenner was rushed to the King's Daughters Hospital, where his burns were dressed. Parker escaped with a burn on one hand.

The plane was badly damaged. Both of the left wings were destroyed, the fuselage was gone on one side and the framework badly charred. The motor, however, was in good condition.

Fenner brought suit for $3,000 in damages against Parker and against Loren Smith and Van Cleave (the owners of the plane).

An out of court settlement was reached and the case was dropped on November 16, 1921, when the defendants agreed to pay Fenner $600 and assume all costs.

Meanwhile, Parker finally made it into business on August 12, 1921. The first carload of airplane parts and supplies was unloaded at the company storeroom located in the Capen building on Railroad Street (the former site of Gardiner Implement Company). By September, five students had enrolled in the Parker School of Aviation, including one girl.

The Parker headquarters soon became a mecca for students and prospective airplane owners alike. Dr. H.O. Cobb, a dentist, caught the fever in earnest and bought a plane to learn the ins and outs of flying. Frank Clergy and John Parks bought another — a monoplane. Parks had considerable experience in flying and wing walking.

John Barker, a Milwaukee Railroad fireman, was one of the advanced students. On October 4, in his third trip, Barker flew the machine without the assistance of the instructor.

Parker operated the aviation school at the Bender field just east of Perry. A program prepared by a number of pilots was given there on October 9. It was estimated that more than 400 cars were parked along the road, the line extending for almost a mile. Unfavorable weather marred the program, but five planes were in operation most of the day and many Perry people took their first ride in an airplane that day.

Extra copies of *The Perry Chief* and materials advertising the big air show to be staged by Parker Aircraft Company were delivered to all the surrounding towns by a plane piloted by Parker.

Thirty-nine people with five planes and ten autos put on a show at the Tri-County Fairgrounds. The admission was fifty-five cents for adults and thirty cents for children. In addition to stunt flying and taking passengers up on flights, there was also auto racing against airplanes. As the cars sped around the race track, planes flew low over them in a race of three miles.

Perry's interest in flying seemed to fade after the air show. But a herd of cattle in the neighborhood of Bagley got their first taste of the flying business shortly thereafter.

Two Des Moines men were forced by weather conditions to land in a farmer's pasture. When the flyers returned to their plane two hours later, they found the cows had broken out of an adjacent field and proceeded to feast upon the tail of the plane, the wings, and half of the fuselage. It was the dope used to coat the plane's fabric skin which the cows had found to be so tasteful.

What happened to Parker is not known. It was reported in November 1921, that he was in critical condition at his home following an assault by a brakeman on the Des Moines Railway.

The fracas occurred over a delay in repairing a car, no mention was made of planes. Witnesses said Parker was struck on the side of the head and was unconscious for more than an hour.

The brakeman gave himself up and was held under $1,000 bond. Bail was secured, but the hearing was postponed awaiting the outcome of Parker's injuries.

A Wild Ride (1921)

Des Moines aviator Johnny Walton came to Perry on July 29, 1921, to give exhibition flights. He was compelled to make a forced landing when some motor trouble developed just after he had taken to the air with a passenger. No one was hurt in the incident, but the machine was slightly damaged and a number of spectators had a bad fright.

Walton, with Miss Clarice Oldham as passenger, got away all right and had started south for a circle of the city, when the motor stopped. Walton was high enough to "volplane" to earth, but did not have time to pick out a landing place.

The best thing he could see was Robert Hastie's cornfield and the machine came down there seventy-five yards north of Park Street. Help was sent for and the machine was made ready for flight the next day. Another plane was also brought in for passenger service.

Chapter Twelve
Organizations

Young Men in Young Perry

Although the order of appearance is not known, the names of the young men of Perry shown here are: Charles Parker, Dr. Will Miller, Fred Thornley, Doc Dunlap, Harry Pattee, Ernie Lester, John Gray, Fred Leonard, Harry Conley, Bob Cardell, Tate Roush, Ed Aiken, Carl Calvin, Sam Hubbell, Charles Wilson, Floyd Bailey, Guy Crane, and R. Longshore.

Salvation Army (1893-1898)

The Salvation Army first began working with the wicked in Perry in August 1893. The following year, meetings were being held in the town hall with the establishment of a corps the eventual goal.

Mrs. Selma Green, who was born, lived and died in Perry, told of seeing these people marching on streets with their drums and tambourines, then back to their building expecting the people to follow them.

During mild weather open air meetings were held and the uniforms, flags and drums all added to the novelty of the appearance. The streets became filled with people who were entertained by this group and sometimes by Perry's Juvenile Band.

On one such occasion when the crowds overflowed into the streets, the meeting was disrupted and disaster narrowly averted. A horse, hitched to a driverless buggy suddenly whirled onto Second Street from Willis Avenue, and went tearing up the street at breakneck speed, scattering people as it went.

Fortunately, no one was injured, but numerous would-be helpers, without good sense, began waving their arms and yelling, frightening the horse even more. Then they started out in hot pursuit, bicycles and boys, buggies and men, but the horse ran on.

A man on horseback finally captured the runaway still hitched to the buggy and led it back to its owner. The horse had bolted just as Charles Marckres was about to get into the buggy. Marckres was pulled some distance by the lines before he fell, receiving severe bruises on his arm.

In the winter, meetings were held indoors. On New Year's Eve, 1896, a watch night service was held in the Salvation Army barracks. Between religious exercises and the eating of oysters, a good time was had by all. The following Sunday, they also held quite a jubilee. A large audience was present and a number of soldiers from Angus attended.

It wasn't long after this that the corps closed out at Angus. At one time it had flourished, but the officers became lax and did not hold regular meetings. The people grew tired of the irregularity of meetings and so the Army died a sudden death.

The Army was still drawing large crowds on the streets of Perry in 1897. The leaders were sometimes accused of not using good judgment in their choice of locations. When they held meetings in front of the post office at 7:20 p.m., just at mail time, with spectators completely blocking the sidewalks, complaints were filed. Marshal Dave Willis had to be called upon to open a passageway and even he had difficulty keeping it open.

Whether it was a carry-over from the Billy Sunday, month-long revival meetings of 1898, or for some other reason, the Salvation Army entirely withdrew its corps from Perry in October of that year. For five years they had done excellent work among the people and many regretted the corps had not been better supported.

The Thelma Club (1895-1900)

One of the most popular organizations in early Perry was the Thelma Club. The date of its founding is not certain, but it must have been about 1895.

One cannot even guess why the large membership of prominent and social men of Perry would choose such an unusual name. It was said that if it were not for the Thelma Club and the railroad, Perry would not be much of a town.

Many stories in Perry newspapers were devoted to the club's meetings and activities. New members were taken in at a rapid rate and the initiation ceremonies concocted for their benefit were reported to result in a great demand for the arnica plants.

Club parties were grand affairs. One of the first mentioned was held at Chandler's Hall with music furnished by the Marshalltown Orchestra. No small undertaking for April 1896.

Club members held annual field days. The second was in July 1896, and was a memorable one. It was estimated that a crowd of more than 2,000 gathered at the fairgrounds. Every effort was made that day to run the best races before the rain came, but to no avail.

It had looked rainy all afternoon, but at noon when it showed signs of clearing, the parade was started. Russell's Military Band led the procession, followed by the Thelma Club members in their white duck suits. Scholes' Light Infantry Band followed. Then came the crowd. By the time the parade made it to the fairgrounds it looked as though it could rain any minute.

Try as they could, only four races could be run before the cloud burst. It was reported in the Bulletin that "some fool started the cry that the grandstand was unsafe" and a near panic erupted. A woman and a girl fainted. One of the refreshment stands blew over and a dressing tent was blown down.

In November, the club took over the entire floor over Wimmers' Drug Store and fitted out the three rooms. The first was used for a reception and reading room, the middle one for whist and other games, and the rear one for a gymnasium and banquet hall.

An initiation service was held in February 1897, followed by a banquet served by Mrs. Walker. Among those taking the vows were attorney Edmund Nichols, Frank Dodson, Arthur Wills, Henry Moody, Frank Cross, Dell Kenworthy, Lewis Crist, George Maroney, Jerry Stoner, Earnest Heightshoe, Sheriff Payne, H.G. Giddings, and John Swearingen. The goodnight chorus was sung in the wee small hours.

The businessmen and Perry citizens gave to the Thelma Club the task of organizing the 1897 Fourth of July celebration. Many people attended the free event and everything went as planned except the weatherman skipped a cog. Part of the forenoon and all afternoon the wind blew real estate several inches thick in the most reckless way.

Then the club seemed to slow down. *The Perry Chief* reported it wasn't dead, merely sleeping. The last of January 1898, it met with little of the old time spirit and decided to spruce up their rooms, take in new members, elect officers, and hold a banquet.

The new slate of officers elected in February consisted of: L.A. French, president; Roy Bailey, vice president; W.H. Fahey, secretary; and Harry Marckres, assistant secretary. H.F. Lods was elected treasurer.

The post of treasurer was of special interest and never conducted without a contest. Every treasurer elected had been married during his term of office; members had come to believe there was something about the office.

Nominations that year were J.P. Lansing, Ed Elliott and George Gardiner. Lansing was married and so not eligible. He dropped out of the race after the first ballot. Though Lods was not nominated by any member, he was clearly the choice of the unseen power which presided over the office and he was unanimously elected.

August 10, 1898, the big day for the field meet dawned bright and clear. All were up early and donned their best bib and tuckers. Thelma colors were conspicuous everywhere. All morning trains bought in large delegations. Others drove from Dallas Center, Adel and other parts. At 9 a.m., the Adel Cornet Band arrived and gave an open air concert on the street for over an hour.

At 1 p.m., the Thelma Club formed in line of parade and marched to the fairgrounds where the events of the day were to take place. Many races were held. At night a great bicycle lantern parade was held with all the wheel men in the city participating. It was a unique closing for the day's events.

A big race meet was planned for the end of September 1899. To stake $1,000 on the success of such a meet in a town like Perry was quite an undertaking. The last day was cold and miserable, with a small crowd, the Thelma boys went into the hole. The members decided to make an assessment for the paying of claims which had accumulated. The future of the club seemed uncertain.

It broke up in the spring of 1900. Furniture and carpets were sold to the YMCA.

Bath, No Lights (1896)

There was an excavation under the sidewalk and into the street in front of the Wild and Rall Shoe Store, and there was gloom inside the store on a Saturday night in December 1896. On these two facts hung a tale.

The water connection for the YMCA rooms was made by tapping the pipes under the store. In the store the lights were furnished by homemade gas, and city water was used in its manufacture. When the YMCA boys turned on the water upstairs, it lowered the pressure down below and the lights would go out.

It was a little annoying for the customers suddenly to find

themselves in the dark, to say nothing about the store owners. To restore lighting, the owners had to close all the gas jets, start the engine, and then light all the jets every time a bath tub upstairs got a new inmate.

Woodmen Take A Trip (1896)

It was a merry crowd when it started in January 1896, but some of the members were a little bit tired and disgusted when they arrived home. The party was made up of Modern Woodmen of Perry and they went over to Dawson on a Saturday evening to visit the camp. They had a fine time until they started home.

There was a freight train at the station when the camp disbanded for the night and a number of Woodmen thought it would be a good thing to ride it home rather than wait until the next day for a passenger train. The freight was not scheduled to carry passengers, but the dispatcher said if the conductor was willing, the Woodmen could ride.

The conductor was suffering from dyspepsia or something akin to it and when they proceeded to board his way car, he objected. W.H. McCammon took him to one side and tried to bribe him by offering him a fine necktie, but the man was stubborn.

Unobserved by McCammon or the conductor, a lot of Woodmen sneaked into the way car and, when the conductor came in and told them to get out, they gave him the frozen face and told him to go hence. McCammon started toward the engine with the avowed intention of purchasing a ride in the cab, but the train started out and left him standing in the right of way, the cold chilly winds of January playing a sad requiem for departed hopes through his whiskers.

The conductor tried to make it uncomfortable for his passengers, but they refused to have it that way and it was an open secret in railroad circles that the old way car was haunted by the ghosts of a crowd of jolly Woodmen.

And that conductor had to carry the crowd without getting a new necktie. It was said he was mad for a long time.

Country Club (1916)

When Perry was young, certain of the population fell victim to golf fever. This was a very popular sport in many cities and some of the local citizenry had indulged in the game in other places. They exposed their friends and neighbors to this fever.

There was no way at the time to promote a clubhouse and properly prepared links, but there was a suitable meadow just south of town. Arrangements were made with the owner, W.W. Phillips, for use of the field.

For a number of years the ground was used rent free. Any nice afternoon, young and old, men and women, could be seen hunting the illusive golf ball and taking off surplus flesh chasing it up and down the hills.

Then the time came for this particular field to be planted to corn, which meant the end of golfing there. When it appeared the golfers were about to lose their sport, a movement to lease grounds was begun.

The long-talked of and much-wanted golf links became a reality in 1916. About twenty-five Perry men — all enthusiastic concerning the organization of a country club — met February 10, in the superior courtroom and decided to form an association, build a clubhouse, and equip the grounds for golf and tennis.

At the meeting, the plan was so favorably received that it was decided to elect temporary officers: John Rude was president; H.C. Modlin, secretary. Directors were: H.M. Pattee; E.D. Carter; John Carmody; H.A. Modlin; and John R. Rude. Scott Snyder, H.A. Nash, and Clark Brown were on the building committee.

The board purchased forty acres of land from A.D. Moore, north of the city, adjoining Chrystal Springs and Park, the property of E.D. Carter. The site was accessible by gravel road year round. M.G. Lyon, manager of the Iowa Railway and Light Company, thought it could be arranged for a line to carry light to the club site. This would also be important to farmers living along the line.

A golf expert, Warren Dickinson, was brought to town in March to look over the site. Dickinson became enthusiastic as soon as he stepped from the automobile onto the grounds.

The only piece of poor road between the city and the proposed club was the lane east from Coleman Corner, a distance of

The First Club House

The clubhouse at the Perry Country Club burned to the ground on the morning of October 22, 1923. It was rebuilt the following year.

about a quarter mile. It was decided to gravel this stretch.

As might be expected, volunteer labor was called upon and there came a morning when some of the club members were seen in town walking as though there wasn't a joint in their entire anatomy. Then it was known for sure who had been helping make the gravel road.

When the 6 p.m. whistle sounded that first day, 130 loads of gravel had been hauled from the pit on the Bell farm just north of Beaver Creek bridge and dumped onto the road. Those 130 loads were hoisted into the wagon a shovelful at a time by men who had not performed a similar hard day's work in years.

The brightest spot came about 3 p.m., when Mrs. Amos Case arrived on the scene with a huge basket of egg sandwiches and hot coffee. At quitting time, the road was only half done. There were nine teams on the job on the morning of March 27, thirteen that afternoon.

The second day found only half a dozen or so club members on the job. The memory of the previous day's strenuous work was too vivid to permit a return to the back-breaking, muscle-aching labor. Those men replaced themselves with paid shovelers and, on this day, 139 loads were added.

Hard physical labor did not end with the completion of the lane. A rock-clearing squad was organized and all members spent some time gathering and loading rocks which were hauled by teams to a place near the clubhouse site. These were to be used in the construction of a cobblestone fireplace in the big main room on the first floor.

Next, a three-ton steamroller was shipped to Perry and every foot of the 40 acres was rolled and smoothed. By May 1916 the budding golf enthusiasts were playing on the new grounds.

On May 3, the building committee closed a deal with Pearson and Son for the erection of a clubhouse. It was a two-story structure with a basement, modern in every way, with water, sewer and lighting systems.

The club was formally opened on July 10, and the fine new building and grounds were turned over to the members. An orchestra was hired and from 6 p.m. until midnight, the members and guests enjoyed a dancing party or card games at the clubhouse. The links were in excellent condition and the tennis courts were the finest in the community. Shade was plentiful and there were many places for the children to play.

The clubhouse was burned to the ground on October 22, 1923, shortly after 2 a.m. Along with the building went all the furniture and fixtures, the household goods of custodians Mr. and Mrs. Ed Mayo, and considerable personal property owned by the members.

This setback did not cool the enthusiasm. On February 21, 1924, the directors announced a new and better clubhouse would be built as soon as weather conditions would permit. And so the club, with increased membership, went on.

KKK (1920-1926)

The Ku Klux Klan was big news in Perry back in 1920.

It was early February when a rumor was heard on Perry's streets that a representative of the KKK was in the city and had approached a number of men soliciting their membership. No one seemed to know who he was, where he stayed, or what he looked like. The reports were so numerous that the Bureau of Commerce went on record as being opposed to the Klan or any similar organizations which resulted in strife.

Their opposition was of little consequence, however, for

about two months later first burning of a fiery cross took place in Dallas County. This ceremony was held near Madrid and it must have been quite a sight to the many spectators who lined the surrounding hills.

At dusk a long procession of cars containing hooded figures drove up and parked their machines in a crescent formation. After a brief ritual, 200 Klansmen stood at attention while a cross approximately twenty feet high was planted in the ground and lighted. Only the crackling of burning wood broke the tense silence, though widespread comment expressed surprise that the Klan was so well organized.

After the cross was consumed, the members of the Klan became a caravan that journeyed five miles northwest of town where a large class of candidates was initiated. Here in a clearing, surrounded by timber, the novitiates took the oath of the order. A heavy guard turned back a number of cars containing curious towns people. The ceremonies lasted until after midnight. The order was said to be adding thirty members a week in Dallas and Boone counties..

All that summer the Klan was active with free public lectures, meetings and parades. The Perry chapter grew rapidly and, according to local members, had 380 members by July. A big ceremonial was held at Beaver Park at which members from Perry and Woodward united.

A farm two miles east of Perry was the site of another gathering on July 30, 1923. The meeting was held in an oat field south of Primary Road 17 and the fiery cross was visible to passing motorists. Hooded sentinels, some on appropriately garbed horses, guarded the field where the exercises were held. A large class was initiated, said to be the largest group ever taken in.

On an evening in September, about 6,000 people packed the Perry fairgrounds to attend a semi-public meeting. The ceremony was opened by a parade of 500 Klansmen in full regalia, headed by six mounted Klansmen, marching around the half mile track. Fiery crosses furnished the light, and drum and bugle corps the marching music. A minister of an established church in Chicago, though not a member, gave the address. A class of 100 candidates was taken into the invisible empire.

The year 1924 saw the Klan grow even stronger. Early in May 276 men were taken into membership and eighty women joined the auxiliary. This meeting was scheduled to be held in a pasture southwest of the city, but because of extreme cold, was changed to an indoor meeting. White robed and hooded figures patrolled the vicinity of the meeting and hooded figures were also stationed at roads leading into the city to direct members to the meeting place.

On June 2, 1924, the Klan parade and semi-public meeting attracted the largest crowd that had ever visited Perry. A check of cars during the hours just before the parade, showed about 2,000 parked in the city limits while a similar check at the fairgrounds showed an even greater number of cars there.

The parade was staged at 9 p.m. Nine Klansmen on horses headed the marchers followed by a forty-piece band and about 650 Klansmen and Klansladies. A number of decorated automobiles were interspersed throughout the parade. The witnesses and marchers were all orderly and the crowd and traffic were handled well by the police. The crowd of Klan members attended the ceremonial at the fairgrounds after the parade. A display of fireworks followed the ceremony.

The power of the Klan was being felt for it was reported that with a thorough organization in every precinct in Perry, the Klan had made a clean sweep of the election of 1924. Tickets which were regarded to be composed almost entirely of Klansmen and Klansladies were elected to represent the city at the Republican county convention.

Two big events in the history of the Klan in Perry in 1925 were the first Klan funeral, and a statewide Klanklave.

One of the largest crowds ever to attend a funeral was present at the services in the Christian Church for a prominent farmer. The local order of the Klan was in charge of the services at the cemetery, carrying out the ritual of their order.

The Klanklave was held at the fairgrounds and the city council granted them permission to hold a parade. This was staged despite cold and disagreeable weather. While attendance did not meet expectations, the apparent interest of the crowds caused concern among many. There were two bands, two drum corps, two floats and about 375 robed Klan members in the parade. The bands and drum corps wore special uniforms and the parade was enlivened by many red torches.

However, a similar parade held in Minburn that fall received different treatment. Four Minburn residents, George McLellan, Lyman Hill, Oscar Howard, and Jimmy Duffy were implicated and warrants sworn out against them for disturbing the peace. Duffy was a black lad who skipped and was not apprehended in time for the trial. The three other lads were fined $10 and costs in Justice Shirley's court for "rotten egging" the procession.

The parade was headed by a drum corps and it was this part that was the special target of the egg throwers. Drums and white robes were bespattered with broken eggs and the decorum of the marchers was somewhat disturbed by the yellow streams which decorated them.

The power of the Klan began to diminish. At the city election of 1926, a ticket not headed by that organization was elected, the first Klan defeat in several years. This was felt to mark the downfall of the Klan as a political power in Perry. The voting in the election seemed to be on the basis of Klan and anti-Klan issues.

Later, on April 25, 1926, an attempt was made to burn a fiery cross on the yard of *The Chief* editor Herbert Adams, but it fizzled out. It fell over when being lit. The cross was placed there by some young men who drove up in a Ford coupe, but were so anxious to get away before their identity was discovered, that the intended effect was lost.

There was still mention of the Klan ten years later, but the interest of the public had waned.

Chapter Thirteen
That's Entertainment

The Fairgrounds

The Tri-County Fairgrounds located on the southern edge of Perry was on land the Tri-County Fair Association bought from Fred Moore in 1920.

Three Times and Out (1875-1929)

Three times Perry tried to build a permanent fairgrounds and all three times failed.

A plot of forty acres just west of a then-smaller Perry was secured for a fairgrounds in the summer of 1875. A few citizens had bargained with Judge Henry Thornburg starting in May, with the agreed-upon price being $30 per acre. A clear title was obtained in July 1875.

Immediately men with teams went to work grading the low places. A track was surveyed the last week of July and completed the last week of August. The name adopted was the Perry Union Agricultural Association. There apparently was no record of a fair being held here by that organization.

The second fairground came about in October 1886, when a company of ten citizens leased the Foster and Heaton ground east of Perry. Articles of Incorporation were drawn up and officers elected. They were: Fred Knell, president; Steele Kenworthy, vice president; George Heaton, secretary; C.H. Ainley, treasurer. All but fifteen shares of the company had been sold.

Work commenced for the launching of the Perry Agriculture Association or District Fair. It was composed of citizens from Dallas, Guthrie, Greene and Boone counties.

A track was commenced in October; an amphitheater built in April 1887, located on the north side of a high point overlooking the surrounding country. Stables, sheds, pens and other structures for stock were erected on the south side. Between the track and in front of the grandstand there was a baseball diamond suitable for the playing of match games. The Middle School is located on part of this land.

The first fair opened on October 4, 1887. Fairs were held there on the beautiful grounds in 1888 and 1889. That third fair was a decided success, both in the number of exhibits and in attendance.

There was a case in court in April 1893, wherein the association was fighting off creditors. The mortgage holder sought foreclosure. The association claimed the foreclosure proceedings were not legal as notice was served on the wrong officers. A settlement was reached.

A fair was held there again in September 1898. As there was no state fair that year and not many smaller fairs in the region on account of the Omaha Exposition, it was thought the fair in Perry had a good chance of being a success.

By April 1903, this association had folded its tent, too. The association disposed of the land to a man whose business it was to buy real estate and subdivide it.

J.E. Barteley and Sam Block of Tipton came to Perry looking over the grounds and the city. They had come once before to negotiate for the fairgrounds, but had been frightened off by the price asked. They came this time to consider an offer of the grounds at $8,000. After studying the business conditions and the real estate situation, they concluded that Perry was ripe for a newly platted addition and that the fairgrounds were the best available site to be had.

County surveyor Henry Brady divided the land into fifty lots for Barteley and Block. Brady also laidout streets and alleys in compliance with city plans. Barteley and Block paid the association $1,000, and agreed to pay the balance as soon as the land and approved abstract were delivered.

The tract became known as the High View Addition. Lots were auctioned on May 26-27, 1905. Had not a heavy rain came up on the first day, every lot would have been sold. As it was, five lots were sold in ten minutes, prices ranging from $80 to $110. The buyers were: Howard Rouse, A. Appenzeller, H. Brady, J. Tyre, and G.W. Thompson. The number of lots sold over the two days was 126 and the aggregate amount was $9,359, including the price of the buildings.

The feeling persisted in some circles that Perry needed and wanted a permanent fairgrounds. In 1916, the Bureau of Commerce began plans for the project and visited several appropriate sites. Among them were: the Alborn tract on East Tenth Street; Fred Moore's farm on Third Street; and the Pattee land on West Willis. Three years later H.A. Pattee, chairman of the special committee, finally started the ball rolling towards the eventual goal.

The Tri-County Fair Association was formally launched at a stockholders' meeting held at the Elks Club on April 22, 1920. About 100 backers attended. Architects from Des Moines were called in to prepare specifications for the track and other work.

A deal for the Fred Moore land at the southern edge of Perry was closed. The association later bought more land from Moore, approximately 20 acres lying west of Third Street and the east of First Avenue. South Third was a private lane owned by Moore and it was closed during fairs and shows. The private lane north of the site was maintained as usual and served as an entrance to the grounds.

Three tractors, seven teams, twenty-five men, an active executive committee, and the 400 stockholders combined to push the project. Piers for the amphitheater were poured under the direction of R.E. Shackleton. Pearson and Son had the contract for the amphitheater and the National Wood Works Company had the contract for the stock pavilion and barns.

The first attraction at the new grounds was a round-up on August 11, 1920.

The first Tri-County Fair was held over four days beginning September 15, 1920. Fairs were held regularly for the next nine years. All but one were scheduled about the same time in September and, just as regularly, the weather did its best to spoil them.

After the close of the third annual fair, during which threatening skies and cold weather had taken their toll, a fund raising campaign was held in April 1923, to aid the association. A sum of $9,000 was raised and the grounds and buildings were saved for the community.

Adverse weather conditions managed to spoil at least one day of three of the next four fairs, producing lower attendance which led to reduced revenues. Rumors began circulating in 1927 that discontinuance of the fair was contemplated, but on July 14, it was announced by the board of the association that the eighth annual session would be held for five days beginning on September 12. Again, rain managed to cause a postponement of one night's performance.

The grounds seemed hoodoo-ed. Even the July Fourth celebration planned for 1928 and which opened on July 3, suffered from a storm the night before, which did considerable damage to the midway. Several concessions and one tent show were blown down and several damaged. Some did not even attempt to open on the Fourth.

Early in June 1928, the stockholders met in the Municipal Building for the purpose of deciding whether or not the project should be continued or turned over to the holder of the mortgage. A new board of directors was chosen, but until they could legally take their seats, the old board retained control. Because of the lack of time, fair dates were set for the first four days of October 1928.

Ironically, the October fair opened with bright sunshine and wonderful Indian summer temperatures and closed with one of the most successful fairs of its nine years of existence.

Then came fair time of 1929 and bright sunshine broke through rain clouds which had hung over the city for several days auguring well for the tenth annual fair. But receipts and funds of the fair were attached by a court action filed by a local farmer seeking to collect on two notes plus interest. These notes had been owned by the Security Savings Bank but, following the bank's failure, they were included in a group which had been purchased by the complainant.

This action tied up all funds. Premiums could not be paid and the fair expense couldn't be settled until a decision was received by the court. Four of the directors gave personal checks of $100 to insure payment of prize money.

Voluntary petition in bankruptcy was filed by the Tri-County Fair Association in January 1930. While listed as voluntary, the action was practically forced upon the directors because of lawsuits then in the courts and others pending.

It was reported that nothing had been paid on the $9,000, due Moore on the land on which the buildings were built.

Jack Bruce bought the grounds and buildings at a sheriff's sale in February 1932, for $8,000. The sale resulted from a judgment granted Moore against the trustees for $8,000. The deed had the usual one-year redeemable clause.

George Cronkhite, local contractor, was high bidder in February 1933 for the buildings, which were sold to satisfy a judgment held by H.M. Shively, trustee. Cronkhite converted the big cattle barn into a modern dance parlor, beverage parlor, and night club known as Betty Lou Gardens.

Later Mark Hanlon became the owner and the Betty Lou Gardens was converted into a skating rink; then, after a time, to a dance hall and tavern called the Burro Barn.

The last vestige of the fair was wiped out on October 31, 1964, when the remaining building was destroyed by fire. It had been used mostly for storage since 1952.

Smith Opera House (1883)

The growing Perry was not one to do without a place of entertainment. After H.L. Davis and M.A. Crocker rented the Union Hall for their billiard parlor in September 1883, Isaac Smith purchased two business lots owned by W. Karger opposite the new Commercial block on Second Street. He let the contract for the erection of an opera house there that December.

Plans called for a 50- by 120-foot two-story building of veneered brick with the lower story divided into two storerooms with fourteen-foot ceilings. The second floor was to be the full size of the building with a twenty-foot ceiling. The roof was to be self-supporting; consequently, there would be no visual obstructions in the room.

It was Smith's intention to make the upper story into one of the nicest opera houses in this part of Iowa. The material for the opera house was being piled in February 1884, in order to start construction as soon as the weather permitted. But, some parts of the project proceeded despite the weather. Carpenters built the wooden frame ahead of time so as not to hinder the work when foundation and forming work began.

A cyclone wrought destruction on the partially completed structure early Sunday morning April 27 1884. The roof was just being constructed and the building otherwise enclosed, except for the windows in the front and back, which had not been put in. The floor had not been laid and the workmen had only commenced to thoroughly brace the building.

The wind twisted the second story loose and, as it fell to the south, it forced the lower floor to the North, crushing it and leaving the not badly damaged second story partly upon it. Some felt the building would not have been safe even if the wind had not destroyed it.

The contractor, Sam Heightshoe, said the Opera House was being built on the same plan as the Commercial block, only stronger. S.E. Smith, who furnished the hardware, said the 2,000 pounds of nails and 800 bolts used on the building indicated to him that the contractor and proprietor meant to have it strong enough. It was a hardship for the owner, costing him $1,500. The debris was hauled away and he said he would rebuild, making the walls solid brick, instead of veneer.

By May 9, 1884, Smith's plans were official. The opera house would be rebuilt and the solid brick walls would contain a good many reinforcement rods to strengthen the structure. The second story had hardwood floors so it could be used for a skating rink as well as an opera house. The last of August, a scenic artist was at work on the Opera House's scenery.

Smith's Opera House opened on September 1, 1884, with a grand ball. The evening was warm and the room well-filled; nevertheless, all heartily enjoyed the occasion.

Medicine Show (1889-1916)

Medicine shows are part of the lore of the west. These shows traveled through towns and villages, entertaining people to attract crowds, then dispensing their own particular remedies. Perry was the birthplace of one such show.

Dr. Condon had been a dentist in Perry for five years when Dr. A.W. Trout came to town in 1884. Early in his medical career Trout had begun to use medicines of his own special compounding. So great was his belief in their merit, that in 1889 he organized and became president of The Dr. Trout Panama Oil Indian Company. That same year, Dr. Condon sold half of his interest in his thriving practice and joined the company as treasurer. Ed Forgrave was named manager.

In September, the new company started north, planning to make Humboldt the first stop on its tour. Along with a goodly supply of medicine, the three proprietors also took three others whose duty it was to give a comedy or musical show for the amusement of the crowd. This was to ensure good humor in the crowd so as to facilitate the sales of the Panama Nerve Oil and other medicines.

The first lesson they learned was that medicine — good or bad — couldn't be peddled without a license. They had only been in Humboldt a short time when the state pharmacist descended on the entourage demanding they show a license. In the hectic activity of getting the show on the road, this item had been overlooked. The necessary amount was immediately produced, a license procured and the show went on.

The last part of September it became necessary to quit the road to revitalize their forces with rest and relaxation for three or four weeks. According to the newspaper report, "the great Panama Medical wonder, the lightning tooth extractor, the Corkological dude, the little female impersonator and the black-faced magnet wiped the sweat from their brows and took their own medicine for a while."

That October they gave a show at the Opera House, charging ten cents and fifteen cents admission. Then the company started out again, this time for Pleasantville. On November 8, the Trout Medicine Company went into winter quarters and all returned to Perry and to their regular lines of employment.

Three years later, the show was doing an immense business and with the end of September came the end of the tenting season. At this point, the show shifted its venues to music halls and opera houses. B. Roy Emms traveled with the troupe in 1892 and 1893.

Evidently Dr. Trout left the company about this time, for in 1894 Dr. Condon was still taking the Panama Medicine Show on the road. Also that year, a reporter wrote of a visit to Dr. Condon's office in the Union block where the medicine was made and prepared for shipment. The doctor had large drug orders from firms in the east and thousands of testimonials from those who had benefited from the Panama remedies.

Dr. Condon left Perry in about 1897, as an item appeared in the newspaper stating that he was then located in Springfield, Illinois, for the winter.

The Chief had no record as to when Dr. Condon died. Dr. Trout remained in Perry serving residents for forty-one years. He died on January 8, 1925, at the home of his daughter, Mrs. F.C. Hamlin of 1825 Willis. He was eighty-one years of age and the grandfather of V.T. "Snick" Hamlin, the creator of Alley Oop.

Perry's Juvenile Band (1892)

John C. Scholes organized a juvenile band in Perry on November 1, 1892. There were 14 members ranging in age from 13 to 17 years. Under the professor's leadership the band made splendid progress.

The band held its first fair at the Town Hall February 27 through March 1 to raise money for uniforms. The event was a grand success — receipts for the first two nights were $200. On March 2 the band fashioned a new program from parts of the first three nights' entertainment for a show at the Opera House. After just four nights of playing, the band could afford uniforms, and good ones, too!

When Scholes and Miss Della Battles were married by Rev. J. Delmar Andrews in the bride's home on May 31, 1893, the juvenile band was out in full uniform to perform a rousing serenade.

The band also occasionally entertained the public with concerts on Second Street.

For some reason not made clear in the newspapers, the Scholes band was succeeded by the B. Roy Emms Juvenile Band, organized in February 1898. Emms' band made its first public appearance in July 1899. Dressed in red sailor suits, the little fellows looked "just too nice for anything" and played beautifully.

Band members were: clarinet — R.C. Logan, Willis Correy, Joe Ahrens; cornet — J.B. Logan, Glenn Ross, John Rogers, Charles Braman; alto — Phil Dodson, Rick Bandy, Edwin Schiller; tenor — John Rude, Glenn Bandy; baritone — Harry Heaton; tuba — Clarence Willis, Wilmot Blakeslee; bass drum — Harry Bruce; side drums — Earl Riffle.

The boys presented their leaders with a beautiful mounted baton with their compliments in January 1900. That spring Emms went to Chicago to buy new instruments for the band, which had been gaining favor in Perry and surrounding towns.

The new instruments were beauties, having been purchased, in part, with surplus funds from the Encampment. They were to remain the property of the citizens who had contributed to the fund. A custodian was appointed to keep track of them and every boy who left the band had to turn in his horn.

Emms' Juvenile Band was still favoring the promenaders along Second Street with open air concerts in 1902.

The Juvenile Band

This picture of B. Roy Emms Juvenile Band was taken about 1904. The members identified in the picture are: Back row — Louis Doss, Coy Eckman, Otto Ortt, Arley Needham, Dr. B. Roy Emms, Silvia Glucklick (a girl!), Edgar Knight and Dale Miller; Middle Row — Harry McLaughlin, Harold Wildman, Horace DeGrush, Fran Braman, Gaylord Courtney, Israel Hern, Lester Job and Grant Eckman; Front row — Frank O'Brien, Nathan Cave, Clarence Miller, Jacob Hern, and Fred Briggle.

The band struck it rich in 1906 when the Fire Department let them have the use of the lower floor of the new engine house for their regular practice. The room was heated, lighted and excellent for their purpose. The only string attached to the Fire Department's offer was that the band not destroy the property in the room.

The fate of this band is lost in the pages of the old newspapers — if, indeed, it was ever mentioned.

There is a picture of B. Roy Emms Juvenile Band donated to the newspaper by Wade Modlin. He thought the picture was taken about 1904. It was not the first band, as these were not "cute little fellows in red sailor suits," as described in local accounts. These boys were in dark suits.

The Circus Comes to Town (1894)

In order to see the Ringling Brothers' Circus these days it is necessary to go to a large city. This was not always the case. There was a time when this circus included Perry on its schedule.

Everyone was pleased in 1894 when the announcement was posted that the Ringling Brothers' Circus would be putting on a show in Perry on June 4. The advance agent had given the city $50 for the privilege of spreading their tents.

Stevenson and Leonard, owners of a butcher shop, had the contract to furnish the circus with 1,500 pounds of meat for the show people.

About 4:45 on a Sunday morning, the first of the three trains required to transport the equipment and animals pulled in to Perry; within fifteen minutes all three trains were in town. A large crowd gathered even at that early hour to watch the proceedings. Many people felt that the unloading of the trains and the setting up for the circus was as interesting as the show itself.

Within two hours, the large menagerie of cooking, dining and horse tents were raised. Coffee was boiling in large pots. The tables were set with clean cloths and the hungry men were fed. The horses received equally good treatment.

It was reported that there had never been such a large collection of fine horses in the state before. A blacksmith's shop with three anvils was set up next to the horse tent.

Attendance that afternoon was remarkably large. In the evening, it rained, not only cooling the atmosphere, but also the ardor for the show — attendance was off.

Exhibitions were given in the three rings on two elevated stages and upon a quarter mile track under the largest canvas pavilion ever erected in Perry.

Some in Perry actually knew the Ringling brothers. George H. Covey was born in a little town on the Illinois-Wisconsin border. As a boy he and his pals, the Ringling boys, Alf and Otto, were always playing circus. They put on shows for which they charged pins.

Years later, when the circus tents were pitched on a large lot near the Haskins' home in Perry, the Ringlings stopped and asked permission to water their horses. Covey asked the unsuspecting brothers how many pins were they charging. Recognizing their boyhood friend, a grand reunion ensued.

Two years later in 1896, the advance agent was in Perry again and announced that the circus would arrive on August 3. Perryites were elated, as the show was now a prime favorite of the town.

Early that Sunday morning of August 2, nearly all the town gathered at the Rock Island depot to see the circus come to town. Two long trains drawn by heavy engines from the main line brought the show east from the Atlantic. The Ringling Brothers had made great strides in show business since their first appearance in Perry.

The next morning, the town began to fill with people who came from every direction not only to see the parade, but to soak up some of the circus experience.

The great tent was crowded to capacity. The opening grand march with its accompanying "living pictures" was of special interest, but so was the menagerie, which included several rare species — a great giraffe and a hippopotamus.

Some local men were well acquainted with Colonel Harry Cooper, the tall man traveling with the circus. They knew him when he was a miner in the iron-stone mines of Brotten in England. When young Cooper had become ill with typhoid fever and grew eighteen inches while ill. When he recovered, he was ashamed of his great height and walked stooped in order to look shorter. Then a showman ran across him and used him as a museum freak, paying him a good salary. He was brought to America by P.T. Barnum and had traveled with shows since his arrival. Some of the Angus men who were his playmates as boys had an opportunity to visit with Cooper.

Will M. Maupin wrote an article on the Ringling Brothers' Circus which appeared in the *Omaha World Herald* in September 1899. Maupin wrote that when the Ringlings started out, they were in a tent show with a few animals for the menagerie. They attracted the attention of old "Yankee" Robinson, a retired showman. He recognized that the Ringlings had the right stuff in their make-up to make a success of the circus, so he went in with them. They started with the policy of a clean show, keeping faith with the public, and constantly bettering the attractions. While with the Ringlings, Robinson died. He was buried at Jefferson.

Maupin said that he was doing newspaper work in Perry when the Ringling Brothers brought their circus to town; it fell to him to report on the show.

While eating dinner with Alf and Otto Ringling the discussion fell on politics, which was beginning to get red hot at that time. Maupin remarked that he knew William Jennings Bryan quite well. The two Ringlings asked many questions about Bryan and they were incredulous when Maupin prophesied that before the campaign was over, Bryan would set the country afire with his eloquence and personal magnetism.

In September 1899 Alf Ringling stopped in at the World Herald office in Omaha and he and Maupin renewed their acquaintance.

"You are the man who told me about Bryan over in Perry," Alf said. "Well, I didn't believe it then, but our show made a territory well covered by Bryan in that campaign, and I want to tell you that that man is a wonder. You didn't begin to tell it all."

Bryan had become a national figure of great importance in the political field of his time. He had run for president in 1896 but had been defeated by William McKinley.

The Ringling Brothers' Circus soon became so large that only cities had the facilities to accommodate them. But there were still other circus and tent shows which stopped in Perry.

Dailey Brothers Circus Arriving by Train

The Dailey Brothers owned one of the circuses that came to towns like Perry after the Ringling Brothers Circus outgrew small towns. This circus is shown arriving on the Milwaukee Railroad tracks.

R.M. Harvey and the Circus (1894)

Perry had another connection with show business near the turn of the century, this through R.M. Harvey. Along with his brother A.M., Harvey had come to Perry from Cambridge, Iowa. In 1893, the Harvey brothers owned *The Perry Chief*.

The Harveys worked out an unusual way of sharing their ownership of the paper. A.M. would take leave from the staff in the winter to study law at Drake. R.M. took over until the spring, when he would leave for his duties as a contracting and advertising agent for shows. He had begun with the Kirkhart Wagon Show, then moved on to the Great Wallace Shows for years.

R.M. Harvey became so well known in this business that *The Billboard*, a journal of the show fraternity published at Cincinnati, gave him a place of honor on its front page and printed a profile of him in 1896-1897.

After the Harvey brothers were no longer in the newspaper business, R.M. was able to secure much show advertising printed at the local plant. These were four-page heralds especially designed for each circus or show and were mailed out daily. In the summer, the old flat bed press ran day and night to fill all the orders.

R.M. Harvey also wrote a series of articles for the newspaper called "Under the Big Top," in which he related his experience in the show world.

He spent most of his 90 years with the great names of the circus world and died in the Perry hospital in December 1959.

Shaker Doctor Comes (1897)

All Perry waited expectantly for the coming of the Shaker Medicine and Concert Company, which was scheduled to appear at the Breed Opera House on May 24, 1897.

This was a once-in-a-lifetime chance as the company had the reputation of being the very best on the road. It was guaranteed to shake the sides of Perry citizens with laughter. In addition, the Shaker doctor's reputation as a physician stood at the head of the medical profession. Some of his cures were called miraculous.

The Shaker society was organized in England about 1706

and came to United States in 1774. It received its name because religious zeal and inner emotion caused members to quiver and shake. The first American society was organized at Watervliet, New York.

The Shakers were the first producers of commercial seed in the United States, invented the circular saw, cut nails, washing machines, flat brooms, and metal pen points. Furniture made by the group is highly prized and admired.

The concert opened to an overflow crowd. Many were turned away. Adults were admitted free, but children in arms were not admitted. When the Shaker doctor gave his scientific lecture on the stomach, he handled the subject with such skill that the audience listened with rapt attention. They were sorry when the presentation was finished.

It was said that many Perry people benefited from the use of Shaker medicine and the doctor's office in the St. James Hotel was crowded daily.

Five days later the Opera House was still thronged with people, the house being packed long before curtain time. That night, some beautiful articles were given to holders of tickets with lucky numbers. Mary Barker received an album; E.S. Dayton, a silver ice pitcher; Thomas Moffitt, an elegant five-bottle silver caster; and Mrs. A.C. Perrott, a twenty-seven-piece set of silverware.

A *Chief* reporter interviewed the doctor, one Louis Turner, in his room at the hotel. The doctor explained that Shakers were seceders of Quakers and were communists in the strictest sense of the word. Their first law — and all were unwritten — was give your heart to God and your hands to labor.

The doctor was a fitting illustration of the sect he represented. Though seventy-six years of age, his eyes had lost none of their luster, and his face betrayed no sign of age, his mental faculties were unimpaired, his step strong, his posture erect, and his head well poised. The reporter left charmed by the Doctor and no longer surprised that the public took such an interest in him and his famed remedies.

The June 2 program was interspersed with amateurs taking part. They were: Miss Undine Andrews, a singer; Arthur Sipes, doing black face comedy; Miss Blanche Johnson, performing an instrumental solo; Miss Hazel Hoblet, with a vocal; Misses Parker and Zimmerman, with guitar and mandolin duet; Miss Florence Buckingham doing elocution; Miss Myrtle Heiss, performing instrumental solo; and the Orange Brothers, in a tumbling act.

The Doctor presented Miss Buckingham and Miss Hoblet the prize. Prize winners and their gifts were: Tom Willis, five silver casters; Will O'Malley, decorated lamp; Lidden Herron, a solid silver cracker jar; Harvey Hanks, water set; Arthur Smith, lamp; and Mrs. Frank Long, the dress pattern.

During the Shaker Medicine Company's stay in Perry, many people were given beautiful presents. Consequently the Opera House was crowded to the doors each night. June 11 was the best of all. First it was old people's night — all children were barred and the oldest lady and man (Mrs. Philbert, age eighty-five, and Thomas Bailey, age ninety) each received a rocking chair. Also that night, every purchaser of medicine received a present from the doctor. The show closed on June 12.

Silver-tongued Orator (1902-1916)

William Jennings Bryan was just one of the famous and important people to visit Perry over the years.

It was a warm and sultry night in June 1902 that the famous silver-tongued orator from Nebraska spoke at the Christian Church. It was said that a good lawyer had been spoiled when Bryan went into politics, as he was so powerful in any argument and could always state facts and figures to make his case. However, this night was too warm to listen to a political speech and little interest was shown.

Bryan had arrived in Perry that morning, but had indicated to W.M. Tarr, chairman of the lecture course committee, that he didn't want any demonstration made. Tarr quietly told H.A. Nash who could always be depended upon to keep a secret. But some of the influential Democrats saw Nash going towards the depot about train time, so they, too, sauntered down that way.

When Bryan stepped off the train, he was met by Tarr and Nash, along with Mayor J.E. Wilson, L.V. Harpel, P.C. Rude, L.M. Resser, H.T. Munn and others. John Shortely had come in on the same train and had met the distinguished orator in the sleeper and had engaged in a long visit with him.

Bryan was escorted to the St. James Hotel over Perry's finest concrete walks, and was shown the high buildings along Second

Bryan Stumps in Perry

*William Jennings Bryan spoke from the steps of the library on October 6, 1908,
as the Democratic nominee for president in that year's national elections.*

Street. In the afternoon the Elks gave him the use of their parlors,
where he held a reception for a number of Democrats, Republicans, Prohibitionists and ladies. Among the callers was the Honorable A.U. Coates, who was later to become Perry's contribution
to the Prohibitionist Party as their nominee for vice president.

It was not surprising that the Elks were so hospitable to Bryan
— he was a brother Elk. Two years earlier, in May 1900, some
Perry Elks traveled to Lincoln, Nebraska, to attend the installation of a large lodge in that city. The Perry Elks who went to
Lincoln were: W.C. Kelley, A.D. Monroe, Tom Granshaw, George
Saucer, Earl White and J.I. Kelley. The Lincoln committee met
them at the depot with the patrol wagon and led them uptown
under a police escort. Bryan was a charter member of that new
lodge and was on the program of toasts at the elaborate banquet.

Bryan was in Perry again on October 6, 1908, as the Democratic candidate for the presidency of the United States. He arrived over the M. & St. L. from Des Moines and was met by a
crow of enthusiastic admirers, a big delegation of high school
students and the Perry band.

Bryan was taken by auto to the Library, where a platform
had been erected for the occasion. John P. O'Malley acted as
master of ceremonies and John Shortely introduced the speaker.

Several thousand had gathered to see Bryan and they stood at attention for his ninety-minute lecture.

Bryan was never elected president, but it was often said that if women had had the right to vote at that time, the story would have been different.

Bryan was in Perry yet another time and spoke to a crowd which filled the Methodist Church to overflowing on May 12, 1916. He was an advocate of equal suffrage and his convincing and impressive speech was frequently interrupted by applause.

He took time in the latter part of his speech to advocate temperance and prohibition, and his attack up liquor was thorough and forceful. This appearance by Bryan in Perry had been announced by the Political Equality Club. Dinner was held at the Pattee Hotel, with a number of local people, followed by a reception in the lobby. H.S. Dugan introduced Bryan there and presided at the later meeting at the church as well.

Pattee Park (1903-1935)

Over the years, Perry citizens have had many different schemes for parks. In 1900, the plan was to convert the rubble-strewn piece of ground in the center of the Triangle into a park by planting trees and adding cement walks.

The old fairgrounds in east Perry were considered a likely spot, but in March 1903 the buildings were sold at auction and the land platted into lots and sold.

Agitation for a park aroused the general interest of the people to such an extent that two sites were chosen by prominent businessmen. Both were along the river and within a 10-minute drive from the city and either could be put in condition for about $500. The people were determined to have a park.

Finally, in October 1903 D.J. Pattee announced that under certain conditions he would deed a tract of land to the city for a park. The ground was part of the Pattee pasture, south of Otley and east of the creamery. A little creek ran through it, making it easy to construct an artificial lake. The primary condition Pattee put on the donation was that the town first had to pledge $1,000 to improve the land.

Pattee did not sign the deed to the site over to the city until

January 1906. The only stipulation he made was that if the city abandoned the park, it was to revert back to the Pattee heirs.

Park Superintendent Newt Hart announced in August 1907 that everything was in readiness to begin excavating a lake. The dirt was taken out and a gravel surface laid on the bottom to make it sanitary and clear.

Two years later Congressman Hull aided the cause by donating shrubs from the government botanical gardens, shrubs from other countries, yet suitable for growing in the United States.

At a meeting of the Park Commission in October 1911 the contract for building the dam and bridge was let. This was in accordance with one of Pattee's ideas — the formation of a lagoon so there would be a place to skate in the winter. It was formally and officially opened on December 18, 1911. About 100 boys and girls gathered to enjoy the skating. The bridge and dam coast about $2,000.

Perry's driving park ceased to exist after the firemen's tournament of July 1913, when Riverview Heights addition was platted. The bandstand and smaller stand which had been used there were moved to the Pattee woods. H.M. Pattee gave them to Pattee Park and the park commissioners had them moved as soon as the new paving on Willis Avenue was opened. This provided a place in the park for band concerts to be held.

A large crowd, including nearly all the school children in the city, was present when a beautiful flag donated by the ladies of the Grand Army of the Republic was formally raised over the bandstand on May 11, 1916.

Two big improvements were on the agenda in 1919. One was to purchase lots on Willis, just north of the park, to make a more suitable entrance with a memorial arch for D.J. Pattee. The other project was the building of a swimming pool. The land was purchased after being voted on at the city election. The entrance was made on Willis and the land was used for a children's playground. The pool was not forthcoming.

The baseball players were given permission to build a baseball diamond in June 1919. They were also given permission to charge admission to the games, provided ten percent of the receipts were given for use of the grounds. The building of the diamond meant a revival of baseball. One hour after the field was finished, on August 8 a real game was in progress.

Changes came in 1922. The lagoon had become a source of

great expense and annoyance. It had gradually filled in and, for the greater part of the year, was a mass of weeds and rushes — unhealthy and unsightly.

So, it was filled in with cinders, ashes, dirt, and clean refuse and seeded over for use as a playground. The course of the creek was straightened and the water still ran over the dam. The new tennis courts were installed by the city with the aide of donated funds from the American Legion Post, which sponsored the games in 1929.

A dedication exercise was held on September 19, 1935, honoring D.J. Pattee. A bronze plaque dedicated to his memory was unveiled. The program began with the raising of the flag, followed by taps, and the high school band playing "The Star Spangled Banner." Mayor E.E. Clothier presented the plaque to the city and Harry Wifvat accepted it on behalf of the citizens.

There have been many changes in the park over the years, but it is still an important part of Perry.

Chautauqua (1910-1922)

Perry was once the headquarters of a thriving home-grown Chautauqua, which was a system of summer school education founded at Chautauqua Lake, New York, in 1874. The idea spread and tent chautauquas began to operate bringing lectures, concerts, recitals and entertainment to rural areas.

In 1910, C. Durant Jones organized a local company for the purpose of bringing Chautauqua's education and social benefits to small towns. In that first year of business, Jones' company visited thirty-nine towns. Five tents were operated simultaneously and thirty-five people were on the payroll.

Many were the headaches connected with the business, chief causes of which were the whims of nature. While playing in Churdan in 1912, a wind storm went over the town, tearing up trees and small buildings. Then it grabbed the big tent and deposited it some distance away.

Fortunately, the storm struck late in the evening, after the crowd had gone home. Heroic work on the part of the tent men, who restitched and repitched the tent and repaired the seats, made it possible for the next day's performance to be held as scheduled.

In 1913, Jones had thirteen Chautauquas in operation. Some of these also ran afoul of the weather. One of his tents was torn to shreds by winds in Graham, Missouri. Tent man Arthur Griffiths of Perry, made the report to the local headquarters. On the heels of this disaster came another storm and another loss in another Missouri town. Another Perryite — Gerald Ostrander — was the tent man.

The Graham incident was just a playful baby tornado compared to this larger-than-life demonstration. No one was in the tent when the storm broke, but the tent was in shreds, 300 chairs splintered, and the piano ruined. Since the only reserve tent had been rushed to Graham, this meant finishing the balance of the four days in the open air.

The circuit closed on a successful season that year. A total of 198 Chautauquas had been held; more than 100 people employed; and there were fifteen complete sets of talent.

In 1914, a young Perry High School graduate joined the circuit. She was Louise Diddy, the late Mrs. Charles Cornelius. That first year was hard for her as she was alone. The next year, eight local girls, all of whom could sing and play an instrument organized a company and toured together for several seasons on the circuit.

Being in a group relieved the homesickness but did not alleviate the hardships of the road. The next day's schedule had to be met, even if it meant traveling all night — mostly by train. Some nights were spent in depots. The iron arm rests on the benches discouraged sleeping, but these girls were all young, slim, and agile, and they managed to wriggle under the arm rests and stretch out on the benches.

The tent raising contest held by the property men on June 1, 1915, on West Evelyn, near the Interurban, proved to be of great interest. Contestants included the Perry men, Gerald Ostrander and Frank Graham. One of the large tents was used and the two men raised it for use in one hour and twenty-two minutes. Two other contestants, Wayne Prichard of Indianola and W.A. Sewell of Kansas, took the tent down and packed it up for shipment in thirty-six minutes.

Mr. and Mrs. Jones opened the 1915 season with a banquet honoring the workers and the talent of the Chautauqua system. At 6 p.m., 120 guests representing twenty states formed a line two blocks long and marched from the Jones College building down

The Jones Chautauqua System

Crowds in Strattford outside a Jones Chautauqua tent in June 1910.

Second Street and to the Congregational Church, where they were welcomed by the King's Daughters. At 4 p.m., the Bureau of Commerce had taken twenty-five auto loads on a drive over the city.

Jones and F.M. Fazel, manager and assistant manager, left for Chicago on September 14, 1916, to attend the annual Lyceum Association International Convention. Jones' Chautauqua was in the front ranks, having visited 325 towns during the season.

This type of entertainment continued to grow in popularity and 1917 was a busy year. The men in the property department worked two months repairing tents and readying them for shipment. Due to the high price of cotton, the value of the tents had doubled. It required almost $5,000 of canvas to handle the Jones Chautauqua business.

The first of June, the annual six-day convocation opened in the Jones Building. During the morning sessions, platform managers and assistants and other employees were instructed in their duties. Model programs were given by the talent during the afternoon and evening in a large tent, pitched just south of the Jones Building.

Convocation week ended with a banquet held at the Methodist Church and given by Mr. and Mrs. Jones in honor of the Chautauqua people. The banquet was served by the King's Daughters. Immediately following the banquet, the workers went to the field.

In the early years of World War I, the group of eight girls were asked to make an appearance at Camp Dodge. The military promised to provide a speaker to share the billing with the girls. The group went to Des Moines on the Interurban, and arrived at the barracks where they discovered that their speaker was John D. Rockefeller.

They played and sang all afternoon, going from one barracks to another and at each Rockefeller gave a talk. He asked the girls where they bought their music. The Rockefeller family had a musical group of their own, and he knew the people in the publishing house where they purchased their music.

Most of the music the girls used on their professional tours was the snappy war music which was so popular. They had one medley, however, which gave them much trouble. For this they had to make a quick change into the long fluffy dresses of the southern belle type. Once during practice something happened that seemed hilarious and from that time on, when they sang "Believe Me If All Those Endearing Young Charms" they would begin to giggle and it was difficult to finish the song with decorum.

It was while the girls were in Graybull, Montana, that the flu epidemic became so bad that they were ordered home. Standing before the depot and seeing the many coffins stacked on the platform was unforgettable. Mrs. Cornelius said she never went out on the circuit after that.

Charles Sinclair, who had once been associated with Jones in the newspaper business, returned to Perry in January 1918, to take charge of the printing department of the Chautauqua. The system did most of its own printing, making nearly all shipments by parcel post. Almost $5,000 was spent annually for advertising material.

In 1920, Jones added six states to his territory so that it covered nineteen states from the Great Lakes to the Gulf and from the Rockies to the Alleghenies.

For the first eight years after the Jones College Building was completed, the office of the chautauqua was housed there, but the advantages of an uptown office were so numerous that it was thought best to change. In April 1921, rooms were secured in the Security Bank Building.

The Jones system opened its twelfth season the first week of

June 1921, but it was not as large as in prior years. Only two circuits were in operation: one a three-day; the other a five-day. In past years, the Jones system had given 2,348 Chautauquas. Articles of incorporation had been filed with the Secretary of State with a capital stock of $25,000.

Then, interest began to wane. The development of the automobile, moving pictures, and especially the radio, were the main reasons for the decline.

Majestic Theater (1911-1916)

In 1911, the Odd Fellows room was remodeled to accommodate the Majestic Theater. An inclined floor was laid and 300 opera chairs installed. There were three aisles so the attendants could seat patrons without disturbing others. The ticket office and lantern deck were lined with asbestos and sheet metal to conform with city and state fire ordinances. A state-of-the-art projection machine was ordered for the photoplay house.

The receipts of the first night's performance were donated to the King's Daughters for their hospital fund.

In the early days of silent movies, the dialog appeared on the screen in printed words. All movie houses had a piano player who watched the screen and played appropriate music to set the mood. It became so familiar that even with the eyes closed, the theater goer could tell what was happening on the screen just by the music being played.

Donald Miller (son of Bill Miller, the implement dealer, and brother of Mrs. George Stevenson) was the piano player for the new picture house. Miller grew up in Perry and graduated from Perry schools. In 1929 he was the organist at the Capital Theatre in Des Moines. In 1948 he was the organist at Des Moines radio station KRNT.

When the Majestic Theater wanted to add a vaudeville, the lodge members made the necessary changes in the building. A stage was built and scenery painted.

The Majestic was almost destroyed by fire on April 3, 1915. For a time the fire threatened the entire IOOF Building. It began in the dressing rooms which were in a frame building at the rear of the brick structure. The door to the main room was open and the fire ran along the burlap walls and scorched the seats. The slanting floor over a flat floor gave the firemen much trouble.

The fact that living quarters in the engine house were not completed and the fire steward, Charles Hollis, had to sleep at home caused a five-to-ten minute delay in the big truck getting out of the station.

The chemical truck driven by Assistant Chief Den Snyder was the first to reach the fire. A line of hose was laid from the hydrant at the corner of Otley and Railroad streets and carried to the rear of the building. The fire was held in check in the frame portion, but the furnishings were ruined. Heat melted bearings on the machine in the projection booth, though it was never on fire.

The theater was entirely rebuilt and reopened on September 1 by the owner, D.C. Pryor. Improvements were made in the rebuilding. On the south side of the lobby, a confectionery store was conducted by U.G. Putnam and Richard Fouch; on the north, there was a roomy entrance. The operator's booth was fire proofed, lined with asbestos and covered with steel. A new projector was installed as were new, comfortable seats for 340 patrons.

Then came four or five changes of ownership in rapid succession. The Majestic closed in May 1916.

First Swimming Pool (1920-1952)

A swimming pool for Perry's Pattee Park had been a topic for discussion in Perry for many years when it was revived in earnest with the offer of R.E. Shackleton to donate the use of all his machinery, equipment, and the services of several experienced men to build a pool for Perry.

Once again, the matter was dropped. The cost for a pool the size Perry needed was estimated at about $8,000, and the money just was not available.

The following year, the matter came up again. Shackleton made the same offer to the board and, this time, agreed to personally supervise the work free of charge. Dozens of other men expressed their willingness to donate labor and cash, and it was felt the project would be completed.

The pool was completed July 29, 1921, and was dedicated and formally opened in mid-August. There still remained side-

Swimming Pool at Pattee Park

The swimming pool was supported partly by fees from the dressing rooms and partly by the taxpayers. Upkeep of the pool was taken care of by the park board and adult fees.

walks to be finished and filling in around the outside.

A required dress code was set for users of the pool. Both men and women had to wear a one-piece bathing suit, with a skirt effect. Tights were positively prohibited. The suits had to extend to within two inches above the knees; the armpits had to be covered in the case of ladies' suits. This type of suit was the standard design used in all public swimming pools and permitted free and easy swimming. Having this suit as the standard made detecting those with improper suits that much easier to pick out.

After a number of near accidents had been averted in the summer of 1923, the council decided to employ a competent life guard during all swimming hours.

The pool was closed in August 1941 on report from the Hygienic Laboratory of Iowa City that the pool was not safe. It was scheduled to reopen the following June after a representative of the State Department of Health had inspected the pool, but by then it was a casualty of war.

Greatly increased demands on city water made it impossible to open the pool, even though approval had been received and the chemicals ordered.

A three-stick charge of dynamite was touched off in the southeast deep end corner of the abandoned pool in April 1952 to make room for a new pool.

Perry voters had given overwhelming support to a $110,000 bond issue for a new municipal pool in a special city election held in June 1950.

Hastie, Founder of Museum and Park

Eugene Hastie was the first to recognize what a great history Perry has had and to do something about it. After spending hours in research and personal interviews, he put it in a book in 1962, so that all could know.

At the age of eighty-two, he was still working hard to find new facts about Perry's past for his little historical booklet about the pioneers and times before 1869.

For years Hastie wrote Bible tracts which were given away. Then in 1938, his first book was published — a history of Dallas County. Following that, a history of the Iowa Assemblies of God Church published in 1948 and a history of Iowa in 1966. He also founded a park and museum, and kept the weather records for more than forty years.

Perry was truly his home. His grandfather owned a 240-acre farm northeast of the city limits which he had obtained from the government in 1855. Here his father, Robert Hastie, was born in a log cabin ten years before there was a Perry.

Eugene Hastie was born on the same farm on January 5, 1890, the log cabin having been replaced by a frame house. Soon afterwards the family moved to a farm south of Perry where he lived until he moved to town in 1968.

Hastie recalled how his father was one of the pioneers who herded cattle on the town site. About 4 p.m., they would start out on horseback to round up the milk cows. Some evenings they were unable to find them, so vast was the open range.

In 1896, Hastie enrolled in the Prairie Flower School, located on the corner north of the John Schnoor farm. The thirty-acre Fahey pond was near enough to the school that the scholars managed to go ice skating in the winter, even during the fifteen-minute recess. There were no grades, just readers. When a pupil

Back to School
Eugene Hastie, left, and G.E. Roberts sit in desks from the old Alton School.

had gone through the fifth reader, that was it.

During those days there was a one-room school house every two miles. They had names such as Strawberry Run (which was shortened to Straw Run), Charity School, Bell School, Coffee School. But none, Hastie thought, was as pretty as Prairie Flower. In southern Iowa, where his wife lived, the school she attended was called Evening Star.

When he was fifteen years old, he was ready to enroll in the Perry Normal School. Here, too, instead of semesters or terms, there was just the prescribed amount of work to cover. Farm boys didn't usually get to start until the first of December when the harvest work was done. They often had to drop out at the beginning of spring work as well.

A framed diploma which hung in the old museum building attests to the fact that Hastie not only graduated in 1908 but also that there was a college in Perry at the time.

Hastie met his wife Lena Brall while visiting an uncle's home in Sidney and they were married on Thanksgiving Day 1913. He had been in southern Iowa in gospel work for a year, and continued in this for seven years after their marriage. This was a few years before the Assembly of God Church was formed.

It was a freak storm which brought Hastie the post of weather observer. The station located at the F.N. Bartlet farm, east of Perry on the Park Street road was wrecked when a small cyclone went through. When Hastie went out to view the damages, Bartlet asked if he would be interested in the work saying, "I think I can get the job for you." The storm had come at a busy time and Bartlett didn't feel he had the time to rebuild the station.

Soon a letter arrived from Charles D. Reed of Des Moines, offering Hastie the job. He was weather observer for forty years and four months. The forty years were up in the winter and the shelter was so deeply anchored in the frozen ground that it couldn't be moved until spring. This was taken to the Perry disposal plant.

His dream of a park and museum began many years before the museum building was actually under construction in 1952. Always a lover of trees, Hastie's goal was to set out as many different kinds of trees as could stand the Iowa winters.

So he planted a garden of trees on an acre of land he formerly put to oats and corn. The arboretum contained one of every tree he could find. He planted the first tree in 1946, a red cedar from the Des Moines River.

The project soon grew to such proportions one man could not handle it and it was sold to the Dallas County Conservation Board in 1966 for about half its value.

Hastie began keeping a diary in 1911. He remembered talking to a Mrs. Clarence McKibben, who had kept a diary for over thirty-four years, and he wondered if anyone would ever equal that. In 1972, when he was interviewed, his diary was sixty-one years old and still going.

The Hasties had four daughters. His wife died in 1964. Eugene Hastie died on September 27, 1983, at the age of ninety-three.

Chapter Fourteen
Stories

Marshal Dave Willis

Dave Willis shown driving Perry's first hearse in 1885. The hearse was built by Carpenter and Son.

Dave Willis, A Man of Firsts

Dave Willis was a much-loved, much-written about Perry Pioneer. For more than 25 years, he was marshal of the city, ran the first bus, the first express wagon, the first sprinkler and drove the first hearse.

He was born in Wayne County, Indiana, on June 24, 1850, and lived there until he was fifteen years old. His parents, Mr. and Mrs. Henry Willis, died during his boyhood, and he came west with his uncles to Perry in 1869. He married Lena Ashcroft, on February 19,1879, and they had four daughters.

In the city directory of 1884, he was listed as an auctioneer, and that his bus line office was at Fred Moore's' livery barn on Willis near Second Street. He was appointed marshal in July 1884 and for his first services received twenty percent of the dog tax collected, half the fee for impounding loose livestock, and $2 for each arrest when the party was convicted and fined.

In April 1887, Willis made arrangements to start a street sprinkling system. He placed his water tank at the city well on West Willis and installed a horse-powered pump. He operated the sprinkler off and on for many years as it was one business which changed hands often.

Later, Willis moved his sprinkler hydrant to the Triangle, but after the library was built, he moved it to the corner of the Lane Building on Otley Avenue because of complaints from the library board. The kick was not the hydrant, but the drinking cup attached to it. Every hour of the day and half the night, a constant throng of people stopped to quench their thirsts. The result was a mud puddle most of the time and a crowd of loafers on the library steps and grounds.

Halloween pranksters often gave Willis trouble. In 1896, he spent the evening trailing a pair of celebrants who were determined to ring the Baptist Church's bell. The rest of the night, he pursued young men who were tearing up the wooden sidewalks and stretching barbed wire along the streets.

About 8 a.m. on April 23, 1898, he captured a man wanted for burglary in Omaha. Willis had received word from Omaha authorities to be on the lookout for the subject who, they thought, would probably be calling for a letter at the local post office.

After receiving that message, Willis kept a close watch, and, sure enough, just before the mail was distributed, he observed a fellow at the general delivery window asking for a letter. The marshal followed the man outside where he told the fellow that they had some business to discuss. When Willis attempted to take him, the man broke loose and took off on a run down Warford and up First Avenue.

The spectacle of Marshal Willis sprinting up First Avenue after the fleeing man, shouting at bystanders to stop him, and firing his revolver at every jump, created such a sensation that the street was soon lined with a mass of excited men.

The fugitive was finally overcome by Ross Green. He was escorted to the police headquarters by the collected multitude. A detective arrived in Perry that afternoon and took his prisoner back to Omaha. He was charged with robbing the house where he was rooming.

In another incident, a man Willis was trying to arrest resisted and struck the marshal a hard blow with a bottle. Judge Gamble struck the prisoner a harder blow, sentencing him to nine months of hard labor at the county jail.

After ably serving as marshal for many years, Willis surrendered his star in May 1901 to his successor, John Resser, who was appointed by the newly elected Mayor Wilson. Willis was again appointed marshal in 1905 and his salary was up to $45 a month.

It was during this second tenure that Willis first reported to work in a brand new navy blue uniform. According to *The Chief,* "it fit him like a saddle on a swayback horse and made him look like a real city policeman. He was not puffed up to have such attractive attire and still spoke to everybody he met."

Willis' reputation was beaten to a pulp when he boasted that he was going to be the only man not an employee of the building crew to climb the fifty-one-foot tower of the new fire engine house. The genial marshal only reached the half-way mark when he became stuck between two joists. It was only with great difficulty that workmen freed the marshal.

In June 1905, while directing the moving of the city jail, Willis broke his left knee cap. The building had nearly reached its new site, when Willis, one of two men helping prop up the building at one corner, lost his balance and fell.

The marshal was carried to his home at First and Lucinda, where Dr. Ross cared for him. This was the first time Willis had ever been compelled to go to bed because of sickness — he was fifty-five years old. After the accident, Willis always walked with a perceptible limp.

Willis had been appointed truant officer for Perry schools in October 1904. Too many people had been dilatory about making their children attend school, so the board appointed Willis.

Willis died in April 1912, after two years of poor health. He was first seized by an attack of stomach trouble in 1910. While he was able to be up and about most of the time, he gradually grew worse. He went to Excelsior Springs in February 1912 hoping the climate and the baths would help. He drew so weak that he had to cut the trip short. He died in Perry shortly after his return.

Graney Bridge (1889)

The bridge over the Raccoon River south of Perry, often called the Graney Bridge, is the third one in the area.

The first bridge over the Raccoon was ordered about two and a half miles south of Perry in 1889. The cost of the iron structure was estimated at $6,290, and opened a very important road to Perry from Washington and Colfax townships — a ten-mile long straight road directly into town.

The bridge proper was completed by 20 September. It was built under the direction of J.C. Andrews of Andrews Brothers, representatives of the Omaha Bridge Company.

Later in September, the editor of the newspaper occupied a seat in one of the company's carriages and paid a visit to the new bridge. The route was directly south to where the laid-out road turned east and then, for the last half mile, wound through the timber that skirted the river. The span across the river was 150 feet and it rose to twenty-one feet above the surface of the water. It was ten feet wide, sufficient for teams to pass and high enough for the highest load to pass under the crossbars.

By the time of the editor's visit, construction on the approaches had just started. They were to be thirty to fifty feet long on each end. Mr. Graney, it was understood, had agreed that, if the bridge was built, he would open the road on either side at his own expense — an undertaking costing about $1,000.

The bridge was closed to the public in 1906, while a new 70-foot span was put in. Great steel casings were sunk and the bridge put in substantial repairs. On account of the high water, the river could not be forded; this meant traffic had to cross at Wolf Bridge west of town.

A new bridge was again needed in the spring of 1912 after the old bridge washed out. Ice chunks had piled together on the north side of the bridge, pushed out piers, and the bridge fell into the river. The mailman Mr. Newlin had just gone across the bridge before it collapsed.

Mr. and Mrs. Guy Haney lived on their farm on a hilltop near the bridge. They could hear the ice cracking and the trees snapping as they rode horseback down to the bridge to inspect it. The telephone wire was broken, so Mr. Haney went back home to call Town Clerk W.W. Phillips that the bridge was out. It was Phillips' duty to report the problem to the supervisors. The road had to be closed, so Phillips sent Andrew Maxwell to the foot of Haney Hill to close the road at that point.

It was not until August that a gang of men started to remove casings and piers of the old bridge. During the entire time the Graney Bridge was out, travelers had to detour several miles out of the way to the Wolf Bridge to get in and out of Perry on the south side.

The road leading up to the old bridge ran along the river bottom and was flooded (and so closed) frequently. For this reason when the new bridge was built, the road was moved a short distance to higher ground.

The river was low most of the summer. It was so low that road supervisor Andrew Maxwell was able to come up with safe and more convenient alternative to the Wolf Bridge detour — he established a ford across the river near the Graney Bridge. Entrance to the ford on the south side was made at the Tim Graney farm and on the north at a place between two small wooden bridges about twenty rods from the old bridge site.

Heavy rains on September 10 caused a delay for the workers

Graney Bridge

This bridge spanned the Coon River for more than fifty years before being pulled down in 1971.

of the Lana Construction Company by raising the river to its highest point in weeks. It also caused considerable trouble in the use of the ford; many rigs attempting the passage were filled with terrorized passengers before they reached dry land on the other side. There was enough water to swim a horse, so people in buggies had to climb upon the seats to keep from getting wet.

Eliza Graham started to town with a basket of eggs, and, as he forded the river, looked after number one and let the eggs fend for themselves. When he reached town, he had about a dozen left, the rest having floated off down the stream as he crossed the river. Many forders came through with a good wetting and there was fun a plenty for those on shore watching from a safe distance. The ford was wide, and no one was in any real danger.

Residents south of the bridge were much inconvenienced because the construction company did not live up to their contract to finish the bridge in time for fall and winter traffic. Rumors were rampant that the company wasn't going to make any money on the bridge, so it didn't care if it was finished or not.

It was pointed out that the Boone County bridges which washed out at the same time had all been rebuilt. Much talk was heard of taking the matter before the board of supervisors for action.

One man consulted County Attorney Winegar with a claim that his community was being discriminated against in being shut off from Perry as a trading point. A delegation from Perry appeared before the board, asking for relief and a large group from Washington and Lincoln townships were also present to insist upon immediate action.

After a year and a half, the bridge was finally opened for use in the middle of August 1913. It appeared to be worth the wait. The new span was considered the best wagon bridge in the county. It had one long span of 220 feet, with no channel support of any kind.

After spanning the river for more than fifty years, this bridge was pulled down on June 29, 1971. The new Graney Bridge had been in use several days at that time. Although the old bridge was supposed to be weakened, several attempts were made to pull the framework over before the steel cable on the crane broke. However, shortly before 10 a.m. the bridge was pulled down into an island, where the steel framework was cut into lengths which could be handled.

Gold Fever (1897)

News of gold strikes in the Klondike, Yukon Territory, did not reach the outside until June 1897, when a steamer loaded with gold reached Seattle.

The news brought a stampede of prospectors in the fall of 1897, and an even greater rush in 1898. Perry and the vicinity were not without their representatives in the hoards.

Lured by the prospect of fabulous gold stores kept beneath the ice and snow, three Milwaukee Railroad engineers — John Conway, John Leaf, and William Baldwin — headed out, determined to make the venture.

The Perry Engineers Mining Company with a capital stock of 6,000 shares at $1 each was formed at a meeting in December 1897. Officers were elected and every share of the stock was sold. E.H. Coltrin was president and Otto Christensen, secretary; directors were Jack Aherns, Ben Stapleton and Frank Liddle.

The company — composed exclusively of railroad men — was organized for the purpose of sending a commission into the gold fields to search for treasure. Three members constituted a commission and, having received a lay-off from the railroad service, were to leave town early in the spring.

Conway, Leaf, Baldwin, and Otto Christensen were selected for the northern trip, with one of the four being an alternate. The three, backed with the capital of the mining company, were to be outfitted for a stay of eighteen months.

Before these men could complete preparations, another Perry man, F. McReynolds, left by train on October 12, 1897, bound for Seattle. It was through his letters to *The Perry Chief* that Perry citizens learned about conditions in the Klondike and Alaska. Not once did he mention the work on their claims, nor did he divulge how much gold they found — if any.

On arrival in Seattle, McReynolds found the town booming. There were crowds in the street, in the hotels, and lodging houses, and each week the throng increased. Ocean steamers left Seattle every two or three days for Juneau, Skagway, Dyea, and other points along the Pacific coast.

Leaf was the first of the Perry Mining Company to leave Perry. He wanted to go through Idaho, where he had some mining interests. Baldwin and Christiansen joined him in Seattle around February, 20, 1898. Meanwhile in January, Sammy Ellis was bustling about, disposing of his property and business in order to leave for the Klondike. He planned to go west in a party of eight who bought a small ship in which they could take a year's provisions and all else needed while there.

Three more passengers were soon on the M. and St. L. heading for cold country. Robert Simpson, Dr. Cockrell, and Ned Riley of Angus. They went via the Canadian Pacific Railroad, to a point some 200 miles north of Vancouver. Then, overland with ponies for about 800 miles, the rest of the trip by river and lake. This was a new British route; taking it cost each many about $350. A later letter about their trip did not mention Riley.

Leaf had a letter of introduction from a Perry man to a Seattle man who was a passenger agent for two or three small steam schooners. He advised them to go on one of the company's ships which he represented. Before leaving Seattle on March 5, 1898, they sent their Perry friends several pictures of them in full Klondike uniform.

McReynolds and the two with him, B.C. Christensen and J. Christensen (brothers of Otto), left Seattle on March 7 on a large ship — the Queen — with 550 passengers aboard. The Perry men had planned to be together and they were hopeful of meeting later.

McReynolds wrote that, after a number of stops, the Queen finally docked at Skagway, a new town at the mouth of the Skagway River. There were two wharves there, and some good buildings of hewn logs. This was as far as the Queen could go and, as nearly all the passengers bound for Dyea, a small steamer was brought alongside and took the passengers the remaining distance of about five miles. There was no wharf at Dyea, so they were transferred to canoes before being carried ashore on the backs of boatmen.

By March 30, McReynolds and his two companions were camped about four miles from "the scale" on Chilkoot Pass, which was so called because the packers weighed in the freight there, before carrying it over the summit, a distance of up to three-fourths of a mile.

The regular packers had stretched a half-inch rope from the scales to the summit and made steps in places for each foot. The climbers then took hold of the rope and began the ascent. After about 1,000 feet, there were ice benches on which to rest. And, rest was needed as the climb was up a fifty degree angle.

It took much more than an hour to reach the top and to look over into the promised land, but all that could be seen were more mountains. Freight was carried up Chilkoot Pass, deposited at the summit, and the porters descended via the nearby Peterson Pass, which terminated at the Chilkoot. It took several days to get all the supplies over the summit.

On April 3, near noon, an avalanche came down the mountainside on the Chilkoot, crushing a number of prospectors who were camped along the trail. A blinding snow storm had raged all day on the summit. As a consequence, many of those in the vicinity were making no attempt to travel. For two days a southerly storm with rain, wind, and snow had prevailed in the area, softening snow.

Snow and ice estimated at thousands of tons swept directly across the trail, which was thronged with gold hunters. McReynolds' group camped within a couple of miles of the disaster and had been over the trail every day the week before. Otto Christensen was with them at the time, having come over from

Lake Linderman to see his brothers.

After paying duty at the summit where the Canadians had been allowed by the United States to establish their custom house, they loaded two sleds on April 7 and headed for the Perry men's camp, a distance of twenty miles, reaching there at about 7 p.m.

Leaf and Baldwin had luxuriant growths of whiskers and the rotund Baldwin had to take a tuck in the waistband of his trousers, so strenuous was the journey. Leaf was the cook and served excellent meals. Otto had decided to clip off his beard as mosquitoes were fighting for possession of the barren spots, so he decided to give them all an equal chance.

The group then moved by sled from the head of Lake Bennett to a camp at Caribou Crossing, some twenty miles away. Sleds five to six feet long and about twenty inches wide were loaded to full capacity, holding at least 1,200 pounds. They put up a mast and sail, as there was a brisk south windand they fairly flew along.

Caribou Crossing had become a city of tents located on a narrow stream about three miles in length, which flowed from Lake Bennett to Lake Fagest. Its chief industry was boat building and every kind of craft — from steamer to skiff — could be purchased.

Here, four prospectors from Sioux City joined the Perry group and they and McReynolds purchased a scow, thirty-one feet long. Baldwin, Leaf, and Christensen had a twenty-four-foot scow and the Christensen brothers also had a boat.

Baldwin decided that theirs was to be the flagship and he the rear admiral, which meant he could manage the rear oar and guide the ship. Otto was captain and master, having had experience with similar crafts on the lakes around Perry. First Officer Leaf was quartermaster and had charge of the bean sack.

A long, wearisome journey was before the men — some 1,200 miles on lakes and rivers where they would just depend on wind or oar.

On June 1, they struck tent and set sail. Only because of adverse winds that day they rowed most of the way home. They were anxious to see home and loved ones but did not regret going to the Yukon or think of turning back.

Then, the letters ceased for Baldwin, Christensen, and McReynolds were back in Perry by September 1898. Leaf remained in the Klondike to look after their claim.

Baldwin and Christensen were on their way back to the north

in May 1899. The night before they left, a number of railroad men gave them a rousing farewell party.

However, all three were home in Perry in July 1899, leaving the Klondike at that time because the river was so high that work on their claims was impossible. It was stated that all three were in splendid health and would return again in the spring of 1900.

Whether they did or did not was not reported. It was doubtful that they did as there was no mention of prospecting for gold again. A few of the men who went made fortunes. The good claims were staked before most of the prospectors arrived.

True Grit (1901)

In 1901, Misses Ella and Lena Willis and their cousin, Miss Florence Willis, left for North Dakota, chaperoned by Ray Heaton. These young ladies all wanted to take up homesteads which had been selected for them by George Heaton.

A small house was all ready for them, including a cow and a chicken. Household effects had been shipped ahead. Mrs. Estelle Willis Pattee (widow of John Pattee), who had a homestead about 100 miles from where the ladies would be locating, accompanied them on their first trip. They would be about 18 miles from Wilton.

The venture showed true grit and enterprise. They were all well-educated and the best and most sensible of Dallas County girls. His two daughters going away left Harvey Willis and his wife alone, an experience they had not had in over forty years, as their home had always been the site of large family gatherings.

Hunt for Horse Thieves (1902)

Horse thievery was not just a problem in the old west. It was serious business in Perry in the early 1900s. In fact, at one time a Society for the Prevention of Horse Thieves was founded in Dallas County.

One morning in August 1902, John Wifvat, a well-known farmer who lived southeast of town, came in to report that his team had been stolen form his barn. Marshal Dave Willis accompanied by Wifvat's son set out immediately in search of the bay mares.

They traveled in a southerly direction without finding a trace of the horses until they reached Redfield. Farmers along the road said they'd seen two men in a buggy leading a span of bay mares pass that way. Following this lead, they reached the timberline west of Redfield, but darkness fell and they went into town to stay the night. During the night, rain caused the river to rise so high that they abandoned the search.

Reaching home, Willis learned that two horses had been stolen from J.J. Gannon's pasture. It had begun to seem that a band of horse thieves was operating around Perry. All during the following week, Willis made every effort to get new leads as to the whereabouts of the horses. He telephoned in every direction and sent out cards.

Rumors began circulating. Two men were reportedly seen near Grand Junction with horses which answered the description of Wifvat's team. Two men on horseback, each leading a horse, which could be Gannon's, were seen northeast of Rippey.

Finally, on a Friday, Willis, accompanied by Will Gannon, took the Rock Island train north. At each station, Willis got off and handed a card giving a description of the men and horses to liverymen on the platform. When he reached Callender, he was told that two such men had sold two horses to a farmer near Moorland.

Willis went to Fort Dodge, secured a team, and then drove out to talk to the farmer. The thieves had traded one of each of the stolen horses for a bronco, a buggy, and a harness. He was able to get a good description of the perpetrators.

On Saturday morning, Gannon headed for home with one of his horses and one of Wifvat's. About six miles north of Grand Junction, he met a team on the road and immediately recognized one of the horses as his, or at least it was an exact mate. He stopped the farmer and learned that the fellow had just traded for the horses in Fort Dodge and it was indeed his. Gannon arrived back in Perry on Thursday, but Willis stayed on the trail.

Willis had set out for Moorland on Saturday and struck the trail again at Webster City. On Sunday night he returned to Perry. Monday morning he left for the country north of Ames to search for the other two horses, not knowing at the time that one had been located. Willis followed the trail from Ames, stayed in Des

Moines on Monday night, and on Tuesday morning reached Indianola.

Willis went to the livery barn and inquired about the men and the horses they had accumulated along the way. He was informed that there was such an outfit camped near the fairgrounds. The livery man also said one of the party had left one of his horses in the barn. Willis recognized the animal as one that had been stolen in Nevada.

While he was still in the barn, the man came in, the very one he'd been hunting for ten days, and, in about half a minute, Willis had handcuffs on him. He was placed in Warren County sheriff's charge while Willis went to the fairgrounds where he found the other man and two boys in charge of several horses. Wifvat's mare was there as well as two stolen at Nevada and the three traded for near Fort Dodge.

Tuesday evening, Willis called upon the sheriff at Indianoloa for the prisoners, but an attorney had been fixing things up a little, and they weren't going to let the men go. But Willis understood his business and succeeded in getting them. The two boys who had been with the horses at the fairgrounds were allowed to go free. They had been hired to take care of the horses.

Willis arrived back in Perry on August 26, with his two prisoners and placed them in the city jail. They were sentenced in Adel by Judge Wilkinson, to a term of five years in the penitentiary.

The Burns Gang (1903-1915)

The notorious Burns Gang created much excitement in the vicinity of Perry in their heyday in the early 1900s.

The gang operated out of Angus, much to the town's consternation, robbing depots, boxcars, occasionally entering private homes, holding up people, and making their name one to be feared. Their ill-gotten goods were peddled to those who could close their eyes to the source and see only a great bargain.

They were never proven guilty of many of the robberies or even the occasional murder laid at their door. In some instances, though, they were caught red-handed.

In November 1903, two men were arrested in Perry and later convicted for stealing two overcoats from the eastbound passenger train while it stood at the station at 10 p.m. The owners of the coats were in the smoker and did not miss them until the train was underway.

They sent a wire from Madrid to Perry telling of the loss and giving descriptions of the coats to the police. It wasn't long before Night Marshal John Mitchell had the culprits in jail. Mitchell knew the men belonged to the Burns Gang and he knew their friends would get them out if they were left unguarded. He woke Marshal Dave Willis to come guard the prisoners while he made his rounds.

On arriving at the city jail Willis smelled burning cloth and found an overcoat stuffed in the stove. It was only possible to save part of the sleeve from the fire. This was enough for one of the owners to identify the coat as his. The other coat had been sold to a bus driver for $4.50. The owner of the coat was brought in from Clinton and the bus driver from Boone and they were able to convince the jury that Burns gang members were guilty of grand larceny.

Judge Nichols retired these two alleged gang member, giving them each a year free board and room at Fort Madison, where they had the privilege of doing some hard manual labor.

At last Tom Burns, the leader of the gang who had eluded capture for so many years, was finally caught in April 1905 when he attempted to rob the Robinson's Clothing Store in Perry.

A.S. McCammon was standing in the door of the Star Clothing Store opposite Robinson's when he saw a fellow enter the store, pickup some goods and sneak out the door. At the hallway of the AOWF Lodge room, the goods were passed to another man who stood in the shadows. Both men hurried north and turned the corner onto Lucinda Street.

McCammon notified his brother, W.H. McCammon, and Dr.John Foltz, and they set out after the men. At the rear of the Coakley-Mitchell Drug Store, the Perry men came face-to-face with the robbers. Hot words followed and McCammon and Foltz were threatened with being shot if they pursued the pair any further. McCammon insisted the fellows drop the goods, which they finally did, but one reached to his pocket as if to pull a gun.

By this time, the police had been notified and were in hot pursuit. Mayor P.H. O'Connor called out John Mitchell to help officers in the search. In a short time, he discovered Burns and one of his pals on Willis Avenue, where the brick livery used to be. Mitchell, not wearing a uniform, was able to get close to them. On being told he was under arrest, Burns tried to bluff his way out. But, when the outlaw looked into the muzzle of a revolver, he decided to "go along."

While all this was taking place, Burns' partner made good his escape, going across the street and entering the stairway of the building which housed the Perry Normal College. A search was made, but he had disappeared.

Burns was taken to Lew Crist's Cigar Store and placed in the charge of Mayor O'Connor. Later it was decided that it would be better to take Burns to the Coakley and Mitchell Drug Store. On the way there, the lawmen and their prisoner met Marshal Dave Willis, who took the prisoner to the city jail.

At about 1 a.m., a call was made to *The Perry Chief* office saying that one of the men was at the Tom Welch Lunch Room near the roundhouse in east Perry. Officer Pryor was found and, with a crowd of about a dozen followers at his heels, he went to the restaurant and made the arrest. Because McCammon could not identify him, the man was allowed to leave town.

The goods stolen were five pairs of pants and five vests, enough to make it a penitentiary offense if convicted.

Even though he had the stolen property when he was apprehended, Burns played ignorant and no amount of questioning could induce him to give out anything that would connect him with the crime.

Burns was the most aristocratic prisoner in the city jail. The surroundings were not to his liking, he demanded a mattress and bedclothes be furnished him.

A hearing was held before Mayor O'Connor and Burns asked that bond of two or three hundred dollars be fixed for his appearance before the Grand Jury.

Burns pleaded his own case while the state was represented by Dallas County Attorney Miller of Adel. The mayor felt it better to fix the bond high enough so that Burns would have to return even if he could to furnish it at all and placed it at $1,000.

That settled it for Burns who went to Adel to remain until the September term of the court. Then, term after term, his case was to have been tried but he always asked to have it put off on the plea that he was not ready. Each time he let it be understood, a lawyer would be retained to fight the case.

When the time came to have Burns up before the judge again

he had no lawyer. He immediately pled guilty and Judge Applegate fixed the sentence at one year at the state penitentiary owing to the fact he had already spent about a year in the county jail.

Over the years Burns had assured local officers that his gang would never operate in Perry. They wanted to sell their plunder here and did not want the town closed to them. Burns reportedly was drunk the Saturday night of the theft at Robinson's Store and his finances low, or he would never have allowed the gang to operate in Perry. This was thought to be the reason for the Robinson's Store job. As it turned out, Burns was caught and his men were free.

It was thought that elements of Burns gang surfaced again in 1912. In April of that year, about seventeen men, including Tom Burns himself, were rounded up in Perry by officers Hart and Hines and jailed. Most of them were caught in the Y (the intersection) of the railroad tracks, but Burns was picked up at Bill's Lunch Car.

Following the wholesale arrests, Marshal Hart contacted the Des Moines police to inquire as to whether the gang was wanted there. A detective was sent to Perry and the string of prisoners was brought before Judge Shortely in the Superior Court.

Tom Burns had the charge against him dismissed. There were no other charges or warrants against him and he had come down from Angus in the evening to do some shopping. Burns would probably have returned there had he not been arrested when he stepped out of the lunch car at Bill's.

Thomas Tiernan and Harry Wifvat appeared for the state against the bunch. At the close of testimony, the officers announced that the state had made no case against any of them except for two for intoxication.

The people at Angus reported that Burns had been keeping straight and working. He was clinging so well to the straight and narrow that people of that section had commenced to forget many things to his discredit and found better things to remember.

Then, that August, a gang of men alleged to be members of the Burns Gang became exceedingly bold again. They maintained a shack at Angus and, while few robberies were reported in this section, it was believed that the men who found shelter there were guilty of illegal deeds in surrounding towns. Tom Burns, the old man, was supposed to be the head of the organization. He was seldom seen, but there was little doubt that he was actually the leader of the group.

For the next three years, this gang of thieves ranged up and down the Milwaukee and Northwestern Railroad lines, robbing boxcars and selling their plunder. Finally, in April 1915, the men were caught and convicted in court in Cedar Rapids and removed from circulation.

This appeared to be the final chapter in the story of crime written by the Burns Gang.

Perry's Famous Cartoonist

Vincent Hamlin, better known locally as "Snick," the creator of the cartoon strip "Alley Oop," is one of Perry's illustrious former citizens. Not only was he born in Perry, but both of his parents were long time residents.

Dr. A.W. Trout, his mother's father, came to Perry in 1884, a physician with thirteen years experience. Snick's mother was four years old at that time. Dr. Trout rented a room over the Chicago Bakery as his office. Snick's father Fred's parents, the A.W. Hamlins, came to Perry from Illinois when Fred was a child, settling on a farm on Park Street.

In 1896, Fred entered the office of Dr. A.L. Brown for the study of dentistry, and, as he was intelligent and had a winning personality, it was predicted that he'd be a success in his chosen undertaking. In June 1899, after a year's practice in Cambridge Fred Hamlin opened an office in L.M. Stoops' gallery in the Clement block. He rented a suite of rooms in the new Bailey and Robinson building when it was completed.

On October 4, 1899, Erma, daughter of Dr. and Mrs. A.W. Trout and Fred Hamlin were married at the bride's home by the Reverend Rosenberger.

The names of Trout and Hamlin appeared many times in local newspapers. In November 1902, Dr. Trout, his daughter and son-in-law, Dr. and Mrs. F.C. Hamlin and their little son Vincent had a miraculous escape from death at the First Street crossing of the Milwaukee Railroad.

They were going home for dinner in a single-seated buggy drawn by the family horse. On reaching the track, train No. 2 was just pulling in from the west, so they stopped. When No. 2 had cleared the crossing, they started across the tracks, only to see the switch engine with the dining car bearing down on them. The horse was turned; the back wheel of the buggy was run along inside of the rail before the engine struck it.

The buggy was overturned and the occupants thrown to the ground. Fortunately, the Trouts and Hamlins had been thrown far enough by the impact that they were not hit by the engine. All were more or less injured, though no bones were broken. Mrs. Hamlin held tightly to her baby and saved his life. Dr. Trout was later granted $450 in a suit against the railroad.

In 1904, Dr. Fred Hamlin moved his dental office to the new Opera House block. In 1908, Hamlin and his father-in-law Dr. Trout closed a deal for a new Holman motor buggy. It was a high wheel machine and was said to take the road at a thirty-mile-per-hour gait.

By the time Vincent was thirteen he had begun to make a name for himself as an artist. He spent most of his spare time drawing. In 1914, one of his pictures was on display in the Reid Jewelry store, which was then located in the Wolf block at the southwest corner of Second and Warford.

It was said that Vincent Hamlin played hooky from school, hiding out at *The Chief* office because they had so much paper. Besides using *The Chief* copy paper, he had a brief career as a carrier boy. According to a letter he wrote to *The Chief* in April 1956, Vincent said he had been forced out of his place in the paper line and retaliated by slamming his paper bag into the folding machine. The citizens were late getting their news that day and he lost his $1.25 a week job. He never found out who carried the route on Willis and Warford that night.

In early 1915 Dr. Hamlin almost lost his eyesight and his car. The car had a prestolite lighting system with flame lights. Vincent had driven it home that evening. After he parked the car in the garage, the motor was steaming hot because of a "scarcity of lubricating oil," according to news reports. When the lad called his father, Dr. Hamlin unscrewed the radiator cap — thinking this would cool the motor faster. Instead, this allowed the "vaporized alcohol" to erupt into the cold air. The flame lights on the car ignited the alcohol causing an explosion that almost blinded the dentist and set the car on fire. Dr. Hamlin had the presence of mind to grab a robe and extinguish the fire.

At the age of seventeen, V.T. (as he liked to be called) was in

France serving in World War I. He was hospitalized while recovering from a poison gas attack and began illustrating letters for himself and his buddies. It was at the hospital that a newspaper man suggested Hamlin try cartooning as a line of work.

Hamlin returned to high school in Perry in 1919. He drew cartoons for that year's Eclipse, then took a journalism course at Drake. He worked for a while with the *Des Moines News* in 1922 and for a paper in Fort Worth, Texas. While covering stories in the oil and cattle country, he became interested in science, geology, and paleontology.

Alley Oop was created in 1929 and in 1933 NEA Service began distributing the strip. Four years about exhausted the stories of the cave man and dinosaurs. It was then that Snick introduced the time machine to take Alley Oop through the centuries with visits with King Arthur, Cleopatra, American Indians, and, in 1956, to Perwa. Here Oop was introduced to people and places in Perry as remembered by his creator.

V.T. Hamlin's mother died in January 1938, at the family home at 1624 Willis at age fifty-seven. His father died in the King's Daughters Hospital in May 1944, at age sixty-four. Dr. Hamlin had been in failing health for several months and had closed his dental office.

V.T. moved to Florida where he made his home until he retired. The cartoonist, visited Perry in 1970.

Flagged Down (1918)

People do strange things in the name of patriotism. They can make a victim out of the innocent, as a young Perry man discovered during World War I.

Marlowe Stotts was a callboy for the Milwaukee Railroad. He was arrested the afternoon of March 22, 1918, because a German flag had been found in his home in the southern part of town.

While it created considerable excitement for a while, there was no way the charge against him could be upheld. It was a small four-inch by six-inch flag, one of a collection of fourteen he had purchased from a local bookstore and had on display on the wall of his bedroom.

It all started when someone remarked he had a German flag in his home. Several young men, bitten by the patriot bug, declared they were going to his home that night to tear it down. They were overheard by a stranger, Marion Stevens from Virginia, a young soldier on furlough who demanded, "You tell me where he lives and you won't have to wait till night."

Stevens was given the address, went to the home, and when no one answered his knock, walked into the house and into the bedroom and took the flag from the wall. He then took it to the mayor's office. Chief Zenor arrested Stotts the flag's owner.

The Perry lad was released when his story was told. Nothing was said about the visiting soldier's illegal entry into the home or the consequences of an illegal search and seizure.

The War to End Wars (1917-1918)

The War to End All Wars has almost been forgotten. But, in Perry, the war was a great cause of celebration — when it started as well as when it ended.

When it was over and peace declared in November 1918, people all over the land celebrated wildly. Perry was no exception.

A few minutes after the message came over the wires on November 11, that Germany had agreed to Allied terms, whistles blew and bells rang, just as they had done in April 1917, when Congress declared war.

In 1917, people were awakened by the night force sounding the roundhouse whistle and every locomotive that had steam joined in the chorus. For several minutes, nothing else could be heard.

Harold Hohanshelt and LaVerne Spearing, employees in the pressroom of *The Perry Chief*, in a spirit of patriotism placed on a flag on a pole atop the water tower. The flag was owned by *The Chief* and had been draped over the press brushing every paper printed that day. After the paper was out, the pressmen decided the city needed a flag on the highest structure.

The new municipal flagpole at Second and Willis was dedicated on June 14, 1918, and the flag which was raised had been purchased by the Bureau of Commerce.

Captain A.D. Haskins was the officer of the day and, at the celebration, veterans gathered at the Milwaukee depot and escorted the Milwaukee employees who attended in a group. All business houses closed.

The parade formed at the depot and was headed by the drum corps, with the old soldiers next, followed by the Reverend Mondamus and his little daughter carrying flags. About 300 railroad employees, the Boy Scouts, and Scoutmaster B. Roy Emms joined in the parade. After the close of the ceremonies, a group picture was taken of the railroad employees.

September 26, 1918, when the great Liberty Loan campaign opened, every whistle and bell in the city was sounded. Everyone was asked to rise, stand at attention, face east for one minute, so that all eyes were directed toward General Pershing and his one million American fighters in France.

A patriotic meeting was held at noon at the roundhouse, presided over by Mayor Wilson. Judge Loren Hayes of Knoxville was the speaker. Short talks were given by R.E. Zerwekh and John Carmody of the Liberty Loan committee.

With the declaration of peace in 1918, people assembled in the downtown district giving it a carnival appearance. As usual the Milwaukee Railroad employees arrived with a band and started a parade. Others joined in with flags waving and noise-makers in hand, marching around the business district for several hours. Fireworks were lighted and people yelled themselves hoarse.

The celebration started at 2 p.m. and continued until midnight without abatement. In the evening a mammoth pile of boxes and barrels prepared for a bonfire was lit.

It was scheduled for 8 p.m., but a youngster couldn't wait and touched a match to it a little early. No one was angry and the rest of the evening was spent parading the streets and attending the pavement dance.

Perry's Chapter of Bonnie and Clyde (1933)

One chapter in the saga of the outlaws Bonnie and Clyde was written in Perry.

Marvin Barrow, age thirty-one, one of the bandit gang of three men and two women lay near death in the Perry King's

Daughters Hospital on July 14, 1933. Barrow had been wounded in a running gun battle with county and state officers near Dexter. He had also been wounded the week before in Missouri when he and another shot their way out of another gun battle. In that battle a bullet had passed through Barrow's skull and doctors anticipated meningitis would result from it.

Barrow's wife was taken to Des Moines by state officers after her husband was brought to Perry. She had been found hiding behind a tree. The other members, thought to be Clyde Barrow and wife and Jack Sherman or Jack Stewart, escaped by fording the river and stealing a Plymouth belonging to Valley Feller, a farmer who was forced to help the woman into the car. Marvin Barrow was unable to flee because of his injuries.

The chase led from the Feller farm, where they had stolen the car, to Polk City where they robbed an oil station. Abandoning the Plymouth, they stole a Chevrolet to make their get-away.

The bandits had stolen a Ford V-8 from Edward Stoner's home on Sixth about 2 p.m. on Sunday. The members of the family heard the car pull away but thought Bob Stoner had taken it. When he came home at 3 p.m., they reported the theft. The car was found literally riddled by bullets in the gun battle; sixty-two holes were counted. It also contained automatic rifles and pistols and a large amount of ammunition.

Suspicion that a gang was hiding in the area was first aroused when John Love of Dexter noticed members of a group coming to Dexter to buy meals, medicine, and bandages. He investigated and found them camped in the woods. Sheriff Knee was notified and the state police department informed. The result was a raid on the campsite.

Several cars of officers went south of the camp and worked back on foot, while others were left near the river in an effort to drive them to the river. Unexpected resistance was encountered and machine guns were fired in all directions right after the first attack. The bandits did go to the river and forded it to make their escape to the Feller farm. One officer was slightly injured. The Stoner car was taken to Adel after the arrest of Mr. and Mrs. Barrow.

In the Perry Hospital, Barrow talked about the killing of Marshal H.D. Humphrey of Alma, Arkansas, and was recognized by the deputy who took part in the fight. The Alma battle was the result of a grocery store robbery. Officers caught up with the

Barrow brothers in their hideout. In the evening gun battle the marshal was killed.

Numerous officers from various localities visited Barrow in the Perry hospital in an effort to identify him. Officers from Platte, Missouri, and Kansas City confirmed the identity of the injured gunman, who was wanted for murder and robberies. At least four murders had been charged to the gang.

After the oil station robbery near Platte, Missouri, the gang was surrounded in a tourist cabin and another gun battle took place. That is when Marvin Barrow received the bullet wound to the head which was expected to claim his life.

Mrs. T.C. Barrow, mother of the injured man, arrived in Perry on July 26, 1933. She had traveled from her home in Dallas, Texas. She was accompanied by another son, L.C. Barrow, age nineteen, and at least two women — Mrs. Emma Parker (mother of Bonnie Parker) and Mrs. May Turner (a friend of Mrs. Marvin Barrow). They left Texas as soon as they read of the gun battle through the newspaper. The shooting had occurred early on a Monday morning.

The local hospital was continually under guard as protection against any effort of gang members to free the wounded man. Bonnie's mother displayed much more concern for her daughter, whom rumors said was injured in her escape at Dexfield.

Marvin "Buck" Barrow was twenty-eight years old, according to his mother, and had been married three times. He had a ten-year-old son by his first wife and an eight-year-old daughter by the second. The whereabouts of the children were unknown, but it was assumed that they were with their respective mothers. Barrow had been released from prison in March, after serving his first sentence for stealing a car. Clyde Barrow had also served a term in prison on the same charge.

Marvin Barrow died in the Perry hospital on July 29, 1933.

The Barrow gang members were pals of Charles Arthur "Pretty Boy" Floyd, the southwest's most notorious outlaw.

The body of Marvin Barrow was taken by train to Dallas, Texas. The mother and her party made the return trip by car. Blanche, Barrow's third wife, was returned to Platte, Missouri, where she was sentenced to ten years in prison for her part in the crime spree.

Chapter Fifteen
The Final Four

PUBLIC LIBRARY, PERRY, IA — 35—

Perry's Public Library

Andrew Carnegie gave Perry $10,000 in 1903 to build the Public Library in Perry. Carnegie's only condition was that the town would agree to maintain the building.

The Carnegie Library (1902)

The steps that led to the creation of a public library in Perry go back as far as 1884 and C.M. Robinson and C.L. Knapp. These two men had received and placed 150 volumes on the shelves of the library located in Dr. Eldridge's office in the Harlen block. One dollar paid to Dr. Eldridge constituted a life membership. Members could take out any book, but only one volume at a time.

In 1894, arrangements were made to open the library in the Perry Business College. This was the result of the first meeting of the board of trustees of the Perry Library Association, held at Mayor Breed's office on September 6. The opening date for the Library was planned for October 1. The books arrived and on September 29, 1894, were placed in the cabinets provided for them in the office room at the college.

Then Andrew Carnegie began awarding grants toward the establishment of libraries across the country. The Perry Council formulated plans to establish a library and support it. The city election in March 1902 was a victory for the Republicans and the library. The former won in two of three wards; the library carried all wards.

The newly appointed library trustees were: L.V. Harpel; S.E. Carrell; A.M. Harvey; P.H. O'Connor; D.D. McCall; Mrs. A.W. McPherson; Mrs. A.J. Ross; Mrs. P.C. Rude; and Mrs. W.H. McCammon. At their first meeting that spring the board prepared a line of action hoping to get the eye and ear of Mr. Carnegie. Representative Hull and Senator Doliver, at the trustee's request, contacted Carnegie on Perry's behalf.

Carnegie's secretary responded, sending a questionnaire seeking the details on the proposed project. The Library Board appointed a committee to respond to the questionnaire.

News that Carnegie would fund the library was announced

on January 16, 1903. He had offered the city $10,000 on the condition that the town would maintain the library.

Then came the quibbling about where to build. There were those who held out against using the Triangle, saying it should only be used as a site for a city hall, although prospects of building one then (or ever, for that matter) did not exist. Others felt it foolish to buy another site when the city already owned one that was free and idle. The location of the library became the most prominent topic of discussion in its day.

By the last of February the site was chosen, all legal steps completed, and notice had been received that Carnegie's money would be forthcoming.

Once the decision to build the library in the Triangle had been reached, the next problem to be settled was over the style and shape of the building. The property figured in this argument as well, since it was a triangular piece of ground. Still, the entire library matter came to a more successful conclusion sooner than any other issue in Perry's history that had been equally agitated.

A building committee was appointed by Library Board president L.V. Harpell in March. The committee was composed of the following members: S.E. Carrell; P.H. O'Connor; D.D. McCall; Mrs. A.C. Ross; and Mrs. A.W. McPherson. The committee charged the architects Nourse and Rasmussen with developing the preliminary plans and sketches.

The board asked for bids on the approved plans on July 1, 1903. The Perry contracting firm of Courtney and Bolt was awarded the contract.

Because the contractors had to place their order for the stone work immediately, they had to know the name to be inscribed. "Carnegie Library" was finally approved by the Library Board as the majority of the board felt it would be base ingratitude not to honor the benefactor for his gift.

Excavation for the building commenced on July 22, and soon workmen were busy laying the footings. In September, the Perry Electric Light and Power Company was awarded the contract for heat fixtures ($852) and Miller Brothers won the plumbing contract ($129). The Millers also were awarded the contract for constructing the cess pool.

In February 1904, a librarian was selected by the full board. There were eleven candidates for the position. A formal ballot was taken and Miss Flora Bailey received the majority of the

Downtown Perry 1908

A view down Willis Avenue in 1908. The Carnegie Library sits in the Triangle at the center left of the photo, the St. James Hotel is at the far right of the picture

votes. Her salary for the first year was $25 per month. As the library grew in size and importance, the board ruled, the salary might be raised.

The new library board also invited the old Library Association (which was no longer active) to meet with them and to take action regarding the books in the old free library.

At 1 p.m. on September 19, 1904, the library was opened to residents of the city for the use of reading rooms and for the checking out of books.

It was formally dedicated on December 10 of that year. The ceremonies were held at the Breed Opera House and it was packed to capacity by those who wanted to hear the governor speak.

On the stage were the officers of the library, members of the board, and those on the program. The high school chorus opened the ceremonies with a song, and Rev. Jesse Povey of the Congregational Church offered the invocation.

Others on the program included: Mrs. P.C. Rude; Allen Harvey; Mrs. A.J. Ross; piano soloist Clara Raife; vocal soloist Mrs. F.C. Clark; Mrs. McPherson, who introduced Judge Nichols, who in turn presented Governor Cummins. Mrs. Cardell closed the show with a piano solo.

When the exercises were completed, a reception was held at the library by the Club Ladies of Perry. The pleasant strains of the Opera House Orchestra inspired conversation and made the time fly.

Several hundred people enjoyed themselves about the frappe bowls in the children's room where Miss Barnard and Miss Swearingen served and in the general reading room where Miss Adams and Miss Roddan served frappe.

During the height of the reception, the lights went out, terminating an otherwise pleasant and profitable evening.

Miss Flora Bailey

Flora Bailey was born October 15, 1871, at Agency and died in May 1952. She came to Perry in 1895 with her parents, C.D. and Elizabeth Bailey from Adel. She attended Cornell at Mt. Pleasant, taught school for a while, then became Perry's first librarian. She retired in 1945 after forty-one years in the position.

First Carnegie Librarian

Miss Flora Bailey was the first Librarian at the Carnegie Library, serving in that post for forty-one years.

Laundry Then a Bank (1899-1916)

At 5 a.m. on September 1, 1899, the fire alarm sounded for a blaze at the corner of First and Willis in the building owned by

Mrs. Hain. The west half of the structure was occupied by the Perry Lily Laundry, owned and operated by Mr. Dietz, who used both floors. The lower east side was the place of business of Hub Shively, proprietor of the pop and bottling works, while the upper floor was the home of John Wittell, a cigar maker in the employ of the Eureka Cigar factory.

The building was almost a total wreck before the Fire Department could get the fire under control. The center of the laundry was gutted, though the washer, wringer, engine, and boiler were saved on the lower floor. Most of the machinery upstairs would be fit to use again after slight repairs.

The pop and bottling works lost nothing but the extracts, for little fire or smoke reached there. Wittell and his wife saved nearly everything but a few clothes, though there was considerable loss due to rough handling of goods.

The fire started on the interior but spread rapidly to the roof and side walls. The building was veneered, but, not withstanding the amount of woodwork in the building, after the first wild rush of fire, it seemed to burn slowly. The fire cooled considerably and quickly so that by the time the department arrived on the scene, smoking embers were the only evidence that the fire had affected the frame of the building.

This structure was an old landmark erected in 1874 and first used as a mill. It was built before the streets were established and it stood about ten feet out into First Avenue. Notices had been given years before to move it east by ten feet and the city purchased the ten feet for that purpose. The owner signed an agreement to move the building within five years. The time had been extended again and again and it appeared doubtful that the move would ever take place.

J.C. Bryan closed a deal with Mrs. Hain on September 22, 1909, for the corner lot. Bryan had a new brick building erected on the lot to house the bank he organized in late 1912.

The first dirt was moved on April 29, 1913; the excavation was made to a depth of about seven feet. Plans were prepared by architect Morrison of Des Moines on which the contractors based their bid estimates. Jacobsen and Stombeck were the low bidders, and the contract awarded to construct the building on June 17, 1913, was in the amount of $10,000.

Plans called for a three-story structure with a brick exterior trimmed in stone; the counting room for the bank was to occupy

Security Savings Bank

J.C. Bryan's bank soon merged with another and moved to a location on Second Street. The bank building was sold and the city leased it for offices.

the entire first floor. The second floor was designated for the officers and apartments, with the third floor unfinished until needed. The fittings were the work of Charles Timeon and Son and were a splendid showing of Perry craftsmanship.

E.D. Carter bought the bank building in June 1916, from Albert Hill of Cambridge who had owned it for about three months. In early 1920, the City Council moved from the library basement into the bank building.

At a special meeting held on January 3, 1928, the city finalized its purchase of the building. The price was $15,000.

The Pattees in Perry

The history of the Pattee family in Perry begins with William Harrison Pattee. He traced his ancestry to 16th Century England, with one of the family members having been a physician to Charles II.

William Pattee was born in Vermont on March 21, 1812. His father was Lorimar Pattee who had served under George Washington in the Revolutionary War. His future wife's grandfather also served in that war and died in the charge with Starke at the Battle of Bennington.

On March 16, 1836, William Pattee and Caroline Fay were married in Franklin County, Vermont. Each was the youngest of a family of ten. Eight children were born to them, five sons and three daughters. The sons were David J., Hubbell, Ira, John and Wallace. The daughters were Marilla R. (Mrs. A.N. Ballard), Capitola (Mrs. Z.N. Fidler), and Amelia.

David J. was the most prominent Pattee in Perry's history. For forty years he was the town's "first citizen." He was president of the First National Bank, pioneer merchant, largest holder of real estate. He was also an early postmaster and mayor for thirteen years. In 1883 he was elected to the Iowa House of Representatives and re-elected in 1885. It was quite a rise from a humble start. David had come to Perry as a young man without any means other than his energy and ability as capital.

David J. Pattee was born December 22, 1839, in Chittenden County, Vermont. He graduated from public school in Georgia, Vermont, and attended the academy there. He took part in the Civil War, serving under generals McClellan, Pope, and Burnside. In the Battle of Harpers Ferry, Pattee was taken prisoner. He was later discharged because of ill health and wandered west, drifting to Des Moines. Here he went to work for Rawson and Osgood.

Pattee re-enlisted in the 47th Iowa, was commissioned a lieutenant and served until being mustered out. Returning from the war, he resumed his duties with Rawson and Osgood. He came to Perry in 1867, erected a building and opened a general store west of what became Perry, operating under the name of Rawson and Pattee. He shortly bought out his partner Rawson.

When the Fort Dodge Railroad came through east of his store in 1868, Pattee put his store on wheels, sold goods as he traveled, and brought the building to the west side of the Triangle.

Later he left the mercantile business and went into real estate and loans. He took an interest in banking and soon formed a private bank in partnership with O. Mosher. He purchased the First National Bank in 1885. In 1877, Pattee was elected mayor of Perry and served his two terms in the Iowa legislature in the middle of the next decade.

In 1872 Pattee was married to Sarah Isabelle Moore, only daughter of Mr. and Mrs. J.H. Moore. The D.J. Pattees were the parents of six children, one of whom died in infancy. The children were May, Harry, Martha, Ada, and Willie.

In 1874, Pattee and Moore purchased 188 acres from Joseph Wolf just south of Perry and moved their stockyards there. The sale price was $6,000. In 1876, Pattee built a new house on the farm. Before moving there, the family lived for a time on Otley Avenue in what was called the Ling house.

In 1883, Pattee began construction of a home on the southwest corner of Fourth and Warford. The family moved into it in time for Christmas in 1884.

Sarah Moore Pattee died on February 12, 1902. She had gone to the Women's Christian Association Hospital in Council Bluffs where an operation was performed. She died one week after her arrival there. D.J. Pattee came home at once on the No. 4 and was met at the depot by members of the Gerard Commandry. Knights Chandler, Thomas, Holmes and Swearingen, who escorted him to his home.

Harry Pattee came home the next day with his mother's remains. About 200 citizens met them at the station. Fred Dodson had a carriage waiting for Harry, who was quickly taken to his home. The people marched in double file ahead of the hearse. The pall bearers (John Shortley, Howard Rouse, F.M. Hoeye, Homer Moody, Bert Holmes, and H.C. Modlin) walked beside the hearse.

The services were held at the Pattee home. The house was filled and scores stood on the porch and walk. Many had to leave for fear they might expose themselves to the chilly air and get sick. All businesses in Perry were closed during the hour of the services.

Harry Pattee was the typical rich man's son. The family had a home on Lake Okoboji where Harry had a yacht, the Fair Wind, which he entered in races. He attended an Eastern college in Poughkeepsie, New York.

Tragedy again struck the D.J. Pattee home in 1903. Son Harry was shot a little after 2 a.m. on January 17. He and his sisters had returned from a dance and had gone quietly to their rooms. Harry had undressed but not retired, when he heard a racket in the back yard and slipped down the backstairs to check it out.

As soon as he opened the kitchen door, he saw a man. There

was another man on the porch on a ladder. He struck Harry a blow, then pulled a revolver, shot him once and ran west down the alley. Harry staggered into the kitchen and called his father who found his son leaning against the door frame. D.J. Pattee phoned at once for Drs. Ross and Trout and notified Central about what had happened and had the authorities called.

It was thought that the burglars were after meat (D.J. Pattee had just had two hogs butchered) and that they were local men, as they knew where the meat was. Harry had noticed when the men ran from the house that they threw the revolver away. Following his directions, Marshal Dave Willis and Frank Dodson found the gun in a manure pile at the barn on the back of the lot. Harry also said one man was short, the other tall.

Both doctors stayed with the victim throughout the day. The bullet had lodged in his breast, but it was not at once probed for or even located, but the doctors were certain it had cut or entered a lung.

Suspicion immediately centered on Steve Crandal. He was an ex-convict and was awaiting sentencing for stealing a hog two months earlier. His father, while admitting his boys were bad, staunchly declared that his son was not guilty of this crime. He stated his son Steven had hauled a load of coal from Angus, tended his team and spent the night with him.

The day following the shooting, Crandal appeared before Justice Lods as promised to receive his sentence for the earlier scrape and was lodged in the city jail until he could be taken to Adel to serve out the thirty-day sentence. If he were to be convicted of the shooting, it would have to be proved that he was out of his father's house.

Within an hour after the shooting, Dave Willis was in communication with different points to secure hounds. When it was certain the hounds would arrive, Willis requested Company B of the State Militia to report and twenty-eight members answered the call. The purpose was to preserve order and to keep curious people away. Another purpose was to patrol the Pattee residence in order to enable the dogs to take the scent.

It was the first time hounds had ever been used in Perry. Word got out and by the time the dogs arrived, the streets were crowded with a mass of humanity. Around the Pattee property the streets were nearly blocked. The dogs, with their owner George Huffmeier and Deputy Sheriff Rhinehart of Newton, arrived on the Rock

Island.

The dogs were taken to the Pattee house and, after two false starts, seemed to pick up a scent that satisfied them. Held back by the keeper and following a devious course, they finally arrived at the old pest house north of the cemetery where Crandal lived. D.J. Pattee, riding in a hack, had followed the dogs.

Huffmeier and Rhinehart had dinner at Ling's Cafe where they had a consultation with Marshal Dave Willis and Sheriff Hanes. The dogs were taken to the Stewart House where they were fed three pounds of good steak.

Harry Pattee expressed a desire to see the hounds, so they were taken to his home and to the side of his couch.

That evening Crandal, chained with another prisoner, was taken from the jail and marched to the depot. A large crowd had been milling about the jail and followed the officers and their prisoners to the depot. They stormed the depot, even threatening to drag Crandal off the train. There were ropes a plenty with the mob and a lynching might have occurred had there been a mob leader. Crandal was one frightened man.

If Steve Crandal was the short perpetrator, who was the tall one? There were no ready clues. Several suspected parties were rigidly examined, but no information was received and no arrests made. The guilty party was never apprehended.

The shooting made news for months. Harry's life hung in the balance and long daily reports were issued in *The Chief*. D.J. Pattee offered a $500 reward good for a year's time upon the arrest, conviction, and sentencing of the guilty party.

When Company B was called out, talk started that this was an irregular and illegal proceeding. There had not been sufficient time to notify the governor, so the boys were ordered out by authority of the sheriff, which was in accordance with the law. The moot point was that if the governor issued the call, the state paid the expense. If the sheriff made the call, the county had to pay. The amount of the bill presented to the County Board of Supervisors was $44.50.

When Crandal was in jail, the county had to support his family and feed his stock. On January 21, 1903, Justice Lods decided that it was a useless expense to feed three head of horses which were weak and poor. Therefore, a committee of Dr. H.M. Stevenson, H.H. Davis and Dave Willis was sent to investigate. On their recommendation, two of the horses were shot and the third put into the care of the elder Crandal.

In February Governor Cummins offered $300 in reward money, making $800 the prize for information leading to the apprehension of the guilty one.

Steve Crandal was released from jail in Adel after 30 days. No formal charge was lodged against him for any connection with the Pattee shooting and none was ever filed.

Weeks later, Harry was still in bed. On March 19, Dr. Trout and Dr. Schooler of Des Moines performed an operation. Three months later, Harry was able to go out riding for the first time. As soon as he was able to travel, Harry and his father took a long trip out west. When they returned to Perry in June, Harry was much improved.

Harry Pattee and Grace Clark were married at the home of her parents, Mr. and Mrs. A.W. Clark, in Papillion, Nebraska, on December 16, 1903. That evening the newlyweds arrived back in Perry to their new home — a gift from D.J. Pattee — a beautiful residence on Willis Avenue known as the Swearingen home. D.J. also gave them deed to a 240-acre farm west of Perry known as the Ballentine farm. Harry worked as a teller in the First National Bank of which his father was president.

After a number of weeks of painful suffering related to the wound he suffered in the break-in at his father's home eighteen months earlier, Harry submitted to another operation in July 1904. It was performed at his home by Dr. Schooler of Des Moines who was again assisted by Dr. Trout. A number of pieces of rib which had been causing abscesses were removed.

D.J. Pattee died in Perry in July of 1912.

Harry then became the president of the First National Bank. He seemed to attract trouble. He was laid up at his cottage on Omaha Beach at Lake Okobiji with a broken hip, the result of an auto accident, in 1922. The hip did not heal and he was taken to the Mercy Hospital in Des Moines in November. In December, the Pattee brothers disposed of their interest in the bank.

On January 6, 1923, Harry was back in the Des Moines hospital for serious surgery to graft a bone in the hip. He had been bedridden most of the time since the auto accident. By the last of January he was on the road to recovery.

Harry and family moved to Corpus Christi, Texas. Harry's wife died there in January 1943. Three daughters survived, Harriet, Jean, and Isabel. Harry died in March 1956, at the age of seventy-six.

D.J. Pattee's other son, Will, was also well known in Perry.
Born in Perry on March 22, 1890, Will, too, was in the bank.
With his brother Harry, Will helped to build the Pattee Hotel as a
monument to their father. He was also a land holder.

Will had the dubious honor of having Perry's first speeding
ticket issued to him. He was fined $5 plus court costs.

He married Gladys Carey Mitchell, a talented musician, on
June 27, 1917, at her home in Lansing, Michigan. Her first husband had died in Denver, and Pattee adopted her daughter, Virginia. Will's first wife, Ruth Dignan, had also died.

Will Pattee was a diabetic. He had hurt one of his legs in a
hunting accident; infection set in and spread to both legs. In April
1960, Will was in the hospital undergoing amputation. He lost
both legs at the knee. His wife died in Houston in September 1964,
at the age of seventy-five. Will Pattee died just eighteen days later.

The Pattee Home

D.J. Pattee announced on March 16, 1883, his intention of
building a new home at the southwest corner of Fourth and
Warford. It was to be brick and the cost was expected to run into
the thousands.

By July of 1884, the residence was under construction and
the foundation laid. Carpentry work commenced in August.

The Pattees moved into the beautiful new residence in December 1884. A. Ammerman moved into the residence vacated
by the Pattees.

A remodeling project was completed in July 1904. The roof
was rebuilt and an elegant porch was added. It started at the entrance on the south, went around to the east, with square corners,
then continued north to the end of the house, terminating in a
circle with a large door. Mammoth pillars ten feet high supported
the porch roof, which extended out far enough to provide considerable shade. There was not another porch like it in the city.

T.A. Phillips purchased the home in 1926 and remodeled the
ground floor into funeral parlors with living quarters up stairs.

In March 1935, after two months of preparation, Mr. and
Mrs. E.E. Niederfrank had made the home into the Maples Tea-

room. New woodwork was put in and light maple furniture was used.

The tearoom was formally opened by new owners Jane and Francis Wilcox on September 5, 1935. About 100 guests called between the hours of 3 p.m. and 5 p.m. to view the changes and to extend their good wishes.

Pattee Hotel

In 1912, the year D.J. Pattee died, his two sons, Harry and Will, completed plans for a very modern and much-needed hotel. It was intended as a building to stand for all time as a monument to their faith in the future of the city and as a memorial to their father, whose activities had so long been identified with Perry.

The land on which the hotel was to be built was the site of Pattee's store, which D.J. Pattee had built and operated in the 1870s. Workmen had begun tearing down this structure in 1905.

Pattee Hotel
The north side of Willis Avenue in Perry's downtown was dominated by the Pattee Hotel. The three-story building is shown in in the center of this photo taken in the mid-1920s.

Lasting Tribute

The hotel built as a tribute to D.J. Pattee by his sons Harry and Will was erected on the site formerly occupied by D.J. Pattee's store on Willis Avenue.

The remaining buildings were moved off in May 1912. Men and teams started to work on the excavation for the hotel immediately afterward. There would be a basement under the entire structure and thousands of yards of dirt had to be moved.

Plans had been submitted to the architect in April, but material was slow in arriving. The contractors were not able to secure enough laborers, carpenters, and bricklayers because there was so much construction under way in the city.

J.C. Mardis and Company of Des Moines secured the contract work on the building, which began in June. The interior decorating was done by G.V. Rowe. The beautiful electric fixtures and system of installation was done by Braman Electric Company. The plumbing and heating plant was installed by Bailey Peppard. Eight firms had bid for the plumbing installation, three of them Perry men, but Des Moines had the lowest bid of $11,001.

It wasn't until the middle of October that workmen began placing the last of the steel in position and the pouring of the concrete began in an effort to complete the framework before cold weather set in. Work in the basement and the first floor was completed by October 16. The plumbing project started in November. Throughout the winter, the interior work was carried on.

The building was as near fireproof as possible, there not be-

Hotel Lobby

The lobby of the Pattee Hotel was modeled after the lobby of the LaSalle Hotel in Chicago.

ing enough wood in it (outside of the furniture) to make a blaze. The floors were all concrete, steel, and tile, and the hallways had no woodwork whatsoever.

In January 1913, Frank W. Wray of Estherville, the landlord for the hotel, arrived in Perry and began conferring with the local dealers for the furnishings.

G.W. O'Malley, of the firm Phillips, O'Malley and Tiernan, went to Chicago and Detroit in February in the company of Wray to select and order shipped the furniture needed. It was the largest single order ever placed by a local store and the men wondered what the wholesalers would think when the rugs were ordered by the gross.

Then Charles A. Graves, proprietor of the Graves Store, took the furniture man's place with Wray in Chicago to select the linens and bedding.

The cost for the furnishings was in the neighborhood of $14,000. The sixty-four guest rooms in the magnificent structure were fitted in colonial mahogany and velvet rugs of a beautiful design. There were shower baths, tub baths, and elegant parlors. The dining room was in early English design and the lobby a replica of the famous lobby of the LaSalle in Chicago. The small dining room on the second floor was a beautiful room for parties and clubs.

The new buses for the hotel arrived on April 30, 1913. They were ordered in St. Louis by E.A. Lester, who was to have charge of the line. It was a handsome rubber-tired wagonette type of bus, lettered in gold and was to haul the patrons to and from the depots.

Ainley's Book Store moved into the east storeroom and was formally opened on May 7, 1913.

L. Dodson, better known as "Grandpa," arrived in Perry on May 28, 1913, from St. Paul to attend the banquet the following day at the new hotel. He went directly to the hotel and asked for a room. His was the first name to be entered upon the new register. Later in the evening, another came in and placed his name above Grandpa's on the page, but the old citizen who had traveled so far was really the holder of the first entry in the book.

The hotel's opening on May 29 was marked by a banquet sponsored by the Commercial Club, followed by a tour of the hotel. A complete telephone system was installed, with a phone in every room and visitors were invited to try out the service when on their inspection tour.

The vacant storeroom on the west was opened for dancing and an orchestra and band were brought to Perry from Des Moines by T. Fred Henry, a famous musician of the day.

The dining room, which extended to the alley and included the northeast corner of what in 1978 was Harland's Hardware, was filled with tables laid for 225 guests. Tables for more than 100 more guests were spread in the lobby.

Tickets for the elaborate banquet were $5 and the eight-course menu included: oranges, bananas , grapefruit, radishes, olives, celery, cream of tomato soufflé; fillet of sole (with tartar sauce); roast stuffed young Philadelphia turkey (with cranberry sauce); larded beef tenderloin; new potatoes en creme; French peas; roman punch; lobster salad a la Pattee; Neapolitan ice cream; angel food cake; devils food cake; and demitasse.

The Reverend Briggs of the Congregational Church gave the invocation. Judge Fahey offered the first toast of the evening and the Hotel Pattee was officially opened. For four hours guests were seated at the tables and three hours of that time were devoted to serving the excellent banquet. Throughout the banquet, the guests were entertained by special music.

That night friends and guests from all over the state joined the Perry people in the festivities. Auto loads of people from Des Moines came to shake hands with the builders.

Less than a year later, the hotel property was sold to the Bosserman Brothers of Murray. It was the largest deal ever made in Perry, a total of $131,700 being involved.

Epilogue

It is difficult to find a logical conclusion for a book that has no plot. To that end, these buildings were chosen for the final four.

They were all Perry show places in their time. Three were built in what was then the heart of the business district. All are steeped in history. Not one will molder away, as so many others have — even though some have stood empty and neglected for a while. All will soon be show places again.

All this is because Roberta Green Ahmanson, a former resident, has remembered her roots. She has chosen these four buildings to purchase, to preserve, to refurbish and to return to their original importance to the town.

The former bank-municipal building on the corner will be remodeled upstairs to office rooms. The downstairs will be readied for a tenant.

The old Carnegie Library has been accepted by the National Registry on their list of Historic Places. It will be a downtown cultural museum.

The old Pattee mansion on Fourth and Warford will be restored to its former glory. The downstairs rooms and part of the upstairs will be given back their original grandeur so that tourists can get an idea of the gracious living in Perry at the close of the Nineteenth Century and the early days of the Twentieth Century.

At great expense the hotel building has been renovated to its past elegance. The constant activities of the many workmen assured the public that this project could be completed.

All this has brought about a great change in Perry, a renewal of pride in the city, and a desire to do something about the remaining buildings. The winds of change are definitely blowing, there is a new spirit abroad in the town.

Index